# Theoretical principles of distance education

Advances in technology since the Industrial Revolution have brought about a new form of education, known today as 'distance education'. The revolution in electronic communications of recent decades has given distance education new status. Today more than 10 million of the world's 600 million students study at a distance. Distance education is now a normal form of learning for those in employment, for homemakers and for those who choose not to go to schools or universities. In the corporate sector distance education is fast becoming a preferred type of training.

*Theoretical Principles of Distance Education* highlights for the first time the implications of these developments for both conventional and distance education. The book explores the problems that distance education poses to the theorist. In a closely planned and balanced study, fifteen of the world's leading scholars examine the didactic, analytical, academic, philosophical and technological underpinnings of distance education, making use of contemporary philosophy, educational philosophy and communications theory.

The book sets new levels for the analysis and study of distance education. It demonstrates for the first time that contemporary educational philosophy, didactic strategies and administrative theory can no longer focus solely on the classroom and lecture theatre but must embrace teaching at a distance too.

**Desmond Keegan** is a leading authority on distance education and the author or editor of several books on distance education. From 1976 to 1984 he was Head of Distance Training at the Open College, South Australia, and from 1984 to 1985 was the foundation Director General of the Italian Distance University Consortium. He is now project manager of the European Virtual Classroom for Vocational Training at the Audio Visual Centre, University College Dublin and the editor of the Routledge Studies in Distance Education series.

**Routledge studies in distance education**
Series editor: Desmond Keegan

**Theoretical Principles of Distance Education**
Desmond Keegan

**Collaboration in Distance Education**
Edited by Louise Moran and Ian Mugridge

**Distance Education: New Perspectives**
Edited by Keith Harry, Desmond Keegan and Magnus John

# Theoretical principles of distance education

Edited by
Desmond Keegan

ROUTLEDGE

London and New York

First published 1993
by Routledge
11 New Fetter Lane, London EC4P 4EE

Simultaneously published in the USA and Canada
by Routledge
29 West 35th Street, New York, NY 10001

Reprinted 1996

*Routledge is an International Thomson Publishing company*

© 1993 Desmond Keegan

Typeset by J & L Composition Ltd, Filey, North Yorkshire
Printed and bound in Great Britain by
TJ Press (Padstow) Ltd, Padstow, Cornwall

*British Library Cataloguing in Publication Data*
A catalogue record for this book is available from the British Library

*Library of Congress Cataloguing in Publication Data*
A catalogue record for this book is available from the Library of Congress

ISBN 0-415-08942-5

*For L. L.*
*Desmond Jnr,*
*Martin and*
*Patricia*

# Contents

viii  *Contents*

# Figures

# Tables

# Contributors

**Cheryl Amundsen** is a professor at McGill University, Montreal, Quebec, Canada. She is cross-appointed to the Centre for University Teaching and Learning and the Department of Educational and Counselling Psychology. Her teaching responsibilities (workshops, seminars, courses and projects) all focus on the improvement of teaching at McGill. Her research interests focus on the study of the teaching–learning process in higher education. Address: Centre for University Teaching and Learning, McGill University, 3700 McTavish Street, Montreal, Quebec H3A 1Y2, Canada.

**A. W. Bates** is Executive Director, Planning and Research, at the Open Learning Agency of British Columbia. Address: The Open Learning Agency, 4355 Mathissi Place, Burnaby, British Columbia Y5G 438, Canada.

**Gary Boyd** is Professor of Education (Educational Technology) at Concordia University in Montreal. Address: Concordia University, 1455 de Maisonneuve Blvd. West, Montreal, Quebec H3G 1MB, Canada.

**Tony Devlin** is Manager of Course Development with Ericsson in Ireland. He holds postgraduate qualifications in Organizational Behaviour and has spent twenty years in software development, most recently in technology-based-training and hypermedia. Address: Ericsson Systems Expertise Ltd, Adelphi Centre, Dun Laoghaire, Co. Dublin, Ireland.

**D. Randy Garrison** is Professor and Associate Dean in the Faculty of Continuing Education of the University of Calgary. He is the former Director of Distance Education and is currently co-ordinator of adult education programmes. Address: Faculty of Continuing Education, The University of Calgary, 2500 University Drive N.W., Calgary T2N 1N4, Canada.

**Chere Campbell Gibson** is Professor in the Family and Consumer Education Department of the School of Family Resources and Consumer Sciences of the University of Wisconsin at Madison. Address: Continuing and Vocational Education, 1300 Linden Drive, Madison, Wisconsin 53706-1375, USA.

**Peter Jarvis** is Professor of Continuing Education, Department of Educational Studies, University of Surrey, Guildford, Surrey, GU2 6TZ, United Kingdom.

**Desmond Keegan** holds postgraduate degrees in philology, philosophy and education. He was Head of Distance Training in South Australia from 1976 to 1984 and first Director-General of the Italian Distance University Consortium. He is editor of the Routledge Studies in Distance Education Series and manager of The European Virtual Classroom project at the Audio Visual Centre, University College Dublin. Address: PO Box 59, Blackrock, Co. Dublin, Ireland.

**Erling Ljoså** is a graduate of Oslo University in religion, science and mathematics. He has worked in distance education since 1970 with the NKS Foundation. He is President of the European Distance Education Network (EDEN) and has been awarded an Honorary Degree of Doctor of the Open University of the United Kingdom. Address: NKS Ernst G. Mortensens Stiftelse, Postboks 5853 Hegdehaugen, 7 N–0308 Oslo.

**Michael G. Moore** is Director of The American Center for the Study of Distance Education at the College of Education of Pennsylvania State University. Address: Adult Education Program, The Pennsylvania State University, 403 South Allen Street, Suite 206, University Park, PA 16801–5202, USA.

**Ted Nunan** is Associate Professor of Education in the Distance Education Centre at the University of South Australia. Address: Distance Education Centre, University of South Australia, Holbrooks Road, Underdale, South Australia 5032, Australia.

**Otto Peters** was Foundation Vice-Chancellor (*Rektor*) of the Fernuniversität-Gesamthochschule in Hagen. He is the author of a series of books on distance education including *Der Fernunterricht* (1965), *Das Hochschulfernstudium* (1968), *Texte zum Hochschulfernstudium* (1971), *Die didaktische Struktur der Fernunterrichts* (1973) and *Die Fernuniversität im Fünften Jahr* (1981). Address: Fachbereich Erziehungs-, Sozial- und Geisteswissenschaften, Fernuniversität, Postfach 940, D-5800 Hagen, Germany.

**Louise Sauvé** is Professor at the Téléuniversité, Québec, Canada, and writes distance education courses, particularly in the Graduate Degree in Distance Education. Address: Université du Québec, Téléuniversité, 2635 boulevard Hochelage, Sainte-Foy, Québec G1V 4V9, Canada.

**John J. Sparkes** taught at Imperial College, Essex University and the Open University where he became the first Professor of Electronics. For ten years he was also Dean of Technology. His address is now 40 Sheethanger Lane, Hemel Hempstead, Herts HP3 0BQ, United Kingdom.

**Benedetto Vertecchi** received his doctorate in philosophy from the University of Rome in 1968. In 1990 he founded the Centre for Research in Distance Education at the University of Rome 'La Sapienza' and the journal *Instruzione a Distanza*. He is the author of twenty books on educational theory and educational evaluation. Address: Dipartimento di Scienze dell' Educazione, Università di Roma III, via del Castro Pretorio 20, 00185, Rome, Italy.

# Introduction

## NEED

Distance education is an exciting new area of education which seems to have something to offer to almost everyone, wrote one of the contributors to this book recently. Linked throughout its history to developments in communications technology, it has benefited from the rapid advances in the 1980s and early 1990s in electronic telecommunications. The 1980s also saw the foundations of the Asian distance teaching universities, many of which already have hundreds of thousands of students. In the 1990s a number of universities have begun to offer professional qualifications at degree level in distance education. Few will query the need to offer a first book on the theoretical principles of this area of education.

A theory of distance education is something which can eventually be reduced to a phrase, a sentence or a paragraph, and which can provide the touchstone against which decisions about distance education can be taken with confidence. It subsumes all the practical research and provides the underpinnings for decision-making.

A selection of the many needs for strengthening the theoretical underpinnings of this form of education are listed here:

- There is nothing as practical as a good theory. It stops one constantly starting from scratch, repeating the endeavours and mistakes of others, and responding continuously to 'crisis' situations without a frame of reference.
- Distance education was born of the wonders of the development of communication technology in the Industrial Revolution. Today that is nearly 150 years in the past, an adequate time for *ad hoc* solutions to be upgraded.
- Theoretical justification would seem to be required for a form of education which purports to make available a parallel provision of

education, equal in quality and status, to that of conventional schools, colleges and universities while abandoning the need for face-to-face communication in the learning group, previously thought to be a cultural imperative for all education.

- UNESCO statistics tell us that 10 million students, most of them adults, study at a distance in nearly every country of the world. This is a sizeable number which justifies theoretical formulation.
- Theoretical justification would seem to be required for offering university degrees at a distance in structures far removed from the theoretical principles of the university as a place where scholars come together for the purposes of knowledge as formulated by Arnold, Newman, and Jaspers.
- Until 1970 distance education was roundly criticized for the malpractice of some practitioners. The move from private to public provision in the last 25 years has muted these criticisms but others have appeared: that it alienates students, that it is contrary to Koranic tradition, that it cannnot give a full university atmosphere, that it is characterized by many of the evils of industrialization.
- Society provides itself with schools, colleges and universities. Distance education students choose not to use these structures provided by society and expect to be awarded their university degrees at home.
- It seems premature to offer bachelors, masters and doctoral degrees in a subject – distance education – whose theoretical underpinnings are noted for their fragility.

## HISTORY

For the purpose of this book the first systematic attempts to grapple with these issues will be set in Germany in 1967.

In that year Günther Dohmen published *Das Fernstudium. Ein neues pädagogisches Forschungs- und Arbeitsfeld (Distance education. A new field of educational research and activity)* through the Deutsches Instsitut für Fernstudium in Tübingen, the world's first distance education research centre. In the same year in Berlin, Otto Peters published *Das Fernstudium an Universitäten und Hochschulen. Didaktische Struktur und Interpretation: ein Beitrag zur Theorie der Fernlehre (The didactical structure and interpretation of university distance education. A contribution to the theory of distance teaching.)*

It is clear that there were researchers who had published on distance education before this date and one would wish to mention Gayle B. Childs from the University of Lincoln at Nebraska, Charles

A. Wedemeyer from the University of Wisconsin at Madison, and Börje Holmberg from Malmö in Sweden. But Dohmen's was the first of many from the research centre at Tübingen and Peters accompanied his theoretical formulation with a 620-page database on distance training programmes throughout the world in 1965, and a 556-page database on distance university programmes in 1968.

Dohmen's work was published only in German and had little influence, but Peters quickly put forward his views in English and his 1969 International Council for Correspondence Education paper brought his theory of industrialization to a world-wide audience. This was increased when the article was chosen for reproduction in the first book of readings on distance education: McKenzie and Christensen's *The Changing World of Correspondence Education* which was published by the Pennsylvania University Press in 1971.

In 1973 Michael G. Moore drew the attention of English-speaking distance educators to the need of theoretical formulation in *The Journal of Higher Education* because 'we continue to develop various forms of non-traditional methods for reaching the growing numbers of people who cannot, or will not, attend conventional institutions but who choose to learn apart from their teachers'. He pointed out the need for:

- describing and defining the field;
- discriminating between the various components of the field;
- identifying the critical elements of the various forms of teaching and learning;
- building a theoretical framework which will embrace this whole area of education.

The work of describing and defining the field occupied the rest of the 1970s. Up to 1978 there was immense confusion in the terminology used to describe the field of study which came to be known as 'distance education'. A plethora of terms was used, discourtesy to the reader was widespread, and confusion reigned as a result. By 1980 a new concern about definition of the field led to writers clarifying whether they were writing about or whether they were not writing about 'flexible learning' or the use of computers in schools or 'educational technology' or some other educational arrangement. Today definitions of distance education may be phrased differently but there is general agreement on the field of study being defined.

The benefits of solving the problems of describing and defining the field of distance education can be seen in the progress of the 1980s. The work of discrimination between the various components of the field and the identification of the critical elements of the various forms of teaching and learning as they occur in distance education was entered into with vigour. Books like Keegan's *Foundations of Distance Education*, Garrison's *Understanding Distance Education*, Holmberg's *Theory and Practice of Distance Education*, Garrison and Shale's *Education at a Distance* and Verduin and Clark's *Distance Education. The Foundations of Effective Practice* move confidently within the boundaries of a disciplinary field and their authors know clearly when and why they move beyond the boundaries of the field of distance education and into other fields of educational research.

Books like these mark what John Sparkes in *Distance Education* (1973) called the general acceptance in the academic community of the emergence of a new set of problems which constitutes the delineation of a new field of study within education. Furthermore, studies like Michael Moore's analysis of the concept 'interaction' in *The American Journal of Distance Education* in 1989, Terry Evans's analysis of the concepts of 'place' and 'distance' in *Distance Education* in 1989, and Philip Juler's on 'discourse' in *Open Learning* in 1990 are mature studies within the field of distance education and have clear presumptions and preoccupations that are not characteristic of the other fields of educational research. What is new is that these studies make important contributions to educational research while saying nothing about classroom interaction or strategies.

With the onset of the 1990s came the introduction of taught degrees for university credit in distance education. The time allowed for building a 'theoretical framework which would embrace this whole area of education' could arguably be said to have expired. Little more than the footings of the framework could be said to be in place and one was faced with the problem of lecturing in a field of study whose theoretical underpinnings were unacceptably shaky. It is this situation that the present book is designed to address.

## PHILOSOPHY

As befits a serious attempt to set the theoretical foundations of a field of study, the reader will find references to contemporary philosophy and educational philosophy. The dominant group in educational philosophy, if one is to judge by the lists of set texts and required readings at English-speaking universities, is the School of Philosophical Analysis represented by Richard S. Peters, Paul H. Hirst, and Michael Oakeshott, with their American contemporaries Israel Scheffler, William R. Perry, and others who are cited in Chapter

7. Deconstruction, Critical Theory and Post-Modernism figure in Chapters 10 and 12, with Scandinavian thinkers from Kierkegaard to Bohr in Chapter 11.

Contemporary philosophy is always a specialist topic as newly won philosophical positions seek to establish themselves as guidelines to philosophical thought or are bypassed and fail to win favour. As this is a book for the general reader and practitioner in distance education a brief introduction to contemporary philosophical positions is of value.

Deconstruction is a contemporary philosophical position, associated with Jacques Derrida from Algiers, which holds that there is no final guarantee of meaning in language and that therefore texts have no ultimate meaning. Thus a work can be shown to deconstruct. Derrida sets out to deconstruct the idea that the meaning of a text can be grasped in some precise concept.

Critical Theory was founded by the Frankfurt School of Adorno and Horkheimer and includes Marcuse and Habermas. Many of the group have Marxist approaches based on the early Hegelian dialectic. Their analysis leads them to a critical theory of capitalist society as basically an administered and manipulated society in which individuals are exploited and ideologies are concealed.

The Post-Modernism of J.-F. Lyotard and similar thinkers builds on and is predated by the critique of totality and the totalitarian state of Critical Theory. It rejects the tyranny of the same and promotes the singular, the particular, and the eclectic by emphasizing the importance of the individual and replacing the collective with the singular.

## PLAN

The plan of the book is to get leading contemporary distance educators to focus on the theory of distance education from differing perspectives. The five perspectives are: didactic, academic, analytical, philosophical and technological. Each perspective is treated by three authors and their analyses are printed in alphabetical order as each is considered to have a different approach.

Part I deals with didactical analysis as befits an educational field. Concepts such as teaching, learning, communication, feedback, interaction, and dialogue are examined as they occur in distance education.

Theoretical underpinnings for the theory of distance education from the academic perspective flow from the fact that a great deal of knowledge about any field of study comes from teaching it, researching it, developing courses about it, interacting with students studying it, and analysing students' views about it. This is the focus of Part II.

Part III deals with analysis: conceptual analysis, educational taxonomies, structural analysis. Thoroughgoing analysis as a necessary precondition for theoretical formulation is just as essential for distance education as for any other field of study.

Philosophical underpinnings of distance education are examined in Part IV, both from the viewpoint of philosophy of education and contemporary philosophy. Thus Chapter 10 deals with the theory of adult education and Post-Modernism, Chapter 11 with service industries and Scandinavian thought, and Chapter 12 with educational design, Critical Theory and Deconstruction.

Theoretical underpinnings for the theory of distance education from the technological perspective form the content of Part V and are based on the essential link between technology and distance education. The array of technologies available today are evaluated, computer-cybernetic solutions are presented, and the role of distance training for transnational and multinational corporations is considered. The final chapter on distance training is of particular relevance as a touchstone for evaluating the theoretical perspectives of the rest of the book because it is the only chapter that deals with the approximately 70 per cent of distance education that lies outside university-based programmes which are the context of most of the other chapters.

## CONCLUSION

It is a pleasant task for the editor to express deep gratitude to all the contributors. Not just gratitude but congratulations too. Congratulations on the success of their contributions, on the precision of their insights, and on the integrity with which they have put forward their views. The theory of distance education is in competent hands. Each chapter contains something new, often startlingly new. Each chapter contains much of value to the distance education practitioner as well as to the theorist. The aim of the undertaking has been to produce a work of quality and the authors have accepted the challenge of quality as expressed by one of the world's leading distance education institutions: 'Quality is never an accident. It is always the result of high intention, sincere effort, intelligent direction and skillful execution' (The Hadley School for the Blind).

# Part I
# Didactic underpinnings

# 1 Quality and access in distance education: theoretical considerations

*D. Randy Garrison*

How shall we treat subject matter that is supplied by textbook and teacher so that it shall rank as material of reflective inquiry, not as ready-made intellectual pabulum to be accepted and swallowed just as if it were something bought at a shop?
J. Dewey, *How We Think*

There is a growing recognition of the worth of distance education as the knowledge base expands and is communicated to the larger educational community. Perhaps the primary reason is the recognition that distance education is, in the final analysis, education. The only real difference is that the majority of communication between teacher and student is mediated. However, this does not necessitate a diminution of the quality of the educational transaction or a reconceptualization of the educational process itself. With the emergence of a variety of affordable communications technologies those in conventional education find fewer philosophical and practical concerns with delivering education at a distance.

The debate around distance education has often been reduced to the issues of access and quality. From a practical perspective they are concerns that must be addressed and balanced when designing education to be delivered at a distance. On the other hand, they often reflect two philosophically divergent assumptions regarding the purpose and viability of distance education. One view assumes that distance education is an approach that is primarily defined in terms of access issues. The other view essentially assumes that in terms of quality standards distance education cannot simulate or approach conventional face-to-face education. Fortunately, it is becoming apparent that both these extreme views are not viable as the theoretical foundation and practical understanding of distance education develops.

The purpose of this chapter is to explore several concepts which weave through an emerging framework or paradigm of distance education. Specific issues around the concepts of quality and accessibility, dominant and emerging paradigms, the teaching–learning transaction, independence and interaction, and communication technologies will be discussed with the intent of informing a potential framework of theory and practice. It should be noted that the focus of the discussion is limited to learning in an adult and higher education context, although much of what is said could well apply to other learning contexts.

## ACCESSIBILITY AND QUALITY

Historically, distance education has been preoccupied with access issues and this has been seen as the *raison d'être* of distance education. Concern for access is the driving motivation for many committed to distance education. Unfortunately, this missionary zeal can blind these educators to issues of quality and paradigmatic shifts that have occurred in how distance education is conceptualized and practised. As a result of new generations of communications technology, such as audio teleconferencing and computer-mediated communication, the image of the solitary and independent learner is changing. Also, innovative approaches adopted by mixed mode institutions that combine conventional and distance education approaches (to the point where it is difficult to label the approach as one or the other) may in effect reduce access marginally for advantages of quality.

The difficulty with assessing the quality of distance education is agreeing on a common meaning or set of objective criteria. Depending on the assumptions and values of the distance educator the meaning of quality will vary considerably. Those educators, working in autonomous distance education institutions with course design teams and taking advantage of the economics of scale, might judge quality from the perspective of the prepackaged print materials. Others in a more traditional mixed mode institution might point to the degree of mediated two-way communication (to simulate face-to-face dialogue) as a measure of quality. Such views in how we interpret quality in distance education are crucial to the direction of future development in the field, both from a theoretical and from a practical perspective.

In a study of the support of faculty for university distance education, Black (1992) states that faculty concerns about the quality of distance education were specifically related to the teacher–student transaction. She states, 'The faculty interviewed believed that dialogue and academic discourse are necessary features of education that must be assured in distance education in order to achieve quality' (Black 1992: 208). This supports the view of Garrison and Shale who argue 'that improving the quality of the educational process through increased two-way communication is likely to have the most significant impact upon the effectiveness of learning' (Garrison and Shale 1990: 128). While the design of print materials and other resources will influence the quality of learning, the overriding impact on the quality of an educational experience is the provision of sustained discourse between teacher and student.

Black concludes her study of faculty support by stating that accessibility and quality 'should be given more prominence because it alone accounted for most of the variation in faculty support for distance education' (Black 1992: 213). Positions with regard to educational accessibility and quality reflect educators' basic beliefs and assumptions regarding distance education. As distance educators we must be prepared to clarify our assumptions regarding access and quality issues. The emphasis we place on the balance and how we define the issues will most likely reflect our beliefs and assumptions regarding distance education.

## PARADIGMS

Distance education is still predominantly a private form of learning based upon prepackaged course materials produced to achieve economies of scale. The primary purpose of this industrialized model (Peters, cited in Keegan 1990) is to instruct as many students as possible regardless of time and location. Access is the driving motivation behind this design and delivery model. For this reason the model represents a particular set of assumptions regarding the theory and practice of distance education. It is the paradigm that, in fact, reflects the roots of distance education and is based upon accessibility issues.

More recently, some educators (Garrison 1989, Garrison and Shale 1990, Thompson 1990) have begun to focus on the quality aspects of the educational transaction itself. The assumption is that education is based upon two-way communication. The focus has turned towards concern for the quality of the educational transaction. Quality was reflected in the nature and frequency of communication between teacher and student as well as between student and student. While access remains an important consideration the two are not seen to be in conflict. In practice, reasonable choices can be made to find the appropriate balance of quality and accessibility. However, issues of quality and accessibility often reflect important but subtle differences in the design and delivery of distance education.

A crucial difference exists when prepackaged print materials are perceived as the primary source of information and learning as opposed to viewing print as a resource to stimulate reflection and discourse. This is not to say that both views cannot or should not be juxtaposed in practice. But if we are to prevent a polarization of distance education beliefs and practice, then we must become clear as to our assumptions. In short, distance educators must be aware of their ideals which ultimately shape practice and impact learners in significant ways.

When learning materials are prepackaged with prescribed objectives for the purpose of sustaining as much self-instruction as possible, then such an approach inherently reflects a behavioural orientation. The difficulty is that this approach is inappropriate to teach higher-level cognitive strategies based upon understanding of complex and ill-structured content areas (Winn 1990). Self-instructional materials are based upon confirmatory feedback intended to guide the student towards a prescribed learning goal. Higher-level cognitive goals, however, demand opportunities to negotiate learning objectives, encourage students to analyse critically course content for the purpose of constructing meaning, and then validate knowledge through discourse and action.

A cognitive/constructivist approach maximizes explanatory feedback which encourages the integration and construction of new knowledge structures–knowledge structures that are not uncritically assimilated in a superficial manner. The student assumes responsibility to construct meaning. Cognitive learning theory reflects understanding as a valued objective – not just as an observable and measurable behaviour. According to Winn, the challenge is to 'monitor and adapt to unpredicted changes in student behavior and thinking as instruction proceeds' (Winn 1990: 64). This can only be achieved via sustained two-way communication which is within the reach of most distance educators in the industrialized world.

Existing communications technology, such as audio teleconferencing and computer-mediated communication, makes it possible to address both access and quality concerns. The danger is to remain within the dominant paradigm of prescribed and prepackaged course materials and simply using two-way communications as optional 'add-ons'. Salomon *et al.* argue that in terms of cognitive effect 'No important impact can be expected when the same old activity is carried out with a technology that makes it a bit faster or easier; the activity itself has to change (Salomon *et al.* 1991: 8). Holmberg's (1990) view of distance education is that things have not changed very much from traditional correspondence. It is suggested that the reason for this apparent lack of change is that the assumptions of the dominant paradigm (i.e., correspondence) reflect a particular view of the teaching–learning process where the educational ideal is a private independent learner. On the other hand, the cognitive/constructivist ideal of an interdependent teacher–learner is emerging as issues of quality (i.e., communication choice) become more prominent. The activity itself is changing with the adoption of new two-way communications technology and reliance on a collaborative mode. For distance educators the paradigmatic choice is between the ideals of assimilating information faster and more efficiently or challenging learners to construct meaning within a learning community.

## TEACHING AND LEARNING

Distance educators have struggled to define satisfactorily their activities and the major reason for this is the ambiguity as to paradigmatic assumptions regarding the teaching–learning process. The problem is that distinguishing characteristics of distance education too often overemphasize the separation of teacher and student. Shale and Garrison argue that this 'perpetuates an undue emphasis for the form that distance education takes and neglects the critical issue that distance education should be about "education" with the morphological constraints arising from distance being simply a physical and therefore methodological constraint' (Shale and Garrison 1990: 25). Although conceptual ambiguities will be reduced considerably by regarding distance education as education at a distance, the challenge still remains to clarify what is meant by an educational transaction or learning experience.

The assumption here is that education represents a special kind of learning. In other words not all kinds of learning are educational. There is a very important distinction between learning that occurs in the natural societal context and that which occurs in a formal teaching situation. Education is a process most simply characterized as an interaction between teacher and student for the purpose of identifying, understanding, and confirming worthwhile knowledge. The transaction between teacher and student represents a mutually respectful relationship. Education is an exceedingly complex transaction for the purpose of transmitting and transforming societal knowledge. Societal values and beliefs are critically analysed and integrated into individual perspectives such that a new consciousness will emerge.

How distance educators view the educational process will to a large extent determine the meaning ascribed to concepts such as independence and interaction. From the perspective of the dominant paradigm independence is the ultimate goal. The ideal is to design a learning package that would maximize independence and con-comitantly reduce the need for interaction. With the focus on independence distance education was able to make advances in terms of accessibility. Independence is seen as freedom to study when and where the student wishes. Interaction is largely defined in terms of how the student responds to the print package. Juler observes 'that attempts in distance education to encourage independence on the part of students usually entail the educational materials assuming . . . a dominance which severely limits the nature and amount of interaction which may occur' (Juler 1990: 26).

The apparent excessive emphasis on independence in distance education, and the resulting ambiguity of the concept, stimulated Garrison and Baynton (1987) to propose the more inclusive concept of control to account for the complexity of an educational transaction. Control, defined as the opportunity to influence educational decisions, goes beyond the rather simplistic view of independence as a freedom to study when and where the student wishes and without consideration for interaction (Daniel and Marquis 1979). Control is achieved in a complex and dynamic interaction between teacher, student and curricula at the macro level and between proficiency, support and independence at the micro level (see Figure 1.1). From an educational perspective control cannot be possessed by only the teacher or student but should be shared in an inherently collaborative process. The balance of control will depend on specific contextual concerns that are constantly changing and being evaluated.

Since the balance of control is constantly changing (due to what has been learned and to changing needs) maintaining this balance in an educational transaction is dependent upon sustained two-way communication. The reality is that as the ability to communicate diminishes so too does the true control of the educational process and, consequently, the quality of the learning. While control is largely concerned with the external management of the educational transaction, it also has an important indirect influence on the internal cognitive process of constructing meaning. Without sustained interaction there is no way to facilitate critical learning. The quality of an

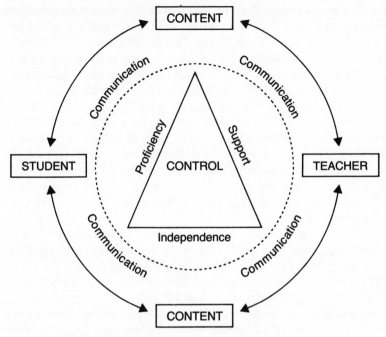

*Figure 1.1*  Control and the educational transaction
*Source:* Adapted from Garrison and Baynton (1987).

educational experience is dependent upon encouraging students critically to analyse differing perspectives, thereby constructing personal meaning and validating that understanding by acting upon it through communicative acts.

The advantage of control is that it is an inclusive concept where both teacher and student roles and responsibilities are considered within a context of communication. If either teacher or learner possess an inordinate or inappropriate amount of control, communcation for critical and meaningful learning is seriously diminished. When an imbalance of control exists, communication is constrained and the quality of the educational transaction is brought into jeopardy. The fallacy is that independence is good and, therefore, the more the better. Unfortunately, all kinds of serious educational learning and motivational problems can evolve when the degree of independence throws control out of proper balance.

It is assumed that interaction is necessary for higher cognitive learning. Cognitive growth or learning is not an autonomous function 'but is the result of the individual's dependency on the communication constraints of the settings in which the individual grows and the patterns of intersubjectivity that the individual's partners invite him or her to establish' (Perret-Clermont *et al.* 1991: 46–7). The primary sources of communication are between teacher and student, student and student, as well as a one-way form of communication from course materials to the student. Students as well as teachers play a very important role in facilitating the cognitive development of fellow-learners. While the control model reflects the immediate educational setting there are many exogenous influences and opportunities for interaction that have an indirect influence on cognition and the validation of knowledge. At some point it may be worth while to expand the scope of the control model to include wider social influences on learning that are perhaps particularly relevant in education at a distance.

In the emerging paradigm, independence takes on quite a different meaning. Independence refers not to an external managerial goal but to a cognitive function. It refers to the student assuming responsibility for constructing meaning in a collaborative or interactive setting. There does not have to be a trade-off between independence and interaction. Interaction is seen as sustained two-way communication for purposes of explaining and challenging perspectives. While accessibility is an important structural consideration, it is seen as a technical issue that can be addressed. The primary focus and concern of the emerging paradigm is interaction and the quality of the educational transaction. It is important to emphasize that students can best create and validate understanding in an interactive environment where concepts are offered, challenged, and acted upon. Perhaps, somewhat paradoxically, the student can best take responsibility for constructing meaning in a rich collaborative environment.

It is beyond the scope of this chapter to consider internal responsibility and external control dynamics of the teaching–learning transaction. However, it must be made clear that accepting responsibility for constructing one's own meaning does not sentence a student to a private learning process. An educational transaction necessitates a sustained interplay between private reflection and external control decisions shared by teacher and learner that indirectly guide the construction of meaning and validation of knowledge. Constructing and validating knowledge requires a responsible learner and a 'critical' (in its best sense) teacher. It is this tension that defines an educational learning experience. Excessive concern with reaching prescribed goals and managing the setting to shape required behaviour will most likely lead to superficial learning outcomes.

## PARADIGMS AND GENERATIONS

The argument thus far has been that the concern for quality in distance education has identified an emerging paradigm based upon two-way communication as a necessary and central component of an education transaction. More specifically the ideal is a collaborative respectful interdependence where the student takes responsibility for personal meaning as well as creating mutual understanding in a learning community. The transaction between teacher and student is characterized by a critical dialogue to understand current knowledge and to encourage the development of new perspectives. In the emerging paradigm the emphasis is on interpersonal and small group communication. Clearly these are ideals but they represent worthwhile and achievable goals in distance education given the new communications technology.

The technology of distance education has been described by Garrison (1985, 1989) as consisting of three generations largely reflecting advances in communications technologies. However, the taxonomy (see Figure 1.1) reflects not simply technological features but also significant shifts in the conceptualization and practice of distance education. Distance education can be seen from the perspective of three developmental stages – correspondence, teleconferencing, and computer-based learning. Before discussing the characteristics of each generation in some detail, it is important to make several points. First, the concept of generation is used to suggest a building upon previous developments. It is not meant to suggest that previous developments are discarded. The reality is that new and current technologies are hierarchically combined to increase technological capacity and choice in designing effective distance education. Second, a clear differentiation is made between technologies capable of supporting two-way communication and media that only send messages one way. Third, pure examples of generations are seldom found. Currently there exists a complex mix of technologies and media that virtually makes it impossible to classify distance methods in terms of one generation or the other. The generations are ideal types but they are useful in understanding the educational applications of the media and to differentiate subtle paradigmatic assumptions.

Communcations technology is the means to address both access and quality issues in distance education. Initially the technology of distance education was used to address the issue of access by overcoming the separation of teacher and student. The first generation of distance education relied upon correspondence and the mail system. In many ways this remains today the primary technology of distance education. This technology is reflective of the dominant paradigm. The great advantages were a cost-effective and efficient method of providing access and meeting the demand for educational services. The downside of the correspondence technology is the dependence upon mail to communicate messages.

The second technological generation, teleconferencing, represented a radical move from the principle of mass access by requiring the student to give up considerable control of when and where to study. On the other hand, what students lost in accessibility they more than gained in quality of interaction. Students were now members of a dynamic learning group where immediate and sustained dialogue was possible not only with the teacher but also with fellow students. Education at a distance was no longer a private affair. With the reality of sustained communication came the realization that education is more than providing access to information. Students were provided with an improved opportunity and climate to analyse ideas, values and perspectives critically and in the process create and validate understanding. In short, teleconferencing represented a 'paradigm shift in the quest to provide sustained interaction and ultimately greater control for both teacher and student over the educational transaction at a distance' (Garrison 1990: 15).

With regard to the computer generation, perhaps the most promising and dominant application is computer-mediated communication (CMC). CMC combines the telecommunications of the second generation with computer capabilities to provide distinct methods of interacting educationally at a distance. The computer's capability for processing and controlling the flow of information may also be used for computer-assisted learning off-line. Until there are significant advances in expert/smart software, off-line computer applications will be best designed to support private learning and thus perhaps seen as an enhancement of the dominant paradigm. On the other hand, CMC like teleconferencing represents a qualitative advance in facilitating interaction at a distance and, therefore, represents an important communication technology in the emerging paradigm.

However, due to the distinctiveness of CMC for supporting an asynchronous exchange of written communication, several issues should be addressed. Communcation by text is by its very nature reflective and delayed. It is therefore very different from the spontaneous and immediate nature of oral communication. Comparatively, one does not inherently represent a higher quality interaction from the other – they simply serve different purposes. In addition, since we have so little experience with this type of interaction many educational questions exist regarding how and when to use it. Feenberg suggests that a decontextualization occurs in computer conferencing and 'it becomes clear that it is not self-sufficient but needs to be supplemented by other means of expression' (Feenberg 1989: 36). Like teleconferencing CMC must be carefully planned and monitored for educational purposes. To enhance the quality of CMC requires the input and direction of a facilitator/teacher to challenge viewpoints, keep the discussion on track, know when to bring the discussion to a close, and to provide a summary. CMC is not seen as a replacement of other forms of communication or as an optional add-on. Its distinctive characteristics must be recognized and considered in its application.

The eclectic collection of hardware labelled ancillary media are differentiated by their inability or inadequacy in supporting two-way communication. They may provide access to information encoded in a variety of symbol systems but, in themselves, do not provide quality two-way communication. This is true of broadcast television which has an attractiveness but an inherent educational limitation. While transmission of a visual image can be an important and even necessary piece of information, broadcast television must be integrated with other forms of communication. Access to visual information may be distributed in a more cost-effective manner using other media. The challenge to distance educators is the integration of technologies and media to meet specific contextual and access needs while striving to maximize the quality of the educational transaction.

There is an inherent risk of losing an educational perspective when distance educators focus too strongly on technologies and become enamoured with new technologies. At the same time it has to be recognized that distance education is dependent upon communication mediated via technology and therefore necessitates an appreciation for technological capabilities while balancing educational needs. It should be reiterated that as generations of technology build upon themselves their distinctiveness becomes less apparent in practice. What must be recognized and addressed consciously are the paradigmatic assumptions that guide the design and delivery of education at a distance. The emerging paradigm necessitates utilizing technologies and media to facilitate an educational transaction that values collaborative and critical interaction while providing access in as affordable a method as possible. Quality is not sacrificed simply for cost-efficiencies and access. Balancing quality and access issues will demand difficult educational decisions.

**CONCLUSION**

In this chapter considerable emphasis has been placed upon quality issues and concerns. Clearly few distance educators would suggest that quality of educational delivery is not an important consideration. The dilemma is that quality is defined in very different ways depending upon one's assumptions and ideals regarding the educational process. Those who view independence as the ultimate educational goal will measure quality in how self-contained the package of learning materials is when supporting the learning process. On the other hand, those who see sustained collaboration as the educational ideal will generally define quality education in terms of the nature and degree of the two-way communication process. These two views or approaches to distance education, which can be documented in practice, have been labelled the dominant and emerging paradigms respectively.

If distance education is to continue to develop as a field of study, then theoretical frameworks will have to be developed that recognize and reflect the differences between the dominant and emerging paradigms – not to artificially create a polarization but to ensure that in the complex world of practice decisions are made with awareness as to the ideals we are striving towards. Education is in essence a social learning experience that is not always compatible with prepackaged course materials designed to enhance private forms of learning. In terms of educational credibility and acceptance the challenge to distance educators is to design and deliver education that is accessible, but not 'intellectual pabulum' to be swallowed without thought. Such a challenge must inherently necessitate consideration and a balancing of accessibility and quality concerns.

There is a growing recognition of the worth of distance education as the field's knowledge base expands and is communicated to the larger educational community. However, the acceptance of distance education as a legitimate field of study and practice will depend upon how education at a distance is designed and delivered. The question is whether our ideals are perceived as being incompatible with the larger educational community. The emerging paradigm reflects a convergence with the general field of education. In the final analysis it is always difficult to justify that distance education is essentially different. A clearer vision is developing that maintains the integrity of the educational transaction and brings distance education into the educational mainstream.

# REFERENCES

Black, E. J. (1992) 'Faculty support for distance education in a conventional university', Unpublished doctoral dissertation, University of British Columbia, Vancouver.

Daniel, J. S. and Marquis, C. (1979) 'Interaction and independence: getting the mixture right', *Teaching at a Distance*, no. 14, 29–43.

Dewey, J. (1933) *How we Think*, Boston: D. C. Heath.

Feenberg, A. (1989) 'The written world', in R. Mason and A. Kaye (eds), *Mindweave: Communication, Computers and Distance Education*, Oxford: Pergamon Press.

Garrison, D. R. (1985) 'Three generations of technological innovation in distance education', *Distance Education*, vol. 6, 235–41.

—— (1989) *Understanding Distance Education*, London: Routledge.

—— (1990) 'An analysis and evaluation of audio teleconferencing to facilitate education at a distance', *American Journal of Distance Education* 4(3), 13–24.

—— and Baynton, M. (1987) 'Beyond independence in distance education: the concept of control', *The American Journal of Distance Education* 3(1), 3–15.

—— and Shale, D. (1990) 'A new framework and perspective, in D. R. Garrison and D. Shale (eds), *Education at a Distance: From Issues to Practice*, Malabar, Fla.: R. E. Krieger.

Holmberg, B. (1990) 'A paradigm shift in distance education? Mythology in the making', *ICDE Bulletin*, no. 22, 51–5.

Juler, P. (1990) 'Promoting interaction; maintaining independence: swallowing the mixture', *Open Learning* 5(2), 24–33.

Keegan, D. (1990) *Foundations of Distance Education* (2nd edn), London: Routledge.

Perret-Clermont, A., Perret, J. and Bell, N. (1991) 'The social construction of meaning and cognitive activity in elementary school children', in L. B. Resnick, J. M. Levine, and S. D. Teasley (eds), *Perspectives on Socially Shared Cognition*, Washington, DC: American Psychological Association.

Salomon, G., Perkins, D. N. and Globerson, T. (1991) 'Partners in cognition: extending human intelligence with intelligent technologies', *Educational Researcher* 19(3), 2–9.

Shale, D. and Garrison, D. R. (1990) 'Education and communication', in D. R. Garrison and D. Shale (eds), *Education at a Distance: From Issues to Practice*, Malabar, Fla.: R. E. Kreiger.

Thompson, D. (1990) 'Some reflections on interaction and independence from research into teletutorials', in T. Evans (ed.), *Research in Distance Education 1*, Deakin University: Institute of Distance Education.

Winn, W. (1990) 'Some implications of cognitive theory for instructional design', *Instructional Science* 19(1), 53–69.

# 2 Theory of transactional distance

*Michael G. Moore*

## TRANSACTIONAL DISTANCE

The first attempt in English to define distance education and to articulate a theory appeared in 1972. Later this was called the theory of transactional distance. What was stated in that first theory is that distance education is not simply a geographic separation of learners and teachers, but, more importantly, is a pedagogical concept. It is a concept describing the universe of teacher–learner relationships that exist when learners and instructors are separated by space and/or by time. This universe of relationships can be ordered into a typology that is shaped around the most elementary constructs of the field – namely, the structure of instructional programmes, the interaction between learners and teachers, and the nature and degree of self-directedness of the learner.

The concept of transaction is derived from Dewey (Dewey and Bentley 1949). As explained by Boyd and Apps (1980: 5) it 'connotes the interplay among the environment, the individuals and the patterns of behaviors in a situation'. The transaction that we call distance education occurs between teachers and learners in an environment having the special characteristic of separation of teachers from learners. This separation leads to special patterns of learner and teacher behaviours. It is the separation of learners and teachers that profoundly affects both teaching and learning. With separation there is a psychological and communications space to be crossed, a space of potential misunderstanding between the inputs of instructor and those of the learner. It is this psychological and communications space that is the transactional distance.

Psychological and communications spaces between any one learner and that person's instructor are never exactly the same. In other words, transactional distance is a continuous rather than a discrete variable, a relative rather than an absolute term. It has been pointed out (by Rumble 1986, for example) that in any educational programme, even in face-to-face education, there is some transactional distance. Seen in this way, distance education is a subset of the universe of education, and distance educators can draw on, and contribute to, the theory and practice of conventional education. Nevertheless, in what we normally refer to as distance education, the separation of teacher and learner is sufficiently significant that the special teaching–learning strategies and techniques they use can be identified as distinguishing characteristics of this family of educational practice.

Even though there are clearly recognizable patterns, there is also enormous variation in these strategies and techniques and in the behaviour of teachers and learners. This is another way of saying that within the family of distance education programmes there are many different degrees of transactional distance. It cannot be emphasized too strongly that transactional distance is a relative rather than an absolute variable. The whole point and purpose of distance education theory is to summarize the different relationships and strength of relationship among and between these variables that make up transactional distance, especially the behaviours of teachers and learners. (It should be pointed out that other variables exist in 'the environment, the individuals and the patterns of behaviors' besides those of teaching and learning. This means there is room for more than one theory. There is need for a theory of distance education administration; a theory of distance education history; a theory of distance learner motivation and so on. The example of distance learner motivation also points out that some theories, such as the theory of transactional distance, are more global than others, and that room exists for more finely focused, molecular theory within the framework provided by a more molar theory.)

The special teaching procedures fall into two clusters; in addition a third cluster of variables describes the behaviours of learners. The extent of transactional distance in an educational programme is a function of these three sets of variables. These are not technological or communications variables, but variables in teaching and in learning and in the interaction of teaching and learning. These clusters of variables are named Dialogue, Structure, and Learner Autonomy.

## INSTRUCTIONAL DIALOGUE

Dialogue is developed by teachers and learners in the course of the interactions that occur when one gives instruction and the others respond. The concepts of dialogue and interaction are very similar, and indeed are sometimes used synonymously. However, an important distinction can be made. The term 'dialogue' is used to describe an interaction or series of interactions having positive qualities that other interactions might not have. A dialogue is purposeful, constructive and valued by each party. Each party in a dialogue is a respectful and active listener; each is a contributor, and builds on the contributions of the other party or parties. There can be negative or neutral interactions; the term 'dialogue' is reserved for positive interactions, with value placed on the synergistic nature of the relationship of the parties involved. The direction of the dialogue in an educational relationship is towards the improved understanding of the student.

Whether dialogue occurs its extent and nature is determined by the educational philosophy of the individual or group responsible for the design of the course, by the personalities of teacher and learner, by the subject-matter of the course, and by environmental factors. One of the most important of the environmental factors – and the one that usually gets most attention from persons both inside and outside distance education – is the medium of communication. As the distance education field matures it is to be hoped that greater attention will be paid to variables besides the communication media, especially design of courses and the selection and training of instructors and the learning styles of students.

## Communications media

It is obvious that the nature of each communications medium has a direct impact on the extent and quality of dialogue between instructors and learners. For example, an educational programme in which communication between teacher and learner is solely by one-way television, an audiotape, or a teach-yourself book, will have no teacher–learner dialogue simply because these media cannot carry messages back from the learner to the teacher. Students usually make internal responses to what is communicated on the one-way medium, but they are not able to make their personal individual responses to the teacher. By comparison, a student taught by correspondence through the mail is able to have two-way interaction and therefore dialogue with the teacher, though the medium slows down the interaction. The dialogue is less spontaneous but perhaps more thoughtful and reflective than a similar course taught in either a classroom or at a computer-mediated conference. It should be apparent that this interactive nature of the medium of communication is a major determinant of dialogue in the teaching–learning environment. By manipulating the communications media it is possible to increase dialogue between learners and their teachers, and thus reduce the transactional distance.

It is worth noting though that, as suggested above, a form of dialogue between teacher and learner occurs even in programmes that have no interaction, such as when the learner is studying through printed self-study materials, or by audiotapes or videotapes. Even in these media there is a form of learner–instructor dialogue because the learner does have an internal or silent interaction with the person who in some distant place and time organized a set of ideas or information for transmission for what might be thought of as a 'virtual dialogue' with, an unknown distant reader, viewer, or listener. By contrast, highly interactive electronic teleconference media, especially personal computers and audioconference media, permit a more intensive, more personal, more individual, more dynamic dialogue than can be achieved in using a recorded medium. Programmes that use such media are therefore likely to bridge the transactional distance more effectively than programmes using recorded media.

There are other environmental factors that influence dialogue and thus transactional distance. These include the number of students each distant teacher must provide instruction to and the frequency of opportunity for communication, usually determined by administrative and financial constraints; the physical environment in which the students learn and the physical environment in which teachers teach (teachers have been known to conduct audioconferences from a telephone in a public hallway and student groups frequently attempt to engage in dialogue through noisy office speaker phones); the emotional environment of teachers, especially the regard, or, more likely, the degree of disregard given to their distance teaching achievements by their administrators; and the emotional environment of learners, especially the regard with which their study is seen by significant persons in their home and work-places.

Dialogue is further influenced by teacher personality, by learner personality, and by content. It cannot be said with certainty that any medium, no matter how interactive its potential, will provide a highly dialogic programme, since it is controlled by teachers who might, for good reasons or bad, decide not to take advantage of its interactivity, and it is used by learners who might not be able or willing to enter into dialogue with their teachers. Finally, experience suggests that the extent of dialogue between teachers and learners in some content areas and at some academic levels is higher than in others where similar media are used. Teaching courses at graduate level in social sciences and education offer opportunity for highly inductive, Socratic teaching approaches, with much small-group work or individual case-study and project work. Teaching basic information courses in sciences and mathematics usually requires a more teacher-directed approach, with considerably less dialogue.

Whatever the dynamics of each teaching–learning transaction however one of the major determinants of the extent to which the transactional distance will be overcome is whether dialogue between learners and instructors is possible, and the extent to which it is achieved.

## PROGRAMME STRUCTURE

The second set of variables that determine transactional distance are the elements in the course design, or the ways in which the teaching programme is structured so that it can be delivered through the various communications media. Programmes are structured in different ways to take into account the need to produce, copy, deliver, and control these mediated messages. Structure expresses the rigidity or flexibility of the programme's educational objectives, teaching strategies, and evaluation methods. It describes the extent to which an education programme can accommodate or be responsive to each learner's individual needs.

As with dialogue, structure is a qualitative variable, and, as with dialogue, the extent of structure in a programme is determined largely by the nature of the communications media being employed, but also by the philosophy and emotional characteristics of teachers, the personalities and other characteristics of learners, and the constraints imposed by educational institutions.

With regard to the media, a recorded television programme, for example, is highly structured, with virtually every word, every activity of the instructor and every minute of time provided for, and every piece of content predetermined. There is no dialogue and therefore no possibility of reorganizing the programme to take into accounts inputs from learners. There is little or no opportunity for deviation or variation according to the needs of a particular individual. This can be compared with many teleconference courses which permit a wide range of alternative responses by the instructor to students' questions and written submissions. These media permit more dialogue and require less structure. A common mistake among unskilled teachers using interactive video or audio is to overstructure their programmes in ways that make them resemble one-way media presentations, and so neglect the potential for dialogue that could be achieved by having a looser structure. When a programme is highly structured and teacher–learner dialogue is non-existent the transactional distance between learners and teachers is high. At the other extreme, there is low transactional distance in those teleconference programmes that have much dialogue and little predetermined structure. As stated earlier (but it cannot be overemphasized), the extent of dialogue and the flexibility of structure varies from programme to programme. It is this variation that gives a programme more or less transactional distance than another.

In programmes with little transactional distance learners receive directions and guidance regarding study through dialogue with an instructor in a programme that has a relatively open structure, designed to support such individual interactions. In more distant programmes, where less or little dialogue is possible or permitted, the course materials are tightly structured to provide all the guidance and direction and advice that course designers can anticipate, but without the possibility of the individual learner modifying this in dialogue with the instructor.

In highly distant programmes therefore, learners have to take responsibility for making judgements and taking decisions about study strategies. Even where a course is structured to give maximum direction and guidance, if there is no dialogue students may decide for themselves whether the instructions will be used, and if so when, in what ways, and to what extent. Thus, the greater the transactional distance, the more such autonomy the learner will exercise.

Since learners are such important actors in the teaching–learning transaction, the nature of the learner – especially the potential to undertake autonomous learning – can have an important effect on the transactional distance in any educational programme. There appears to be a relationship between dialogue, structure and learner autonomy, for the greater the structure and the lower the dialogue in a programme the more autonomy the learner has to exercise.

Successful distance teaching depends on the institution and the individual instructor providing the appropriate opportunities for dialogue between teacher and learner, as well as on appropriately structured learning materials. Frequently this will mean taking measures to reduce transactional distance by increasing the dialogue through use of teleconference, and developing well-structured printed support materials. In practice this becomes an extremely complex matter, because what is appropriate varies according to content, level of instruction, and learner characteristics, especially the optimum autonomy the learner can exercise. Much time and creative effort, as well as understanding of the characteristics of the learner population, have to be devoted to identifying the extent of structure needed in any programme, and in designing appropriately structured presentations and interactions. Much skill is needed to facilitate the degree of dialogue that is sufficient and appropriate for particular learners. To overcome transactional distance in these ways by appropriate structuring of instruction and appropriate use of dialogue is very demanding. It requires the engagement of many different skills and it requires that these skills are systematically organized and deployed. It requires changes in the traditional role of teachers and provides the basis for selecting media for instruction.

In distance education teaching is hardly ever an individual act, but a collaborative process joining together the expertise of a number of specialists in design teams and delivery networks. The typical model is that of the course team of content experts, instructional designers and media specialists, providing structured materials which are then used as the basis for dialogue between learners and specialist teachers (often called tutors). A very rough analogy for this process might be found in the entertainment industry where the medieval troubadours who wrote and sang their own songs gave way in modern times to the television team of writer, singer, producer, camera persons, editors and others. The simile has a very limited application, since there are additional processes that have to be organized in education, such as the need of the learner to have practice, feedback, and counselling.

## Structuring instructional processes

The following are some of the processes that must be structured in each distance education programme.

1 *Presentation*. In most programmes there are presentations of information, demonstrations of skills, or models of attitudes and values. The recorded media (i.e., text, audiotapes, videotapes and computer discs) are usually the most powerful for delivering such presentations. For information with a short shelf life the computer may be preferred over print as a means of rapidly updating information and may also serve as an electronic library for persons who find access to hard copy libraries difficult.

2 *Support of the learner's motivation.* Having planned or been given a curriculum, a programme of content to be taught, course designers and instructors must stimulate, or at least maintain, the student's interest in what is to be taught, to motivate the student to learn, to enhance and maintain the learner's interest, including self-motivation. This is done by various techniques of stimulation within films, recordings and text, through feedback from tutors, and through unstructured, individual, personal teacher–learner dialogue.

3 *Stimulate analysis and criticism.* These are higher order cognitive skills with associated attitudes and values, that learners are expected to develop in higher education. Structuring the development of such skills and attitudes at a distance is especially demanding. The recorded media are often regarded as having special authority, and the student must be assisted to analyse their contents and to challenge them. Ways in which this can be done include hearing experts expose their differences on tape, or organizing discussions by teleconference in conjunction with a recorded or printed presentation.

4 *Give advice and counsel.* The instructional programme must provide guidance on the use of learning materials, on techniques for their study, and some form of reference for individuals who need help with developing study skills and dealing with study problems. Many of these problems can be anticipated and provided through structured teaching materials, but eventually many must be dealt with on an individual basis by telephone, mail, e-mail, and face-to-face interviews.

5 *Arrange practice, application, testing and evaluation.* The students must be given opportunity to apply what is being learned, either the practice of skills that have been demonstrated, or manipulation of information and ideas that have been presented. For this purpose, written assignments delivered by personal computer or by mail are usually important. The tutor is especially valuable in responding to the learners' attempts to apply new knowledge. Even highly self-directed learners are vulnerable in the process of application since they do not know enough about the subject to be sure they are applying it correctly. The well-structured distance education course provides opportunity for dialogue with an instructor as a means of helping the student in this process of reality testing and getting feedback.

6 *Arrange for student creation of knowledge.* The opportunity for students to engage in sufficient dialogue to share with teachers in

the process of creating knowledge has been denied to distance learners until very recently. It is this very important process that promises to be the personal computer's main contribution to distance education.

## Selection and integration of communications media

To deliver teaching programmes that are maximally effective in overcoming transactional distance it is necessary to select the appropriate medium to provide each teaching process, with the appropriateness being dependent in part on other variables in the transactional environment, such as learner characteristics and content characteristics. In general however, some teaching processes can be seen to be more appropriately delivered by certain media.

Table 2.1 suggests, by varying numbers of crosses, the strength of each medium for delivering each of the teaching processes – namely, presentation, motivation, analytic and critical development, application and evaluation, and learner support. The practical significance of this idea is that the course designers apply the idea of dividing the functions of the teacher – and delivering instruction that was assembled by a team of specialists, through numerous media. The learner benefits from the highly structured presentation strengths of the broadcast media as well as from the dialogue possible by correspondence and teleconferencing. (Nevertheless Table 2.1 has to be regarded as a statement of hypotheses, since there is little empirical evidence at present regarding the relative strengths of these media for these processes.)

*Table 2.1* Relationship of dialogue, structure and instruction

| | Media with no dialogue and highly structured | | | | |
| | Pres | Mot | An/Cr | App/Eval | Supp |
| --- | --- | --- | --- | --- | --- |
| Self-study guide | x | x | x | x | |
| Audio recordings/broadcast | xx | xx | x | x | |
| Video recording/broadcast | xxx | xxx | x | x | |
| | Media with dialogue structured | | | | |
| | Pres | Mot | An/Cr | App/Eval | Supp |
| Correspondence | xx | xx | xxx | xxx | xx |
| Video conference | xx | xx | xx | xx | x |
| Audio conference | xx | xx | xx | xx | x |
| PC conference | xx | xx | xxx | xxx | xxx |

*Notes*: *Pres* = presentation; *Mot* = motivation; *An/Cr* = analytic and critical development; *App/Eval* = application and evaluation; *Supp* = learner support.

## THE AUTONOMY OF THE LEARNER

When the theory of Transactional Distance was first put forward it represented a fusion of two pedagogical traditions that, in the 1960s, often appeared to be at war with each other. One was the humanistic tradition, which gave special value to interpersonal, generally open-ended and unstructured dialogue in education as in counselling from which many of the educational techniques were borrowed. The other was the behaviourist tradition, which gave great value to systematic design of instruction that was based on behavioural objectives with maximum teacher control of the learning process. In the early 1970s distance education was dominated by the behaviourists. The importance that was given at the time to challenging the behaviourists' hegemony is indicated by the title of the first paper in which the theory of Transactional Distance was publicly presented (Moore 1972); it was called 'Learner autonomy – the second dimension of independent learning'. In that paper it was argued that university correspondence educators (the term 'distance education' was not yet used) were constraining the potential of their method by neglecting the ability of students to share responsibility for their own learning processes.

Analysis of the data used to generate the concepts of distance, dialogue and structure suggested that there were recognizable patterns of personality characteristics among students who preferred, or who succeeded in, teaching programmes that were more highly dialogic and less structured, compared with those who preferred, or succeeded in, less dialogic and more structured programmes. It also became obvious that many students used teaching materials and teaching programmes to achieve goals of their own, in their own ways, under their own control. The term 'learner autonomy' was chosen to describe this process. Learner autonomy is the extent to which in the teaching/learning relationship it is the learner rather than the teacher who determines the goals, the learning experiences, and the evaluation decisions of the learning programme. A description was given of an ideal, fully autonomous learner (in gender specific terms that would be avoided if the description was written today). This ideal was a person who was emotionally independent of an instructor, a person who in the words of educational psychologist Robert Boyd, 'Can approach subject matter directly without having an adult in a set of intervening roles between the learner and the subject matter' (Boyd 1966). According to Malcolm Knowles such autonomous behaviour should be natural for the adult, who, being adult, has a self-concept of being self-directed. However this state-ment about learner autonomy did not suggest that all adults *were* at a state of readiness for fully self-directed learning. On the contrary, as stated by Knowles, because learners are trained to be dependent in the school system 'adults are typically not prepared for self directed learning; they need to go through a process of reorientation to learning as adults' (Knowles 1970). While only a minority of adults might be practising as fully autonomous learners, the obligation on teachers is to assist them to acquire these skills.

Distance education programmes can be examined to see to what extent the teacher or the learner controls the main teaching–learning processes, and can then be classified according to the degree of learner autonomy permitted by each programme. When this was done with the sample of programmes generated in the inductive study that provides the data for the theory of Trans-actional Distance, a relationship was hypothesized between trans-actional distance on the one hand and learner autonomy on the other. Students with advanced competence as autonomous learners appeared to be quite comfortable with less dialogic programmes with little structure; more dependent learners preferred programmes with more dialogue; some wanted a great deal of structure; while others preferred to rely on the informal structure provided in a close relationship with an instructor. When tested in an empirical study this relationship appeared to exist, but far more testing of this is required before it can be said to have been proved beyond doubt.

## DIALOGUE, STRUCTURE, AND AUTONOMY IN TELECONFERENCE INSTRUCTION

Since the theory of Transactional Distance was written, the most important evolution in distance education has been the development of highly interactive telecommunications media. This is the family of teleconference media – i.e., the use of interactive computer networks and audio, audio-graphic, and video networks, which may be local, regional, national and international and are linked by cable, micro-wave and satellite. Their use has added the possibility of faster dialogue with the teacher and, by computer conferencing, more individual dialogue. These media provide less structured programmes than the recorded or print-interactive media. Above all, the tele-conference media allow a new form of dialogue that can be called inter-learner dialogue. Inter-learner dialogue occurs between learners and other learners, alone or in groups, with or without the real-time presence of an instructor. By audioconference, video-conference, and computer conference, groups can learn through interaction with other groups and within groups. There are enormously significant implications in this potential, in every process of teaching–learning. In particular, such dialogue by learners to learners within and between groups makes it possible for distance learners to share in the creation of knowledge. This engagement of the 'collective intelligence' is what Kowitz and Smith (1987) define as the third and most advanced form of instruction, after teaching basic knowledge and teaching technical abilities. Groups and 'virtual groups' also provide opportunities for exercises aimed at developing skills of analysis, synthesis and critique of knowledge, as well as testing and evaluating. In particular, the personal computer is opening new opportunities through its combined asynchronicity and relative lack of structure. Not only can each individual student interact with the ideas of others, but this can be in his/her own time and at his/her own pace. This is something not available before in either distance education or conventional education. It promises to give all students the benefit of shared learning but to reduce the embarrassments experienced by many students in conventional education, since the slow and reflective student is able to contribute as well as the quicker and more extrovert.

The teleconference media permit learners to exercise and develop autonomy by making presentations to classes and in other ways acting as resources for their peers. Such participation in presentation also reinforces or enhances motivation, including self-direction. Being able to share the activities of teaching, the distance teacher has access to a greater variety of activity than can be accomplished by the teacher alone. Teleconference can provide a more friendly and supportive atmosphere than less dialogic forms of teaching and even many conventional learning environments. It has been a consistently observed phenomenon that students report pleasure at the inter-dependence they develop in teleconferencing. Instructors in tele-conference mode must not overstructure, nor be overanxious about keeping control of the details of the dialogue that develops among students. Persons familiar with writing for academic publication often overstructure, and miss the point that the media being used are powerfully dialogic and therefore permit participation by everyone. Instructors must give everyone frequent opportunities to contribute and be aware of who is not contributing, yet not impose too much pressure.

## THE PLACE OF TELECONFERENCE IN DISTANCE EDUCATION THEORY

The arrival of teleconference technologies offers the opportunity of making a very important modification of figures that were presented in the original theory of transactional distance. A place for teleconferencing must also be found in the typology of programmes that was developed as part of that theory.

In the original theory of transactional distance a series of graphical drawings was used to show relationships between teachers and learners. This was based on Maccia's (1971) figure that showed a conventional classroom as a one in which person A (the teacher) influences persons B, C, D (the students), and was represented as shown in Figure 2.1a.

Following this principle, figures were produced to show distance teaching–learning relationships, with some programmes having lines to show dialogue between teacher and learners, and others with only one-way communication from teacher to learner (see Figures 2.1b–g). In programmes of less structure there were several rays emanting from the source of instruction to represent the greater flexibility from the learner's perspective. (The term 'telematic' was used for 'distance'.)

The modification that is necessary to take into account the impact of teleconference technology is simple, yet has profound implications, as suggested above. It requires a diagrammatic drawing together of the learners into a network or networks that might be independent of the instructor, or at times linked to the instructor. What is shown in these diagrams (see Figures 2.2a–f) is that in all forms of distance education, using such traditional media as correspondence, or highly structured radio or televison broadcasts or tapes, what was before a bilateral relationship between a teacher and a distant learner is

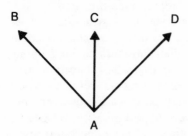

*Figure 2.1a*   Conventional teaching

*Figures 2.1b–2.1g* Forms of distance teaching before introduction of teleconference media

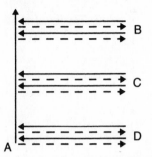

*Figure 2.1b* Telemathic teaching type + D + S (e.g. correspondence)

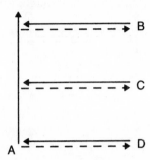

*Figure 2.1c* Telemathic teaching type − D + S (e.g. radio programme)

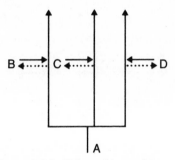

*Figure 2.1d* Telemathic teaching type + S − D (but less structured than Figure 2.1c – e.g. programmed text)

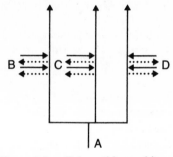

*Figure 2.1e* Telemathic teaching type + S + D (but less structured than Figure 2.1d – e.g. computer-assisted instruction)

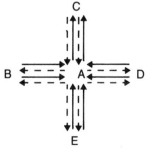

*Figure 2.1f* Telemathic teaching type + D − S (e.g. tutorial)

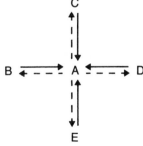

*Figure 2.1g* Telemathic teaching type − D − S (e.g. textbook)

## 36  *Didactic underpinnings*

*Figures 2.2a–2.2f* Forms of distance teaching after introduction of tele-conference media

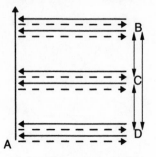

*Figure 2.2a*  Telematic teaching type + D + S (e.g. correspondence)

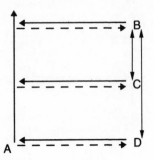

*Figure 2.2b*  Telematic teaching type − D + S (e.g. radio programme)

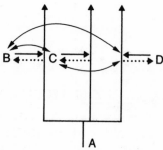

*Figure 2.2c*  Telematic teaching type + S − D (but less structured than Figure 2.2b – e.g. programmed text)

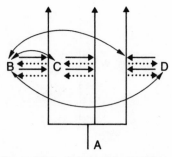

*Figure 2.2d*  Telematic teaching type + S + D (but less structured than Figure 2.2a – e.g. computer-assisted instruction)

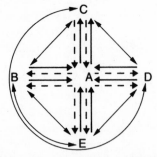

*Figure 2.2e*  Telematic teaching type + D − S (e.g. tutorial)

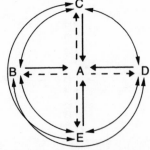

*Figure 2.2f*  Telematic teaching type − D − S (e.g. textbook)

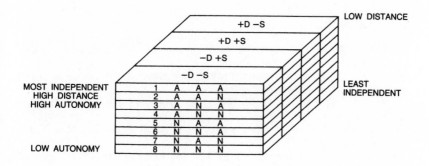

*Figure 2.3* Suggested typology of educational programmes

now a mutilateral relationship that brings an enormous number of dialogues between and among participants.

## THE PLACE OF TELECONFERENCING IN THE TYPOLOGY

The typology of distance education developed in the original theory of transactional distance, as reproduced in Moore (1983) is represented in Figure 2.3.

Compared with broadcast, recorded or correspondence media, learner–instructor interaction by teleconference is more dialogic and less structured. Programmes are −s +d, i.e., less distant. On the original typology they fit approximately above the tutorial and below the correspondence method. What about autonomy? Are learners more able to plan, implement, and evaluate? Compared with self-directed study, no, since there is an instructor who often dominates (or at least influences) planning, implementation and evaluation. Compared with other institutionally provided distance education programmes such as those delivered by correspondence, the higher degree of student participation should result in relatively autonomous learning. There is greater potential for instructors to consult the learner group by audio and video and the individual by computer. There is greater potential for individual self-directed implementation, and more self-evaluation. Above all, there is great potential for peer support and for peer generation of knowledge. Therefore it can be hypothesized that in the hands of progressive teachers, teleconferencing gives opportunity not only to reduce distance but also to increase the autonomy of learners.

## REFERENCES

Boyd, R. A. (1966) 'Psychological definition of adult education', *Adult Leadership* 13, November, 160–81.
—— Apps, J. W. and Associates (1980) *Redefining the Discipline of Adult Education*, San Francisco: Jossey-Bass.
Dewey, J. and Bentley, A. F. (1949) *Knowing and the Known*, Boston: Beacon Press.
Knowles, M. (1970) *The Modern Practice of Adult Education*, New York: Association Press.
Kowitz, G. T. and Smith, J. C. (1987) 'Three forms of instruction', *Journal of Educational Technology Systems*, 15(4) 419–29.
Maccia, E. S. (1971) 'Instruction as influence toward rule governed behavior', in R. Hyman (ed.), *Contemporary Thought on Teaching*, Englewood Cliffs, N.J.: Prentice-Hall.
Moore, M. (1972) 'Learner autonomy: the second dimension of independent learning', *Convergence* V(2), 76–88.
—— (1973) 'Toward a theory of independent learning and teaching', *Journal of Higher Education* XLIV(12), 661–79.
—— (1983) 'On a theory of independent study', in D. Sewart, D. Keegan and B. Holmberg (eds), *Distance Education: International Perspectives*, London: Croom Helm.
Rumble, G. (1986) *The Planning and Management of Distance Education*, New York: St Martins Press.

# 3 Distance education in a postindustrial society

*Otto Peters*

## INTRODUCTION

Distance education has been analysed as a singular product of the era of industrialization (Peters 1967, 1973, 1983, 1989). It could be demonstrated that its structure is determined to a considerable degree by the principles which govern the industrialization of the working process in the production of goods. This means that distance education is also strongly influenced by such principles as, for instance, rationalization, division of labour, the assignment of frag-mented tasks to specialists, mechanization and automation. Some striking similarities are:

1 The development of distance study courses is just as important as the preparatory work prior to the production process.
2 The effectiveness of the teaching–learning process is particularly dependent on very careful planning and adequate organization.
3 The function of the teacher is split up into several subfunctions and performed by specialists as, for instance, in the production process at an assembly line.
4 Distance education can only be economical if the number of students is great: mass education corresponds to mass production.
5 As is the case with the production process, distance educa-tion needs capital investments, a concentration of the available resources, and a qualified centralized administration.

These findings justify the statement that distance teaching is – compared to other forms of instruction–the most industrialized form of teaching. This separates it distinctly from traditional face-to-face teaching in classrooms or in groups which, therefore, to extend the comparison, can be called pre-industrial – that is, structurally similar to the work of a craftsman. Looking at distance education in this way it is easy to maintain that this particular form of teaching and learning is most progressive, as it has adapted to the powerful trends of the era of industrialization – which surely cannot be said of our schools, colleges and universities. Even more, one might also think that this structural peculiarity makes distance education especially conducive to tackling some of the big educational tasks of the future such as, for instance, continuing education for most adults working for a living.

This assumption, however, invites criticism. Do we still live in the era of industrialization? Do we not speak of *post*industrial developments now? Are the principles of industrialization not already in the process of fading out? Is it not, after all, already somewhat old-fashioned to analyse the structure of distance education in terms of industrialization? Will there not be a working world structured differently in many ways? Would it not be more appropriate to inquire into the problem as to whether there are affinities of distance education to postindustrial work processes also? And, finally, if distance education were adapted to postindustrial trends and expectations in the future in order to keep abreast with new societal developments, what would it look like? I shall try to deal with these questions.

Let me, however, make a preliminary cautionary remark before I begin. If we analyse our society in its present state of development we can already discern definite developments breaking away from industrialism. More and more enterprises of the car industry, for instance, are giving up production at the assembly line and are establishing small work groups in which each group member is no longer engaged in one activity but rather in a variety of activities in a craftsman fashion. Opel alone has already established organized teams for roughly 6,000 employees, each of them consisting of eight to twelve members who elect one of them to be their speaker (Eglau 1992: 31). And if we study social, political, and cultural developments we can recognize fundamental shifts in values and value orientation. I only draw attention 'to the emergence and generalisation of subcultures sharing a rejection and critique of the established order' (Wood and Zurcher 1988: 2) as well as to the attempts to create a 'counter-culture' with all its postmodern developments and tendencies in the fine arts.

Although these changes are very impressive, are they really early signs of a 'new era' which might be called '*post*industrial'? Admittedly, there are researchers who have thought so already for quite some time (Boulding 1964; Kahn and Wiener 1967; Bell 1976; Fuchs 1968; Brzezinski 1970; Toffler 1970, 1980; Williams 1982;

Wood and Zurcher 1988; and Peters 1981). And, it is true, some of them even think that these changes have already become very significant. There are observers 'who compare the quality and pervasiveness of this change to the transformations wrought by the industrialising of our society' and refer to postindustrialism as to 'another "revolution" of momentous and far-reaching change' (Wood and Zurcher 1988: 1). And yet, in spite of all this the 'new era' will still remain largely a matter of the future. Therefore, many of the changes in distance education I am going to refer to will necessarily be futuristic ones and, hence, might perhaps not be realized at all. Dealing with them means leaving firm ground and entering the sphere of speculation. However, considering the expected structural changes of distance education will shed some light on the direction to which it might have to develop in order to be complementary to the principles and tendencies of a postindustrial society.

## NATURE OF POSTINDUSTRIAL SOCIETY

What, then, does postindustrial mean? Wood and Zurcher (1988: 22) have suggested that above all society will undergo the following three economic changes:

1  the proportion of labour employed by the tertiary or service sector will dramatically increase;
2  the 'new' technology will emerge;
3  the decision-making structure of the economy, and eventually that in society at large, will change significantly.

The growing *service sector* has already become the major employer of the work-force in highly industrialized countries. This leads to significant changes of work activities and attitudes, and especially of social relations. It may well be that the secondary sector – the industrial production of goods – will cease to be of overriding importance. It could even be that it will be 'forgotten' just like agriculture seems to be forgotten in highly industrialized countries (Kahn and Wiener 1967: 152). The service sector, on the other hand (for instance, banking, accounting, transport, legal, education, health, government, domestic, hotel, gastronomy, repair and entertainment services) will assume even more importance. This means that the quota of highly qualified occupations will definitely become larger, as new postindustrial needs must be met. Because of the knowledge explosion, life-long training and retraining and continuing education will become imperative for them. Bell, for instance, believes that the professionals of the future will never really leave their alma mater as they will have to combine work and academic study (quoted by Peters 1981: 163).

The *'new' technology* comprises the world of computers (mainframe and personal computers, computer networks), communication systems, and further inventions of electronics. 'What counts is no longer raw muscle power, or energy, but information' (Bell 1976: 127). This has already changed many work processes structurally and will continue to do so. As production will use more and more very efficient communication networks 'the physical location of an enterprise is no longer really important' (Norman 1975: 321). And, in addition the work-place of the employee can be chosen at leisure (Peters 1981: 73) – that is, with the help of computer terminals it can also be at his home. This development has already begun. Perhaps the change from industrial technology to 'new' technology will be as fundamental as the change from the craftsman's technology to industrial technology.

The *decision-making structure* will change considerably. 'In the industrial enterprise, power rests with those who make decisions. In the mature enterprise, this power has passed, inevitably and irrevocably, from the individual to the group' (Galbraith 1971: 109). Indeed, the hierarchy will be substituted by groups in which the members make decisions as a group. These groups plan and control their work themselves. Hence, a big enterprise consists of many small decentralized units. There is a high transparency of responsibility. The necessary control of complexity is safeguarded by the sophisticated information system. Democratizing is a dominant trend. Co-determination has a high priority.

What will this mean for the organization of labour processes? The man–machine relation will primarily be substituted by 'a game between persons' (Wood and Zurcher 1988: 12); attention and interest will be focused upon persons everywhere and not upon institutions (Peters 1981: 73).

The central person is no longer the entrepreneur, manager or industrial executive but the professional, for he is equipped, by his education and training, to provide the kinds of skills which are increasingly demanded in the post-industrial society. If an industrial society is defined by the quality of goods as marking the standard of living, the post-industrial society is defined by the quality of life as measured by the services and amenities – health, education, recreation, the arts – which are now deemed desirable and possible for everyone.

(Bell 1976: 127)

Since the employees will render highly personal services, they will also be able to develop and exercise personal skills. Their work experiences will be more completely human and satisfying as they are

*Table 3.1* Management in a postindustrial society

| Traditional assumptions about management | Future assumptions about management |
|---|---|
| *Planning*: An executive function moving the organization | A function for everyone, essentially moving up the organization. |
| *Organizing*: The manager determines how and when work is to be done, assigns it to employees. | The employee determines how and when his work is done within jointly determined deadlines. |
| *Authority and responsibility*: Rests with the manager. He delegates authority commensurate with responsibility. Each employee has one boss. | Authority and responsibility rest with employees who exercise it over their own work. They seek help from managers when it is needed. In matrix organizations employees will have to report to 2 or 3 people. |
| *Staffing*: Management determines the staffing needs and selects employees based on industrial-engineered work systems. | The working group determines the staffing requirements, hires employees, and designates and evaluates managers. |
| *Hierarchy*: There was some limit to the number of people whom one could control. Extent of control was discussed in terms of quantity of workers per manager. | Hierarchy will be significantly flatter since people will be left to manage themselves. |
| *Directing*: The manager directs and motivates the work of subordinates. | Employees are self-directed and self-motivated and turn to management when they need help. |
| *Controlling*: Uses external control systems for management. | Will rely on employee self-control. |

*Source:* Adapted from Elbing and Gordon (1974: 326).

more creative. Work alienation, a typical result of the industrialized production of goods, will diminish (cf. Fuchs 1968: 189).

All of this, of course, will have consequences for the *organization and management* of labour in a postindustrial society. Elbing and Gordon (1974: 326) assume that a number of changes will take place (see Table 3.1).

It is also necessary to outline here significant *changes of values* which have been caused by or are concomitant with postindustrial production processes. They have influenced the *zeitgeist*, the attitudes and behaviour of people and their cultural life at large. More and more we are becoming aware of the emergence of a new type of man – of the 'postmodern self'. This is not a matter of philosophic observation or speculation but can be proved by empirical research. Wood and Zurcher (1988), for instance, have made a quantitative and qualitative analysis of nineteenth-century and more contemporary diaries. In this they have been able to demonstrate definite shifts of values in the following dimensions: from rationality to irrationality, from unemotional performance to emotional expresssion, from institutional roles and standards to individual roles and standards, from societal duty to duty to self, and from achievement to gratification (Wood and Zurcher 1988: 125).

The sense of duty of the nineteenth-century man included 'school work and study of the student' and 'professional and work activities'. The researchers found ideas and themes 'which together constitute an approximation to the values and world-view of the Protestant ascetism' which was described by Max Weber as being one of the preconditions of the rise of capitalism. This means also that they valued 'temperance and moderation' and distrusted and rejected 'creature comfort and sensual experience' (Wood and Zurcher 1988: 126).

It can be easily seen that the new tendencies and trends and the 'postmodern self' have developed as a reaction to, and criticism of, life in the industrial era. This can be illustrated by the following examples, in which the new trends are apparently just the opposite of certain traits characteristic for man in an industrial society.

1 He rejects delayed gratification and restraint, but is more easily motivated to enjoy his work. Therefore, he likes spontaneity, chooses stimulation, and is open for expressiveness (Wood and Zurcher 1988: 13).
2 He is not ready to endure distress, but develops a capacity for joy (Peters 1981: 67).

3 He refuses to do empty routine work, but desires to do something meaningful (Peters 1981: 179).
4 His work is not directed towards materialistic objectives, but rather towards the fulfilment of human values. Consequently, his life will not be dominated by the restless pursuit of profit, but by his wish to develop his personal potential.
5 The objective of his work is not achievement, but self-realization.
6 He does not like self-control, but seeks self-expression.
7 He rejects competition. He does not like to rise in the hierarchy of his enterprise, but is rather interested in a good work climate.
8 He does not like to become isolated, but is interested in social relations. He seeks *inter*-dependence rather than independence (Peters 1981: 67). He is ready to restore 'conviviality' (Ilich 1973: 2).
9 He will not participate in exploiting nature, but rather develop ecologically harmonious life and work processes (Peters 1981: 66).

These observations indicate, indeed, that the postindustrial era will bring about broad shifts in culture and values. Our modern culture may turn post-modern.

## STRUCTURES OF INDUSTRIALIZED EDUCATION

If we analyse the structure of distance education after having dealt with principles and trends both of the industrial and postindustrial period, we can clearly see that distance teaching is still basically an industrialized form of teaching. This is not surprising at all, as the principles and trends of industrialization are still potent in our society and, of course, also in the production of goods. The powerful influences of a development of more than 150 years will not cease to be effective because of the new postindustrial principles and trends referred to, although these latter might become stronger in the future. On the other hand, a closer look at distance education reveals four elements which, indeed, correspond with postindustrial tendencies, not only contemporarily but also right from its beginning: the learner can be dislocated from the class or lecture room to his home or to a working place in his company, as mediated instruction is primarily being used; more than other forms of teaching it calls for the self-reliant, self-directed learner; distance education has always promoted social interactions among the students; and it has a strong affinity towards new electronic media.

1 What is predicted for the production of goods – namely, that the employee will no longer be tied to a given place of work due to

the use of technical communication systems – has been routine in distance education already for more than 150 years. Indeed, the students need not meet their teachers regularly at given places but work independently, the main means of communication being the printed paper and the written letter.

2 In distance education it has always been necessary that the learner takes over responsibilities for his own learning – a function which in other circumstances rests with the teacher or the teaching institution. The learner, therefore, is given the opportunity to develop *self-determination, self-direction* and *self-control* to a high degree. He determines where, when, and how long he wants to engage himself in the learning process. If distance education also comprises contract learning the student is also able to determine or co-determine *what* he or she wishes to learn and *how* to control and evaluate the results of this learning.

3 Although many proponents of distance education expect the development of teaching material which is truly self-instructional – which means that it can be studied without the help of a teacher – it is also well understood that *social interactions in face-to-face situations* are important. Therefore, most open universities have provided for study centres in many parts of their countries. And these study centres very often provide for social interactions, which ironically are likely to be more personal than, for instance, at institutes of higher learning, especially in European countries. Also, when it is difficult to provide premises and tutors for such activities the learners are often encouragd to take the initiative in establishing *self-help groups*. Here again they act as self-determined individuals relatively independent of the teachers and teaching institution.

4 Already, at a very early date, distance education has developed a great affinity with the new electronic communication systems: radio and television as well as the computer are being used. And more and more electronic communication media are integrated into the teaching–learning system. It can be predicted that this tendency will become stronger in the years to come. This separates distance education from traditional forms of teaching and learning which have strong tendencies to resist the use of such media.

We can see that within the structure of the most industrialized form of teaching and learning the seeds of postindustrial developments can already be found.

## EFFECTS ON DISTANCE EDUCATION

If the postindustrial tendencies referred to become stronger and change working processes in the way I have indicated – and, above all, if the post-modern value system permeates our culture – will this leave distance education unscathed? Will distanced education stick to its structure, to its guiding principles and to its accumulated experience which, after all, have established its extraordinary success? Or will it adapt to the societal changes and develop new forms of distance education? Nobody knows, of course. The chances are, rather, that the big distance teaching insitutions in particular will be so bureaucratized and structurally inflexible that this will probably never happen. But it may also well be that definite changes will be suggested and tried out. If so, what would a postindustrial distance education look like?

Before I go into this, however, I should like to suggest that post-modern tendencies have already arrived at the Fernuniversität in Hagen. That is to say if we analyse the attitudes of the students we can see that they no longer correspond to the traditional image of the ambitious social climber who desires to earn more money and to gain more status in his company. On the contrary. When students were asked which criteria of job description they valued most, 'work satisfaction' ranked highest, immediately followed by 'independence of work' and 'personal interest in work' – whereas 'high salary' was in seventh place and 'high status and prestige' only in fifteenth place down at the bottom of the list (Bartels 1986: 179). Accordingly, general and academic goals of study which may help in the process of self-realization are already more important than strictly vocational or professional goals (Bartels 1986: 216). Obviously, the image of the 'typical' student of industrialized distance education must now be shaped anew and adapted to these facts indicating postindustrial influences.

It would seem to be all the more necessary to depict a postindustrial model of distance education.

### Demand

The definite increase of the *service sector* of society will lead to the establishment of many new jobs, just as the process of industrialization in the nineteenth and twentieth centuries created many new jobs beyond craftsmanship. If the key person of the new era is going to be the professional, the role of scientific knowledge and technology will be at a premium and assume even greater importance. This means that, much more than is the case now, schools and institutes of higher learning and providers of continuing education will be a decisive factor in the development of society. As lifelong learning will have ceased to be merely a slogan by then, and will, indeed, be practised widely, and also as many adults will not be able to attend these learning institutions, there could be an even greater demand for distance education than there was in the industrial era in which it developed.

## Students

We must, however, also face the possibility that demand will decrease substantially in spite of this if distance education continues to stick to its traditional industrial patterns. We must ask ourselves whether persons in the postindustrial era will still be ready to undergo the strains of learning at a distance in addition to their vocational, professional and family obligations? Will they have the persistence to do this for many years – up to ten and more years, for example, in open universities? Will they really sacrifice so much of their leisure time which they could use otherwise for their family or recreation? Will not the hedonistic tendencies of the new era distract them from carrying this burden?

Knowing that postindustrial man will not be ready to delay gratification for his endeavours; that he will reject competition in the working world and in learning processes; that he will not be interested in material satisfaction and, hence, does not react to financial incentives but will rather seek wholesome social relations and cultural satisfaction (Peters 1981: 66); and knowing also that the powerful influence of Protestant ascetism will lessen and, perhaps, eventually fade away, these questions must be answered in the negative. Apparently, in distance education the image of the 'typical' student who wishes mainly to improve his vocational status and his income by climbing up in the hierarchy of his company or by changing positions does not hold true any longer. This means that correspondence colleges and open universities will lose the majority of their clients and their traditional *raison d'être*. Possibly, an entirely new type of student will emerge with new value systems, new needs and new priorities. He or she will enrol for distance education for different reasons and seek experiences which so far have not been provided for.

**Objectives**

The dominating goal will be *self-realization*, which will bring about the emergence of the post-modern self which 'chooses stimulation, openess to experience, and expressiveness' (Slater 1970), and stresses personal duty, happiness, and enjoyment (Yankelovich 1981). Furthermore, there will also be the goal of *improving the qualification for a job*, preferably in the service sector. This goal seems to be a continuation of the most important goal of distance education in the industrial society. However, if we take note of and, possibly, appreciate what has been said about the post-modern self, we cannot but assume that this goal will have to be interrelated with the goal of self-realization. Considerable changes will have to take place here as well.

**Structure**

I believe that – seen from a post-modern point of view – the double burden of a full-time job and a long intensive period of learning at a distance will be considered as 'inhuman' for two reasons. First, the students have to strain every nerve for too long a time. Second, the additional demands on them divorce them more or less from their families, their neighbours and friends, and reduce their civic, social and political contacts. Because of this neglect of fundamental personal needs this system will no longer be feasible in its original industrialized form. The only way out is a combination of part-time work and part-time study. Already many young persons like to work part-time only in order to have more time for 'themselves' – that is, for family or social activities – and thus have more time to enjoy life as long as they are young. Why not also use such additional time for learning at a distance in a post-modern way?

As far as continuing vocational and professional education is concerned it might be possible to develop more of those models which are already practised by big international electronic companies and which integrate distance education into the daily work processes. Learning is thus an important element of the job to be performed and does not require additional time and fees and relieves the learner of the double burden referred to.

**Curricular aspects**

When deciding about the contents of courses in distance education it is obvious that we have to realize that people in the postindustrial society will be interested in the present rather than in the future; that they – in a nihilistic manner – will reject the tradition of enlightenment, especially the optimistic belief in the unending progress of society and the confidence in scientific advancement; that they will have given up all ideological schemes and utopian programmes of societal reform; that they will have to find out for themselves what will be 'meaningful' in a given situation, realizing, of course, that – in a pluralistic society – the values they find to be relevant will be different from those of other persons and in no way better. They will have a preference for social relations and social problems; will be open to aesthetic and ethical issues; will seek cultural satisfaction; and will like to live in harmony with nature. A realm of attractive themes can be derived from this new state of consciousness with its reassessment of so many values. Probably, all courses will have to be rewritten.

In addition, courses for qualifying and updating learners for jobs – not only in the service sector – will be influenced by this new understanding. These courses will probably no longer aim at vocational or professional competence in a narrow and one-dimensional sense, but will enable the learner to become aware of the complexity of work situations and of multidimensional approaches to the understanding and mastering of them.

If distance education will not comply with such new requirements it can be predicted that there will be a growing discontent with the curriculum of many courses, as students may think that the contents of teaching and learning are too far away from everyday problems of vital importance be they, for instance, social, political or ecological. Similar arguments to those voiced by the protesting students of 1968 may be aired, but this time for different reasons.

## Methods

So far the backbone of distance education has usually been the sustained and careful study of specially developed and painstakingly prepared standardized *course material*. Tutorials and group work, in which the learners meet face to face with a teacher and fellow students, are usually only complementary. In postindustrial society it may be just the other way round. There might be a growing number of students unwilling to study in isolation from other students and teachers as they are mainly interested in people and social relations. The paradigmatic 'lone wolf' who relies on his own learning strategy and on his extraordinary endurance in order to 'survive', and who considers co-operation with other students merely a loss of time, will cease to be typical of many distance students. Since post-modern students will have a strong desire to develop and experience *social relations*, forms of learning which provide for them will have to be emphasized. As predicted for the working process, the emergence of *autonomous groups* will become the main constituent of the learning process. They could be local or regional and meet face to face, and in addition to this communicate with each other with the help of traditional or new technical media (teleconferencing). They will have a 'critical group size' – that is, the groups are not to have more members than can be managed without a hierarchy. These groups will render opportunities for the development of a wholesome and enjoyable work climate. They will allow feelings of togetherness and belonging. And they will encourage spontaneity and self-expression.

*Self-study*, on the other hand, will only be complementary to the work in these groups. Ideally, it will not be normalized and standardized by special course material but will be 'open' in the sense that the learners themselves acquire the information they need in given situations. Clearly, it will be an important objective of this method of study to enable the students to store and to retrieve information which will be relevant to their learning process with the help of computers and to develop and refine this particular skill.

As post-modern students want to live their lives now and not, so to speak, postpone them for some time in the future, they will look for attractive and pleasant learning experiences which are not only a means to an end but also ends in themselves. They will have to be already rewarded in the process of learning in many ways.

Since postindustrial persons reject dull routine work and prefer creative work in the production process, they are likely to behave accordingly in the teaching–learning process. This means that traits of behaviour such as, for instance, openness, originality, and flexibility will be highly valued and that models of teaching and learning will be preferred that provide especially for this type of acquisition of knowledge and skills.

## Technical media

The impact of the 'new' technology will, without doubt, become stronger. Distance education will continue to rely increasingly on differentiated electronic communication systems. The tools of learning of the home-based student will no longer consist mainly of printed material and books but will also involve the use of audiocassettes, videocassettes, diskettes for the computer, and compact discs. Furthermore, the students will use the telephone (conference call), telefax, viewdata, teletex/telex, datex, videoconference, as well as radio and television in order to acquire the additional information they need for their studies (Wurster 1989: 9). Thus, the ubiquity of relevant information enables them to stay at home for some of their learning activities. This will be considered to be quite natural as more and more workers are dislocated from the production process by means of sophisticated technical media. It is possible that the image of the learner in distance education as an extraordinary person who does not really belong to the mainstream of education will disappear.

**Organization**

Will the expected disintegration of hierarchies in working situations have an impact on the relationship between the learner and his distance-teaching institution and its representatives? Analysing post-industrial trends one cannot but assume that this will, indeed, be the case. It may well be that adult learners with experience of life and work will seek to emancipate themselves from being dependent on a hierarchy of persons in the teaching institute and its bureaucracy. Rather, they will insist on determining themselves what and how to learn. They will try to become autonomous in this field as well. This means that the functions of the teaching institutions will change in so far as they will become primarily service agencies whose main role it is to motivate, to inform, and to advise the students expertly.

This change could also have consequences for the management of learning. Here, I should like to refer again to Elbing and Gordon (1974: 5) who made assumptions about postindustrial management of work processes. It seems to be more than probable that if the principles and trends in a postindustrial society become so strong that they change the management of work processes as indicated in this comparison they might also change the management of learning processes. These changes could take place on the following levels. *Planning*: would be a function of the student individually or as member of a group and no longer mainly decided upon beforehand by groups of experts in ministries or in the teaching institution. *Organizing*: the student determines 'how and when his work is done within jointly determined deadlines'. *Authority and responsibility*: rests with the students 'who exercise it over their own work. They seek help from' teachers, or counsellors 'when it is needed'. *Hierarchy*: 'will be significantly flatter since' the students 'will be left to manage themselves'. *Directing*: students are 'self-directed and self-motivated'.

*Controlling*: will rely on self-control. The definite shifts described indicate that the organization of the learning process in the post-industrial society might become entirely different in many ways.

## Institutional aspects

A great number of distance teaching institutions will probably no longer try to impress students by their sheer institutional greatness and importance. Rather, they will place greater emphasis on the students and students' needs, and focus upon students' learning activities in order to prevent them from feeling dependent, unimport-ant, weak and exposed to a powerful bureaucracy. This will mean a definite departure from a highly centralized organization of the teaching–learning process and a move to small decentralized units which can be made transparent by the means of new technology.

## THREE PERSPECTIVES

When postindustrial models of distance education are discussed and developed in the years to come it will be helpful to have theoretical guidelines at hand and to know about the theoretical underpinnings of the expected changes of teaching and learning. Although the elaboration of such theories is still a desideratum, it seems possible to refer to some preliminary theoretical approaches. I should like to illustrate them with three examples: the *Lebenswelt* perspective, the ecology perspective, and the concept of instructional design.

### The *Lebenswelt* perspective

In order to appreciate the changes suggested by this theoretical perspective one should keep in mind that there was a so-called *realistic or pragmatic perspective* of adult education which was very influential in the Federal Republic of Germany from about 1965 to 1975. It is a good case for illustrating how strongly requirements of a growing industrialized economy also influenced the theory of adult education. According to the theoretical perspective, the main objec-tive of adult education was the increase of vocational and professional qualifications on all levels in order to improve industrial production and to remain successful in international economic competition. Critics of this concept called it 'technocratic', as it instrumentalized the learner and the learning process which thus became mere means to an end.

In the 1970s, however, a radical change took place as the *Lebenswelt* of the individual learner and his subjectivity assumed a high priority. The general goal of adult education was no longer primarily better qualification for better jobs, but personality building. Experts became aware of how important it is for the teacher to explore and to understand the *Lebenswelt* of the learner, both in a biographical sense and in the sense of how the learner perceives, interprets and understands his or her social environment. The main objective became the development of the learner's identity. All of this could be achieved by direct social interaction only. Dialogues and group discussions were considered to be the best means of accomplishing this, with no other didactic instruments being substitutable for them.

This new perspective was developed mainly by experts who were disappointed with the results of the big educational reform schemes of the 1960s and 1970s which were typical outgrowths of an industrialized society. They discovered, instead, the individual adult learner and his situation. Thus, the learner ceased to be just a mere element of a teaching–learning system usually dominated by the teaching institution and instead was located directly in the centre of interest. It was the learner's individuality which counted now. This shift of emphasis must be borne in mind when we conceive, plan and prepare post-modern learning situations for distance education – this can be said although the proponents of this particular theoretical perspective never characterized their approach as post-modern. The new perspective suggests that a teaching–learning system, in which thousands of students study the same carefully prepared, standardized and pretested learning material and are tested according to the same predetermined categories, is clearly an industrialized approach. As such it will not be considered educationally sound at all in a postindustrial society.

## The ecology perspective

This theoretical perspective of adult education was suggested by Siebert (1985: 589). According to him it not only aims at making the students 'environment-conscious' but also at a radical and far-reaching change of the way in which nature is perceived and understood. It rejects causal and analytical ways of thinking in the tradition of Galileo and Descartes which, on the one hand, paved the way for outstanding scientific and technological achievements and eventually for the triumphant advance of industrial society and, on the other, for the 'control, exploitation, and manipulation of nature'.

In the context of this chapter it is sufficient to point out that the rejection of causal and analytic ways of thinking and of empirical approaches based on them can also be related to teaching and learning. The proponents of the ecological perspective are certainly not in favour of teaching–learning systems which are carefully planned, controlled and evaluated down to the smallest detail. That is, they are opposed to the technology of education. Rather, they recommend 'self-initiated, global learning'. They no longer expect relevant learning to take place in traditional institutions but rather in new social movements and civic action groups. They expect that here new forms of learning will emerge which will lead to 'global, interrelated, systemic, complementary and dialectic ways of thinking'. Siebert considers this to be an explicitly post-modern development.

This perspective is usually presented with a sense of urgency as the continued expansion of the industrial systems endangers and destroys our natural environment which is a fundamental requirement of our life. Distance education in a postindustrial society will have to include the ecological perspective in order to help to change traditional scientific and empirical ways of thinking. The new thinking will have to rely much more on qualitative than on quantitative standards and will have to develop nothing less than a new ethic. This means that distance education will have to redefine its objectives, extend its curricular scope considerably, and employ new methods of self-initiated and self-directed learning.

## The concept of 'instructional design'

Flechsig (1987) maintains that the concept of 'educational technology', which is widely used in a number of countries, will no longer be sufficient in a postindustrial era. And, indeed, if we analyse it, we will see that it is a typical product of industrial society. It presupposes that instruction can be planned, evaluated and improved considerably in the same way as the production of goods can be planned, evaluated and improved. Therefore, Flechsig seeks other theoretical explanations and looks for a model of teaching and learning which is open for the new phenomena of the postindustrial society. He calls it 'instructional design'. This model revolves around the concept that teaching is more than handicraft and technique, and more than a system which can be fully determined by scientifically based decisions – namely, that it is an art as well. It also indicates that not all elements of the teaching–learning process can be at the disposal of those who plan and develop instruction – especially not the student's self-determination in instructional matters. The term 'design' is partly used because of its origin in the fine arts. It suggests that the persons who design instruction are fully aware of unpredictable factors of the learning situation, factors which are new and cannot be standardized and reproduced *ad libitum*. This refers to the more pragmatic, but also to the aesthetic, ethical and moral dimensions of instruction.

In order to characterize the new concept some of its more typical features will be specified:

1 Students and their learning take precedence over teachers and their instruction.
2 Teaching does not primarily mean the direct intervention of a teacher but rather the development of favourable learning environments.
3 The educational quality of a learning environment is not only measured with regard to professional norms or predetermined teaching objectives, but also with regard to its functionality, its meaningfulness and the quality of life it brings.
4 Learning environments may have to be separated and isolated from life, but at the same time they will have to represent part of the *Lebenswelt*.

According to Flechsig, the concept of instructional design is a typical product of our time indicating the transition from the modern to the post-modern society.

If developers of distance education want to orient themselves with the help of this concept they will be urged to accept and to implement fundamental structural changes. Obviously, the role of learners will have to become a more prominent one. Their being presented with standardized and prefabricated course material of some length with computerized control will simply not do any longer. We will have to find ways in which the learner takes the initiative in most phases of the teaching–learning process, and this must include more say in curricular decisions and methods of control and evaluation. The planners of distance education will also have to concentrate on the task of dealing with the students indirectly – that is, by developing learning environments which are conducive to open learning situations in which the students are encouraged to become active in organizing and managing their learning processes themselves. And, finally, the planners of distance education will have to deal with the problem of how to transform the learning experience in such a way that it is no longer just a preparation for some specific future goal but also a representation of life itself, with a resultant improvement in the quality of living.

## CONCLUSIONS

Drawing conclusions from the above, the following statements can be made:

1 Distance education is, indeed, a typical product of industrial society. This not only applies to its inherent industrial principles and trends but also to the fact that distance education has been capable of meeting educational needs typical of an industrialized economy and that it could attract and keep highly motivated students who wish to improve their vocational or professional status as well as their income, sacrificing their leisure time for gratifications often delayed for many years.

2 In a postindustrial society the traditional industrial model of distance teaching will no longer satisfy the new needs of new types of students with their particular expectations and values which, seemingly, not only differ from those of the students in the industrial society but are in many cases even the exact opposites of them.

3 This situation calls for the design of new models of distance education. They will probably by combinations of intensified and sustained group work – highly sophisticated ways of acquiring the necessary information for self-study and increased telecommunication between the participants. They will have different sets of goals and objectives. And they will have to rely on self-directing and self-controlling – that is, on students becoming autonomous.

This means that the shift from industrial to postindustrial distance education will be a Copernican one. Slight and superficial alterations will certainly not do.

## BIBLIOGRAPHY

Bartels, J. (1986) *Die Absolventen des Fachbereichs Wirtschaftswissenschaft. Eine empirische Untersuchung*, Hagen: Fernuniversität, Zentrum für Fernstudienentwicklung.
Bell, D. (1975) *Die nachindustrielle Gesellschaft*, Frankfurt am Main: Campus Verlag.
—— (1976) *The Coming of Post-Industrial Society: A Venture in Social Forecasting*, New York: Basic Books/Harper Colophon.

## 58 Didactic underpinnings

Boulding, K. E. (1964) *The Meaning of the Twentieth Century: The Great Transition*, New York: Harper & Row.

Brzezinski, Z. (1970) *Between Two Ages: America's Role in the Technetronic Era*, New York: Viking.

Eglau, H. O. (1992) 'Schlank und rank. Deutsche Industrielle übernehmen die Methoden der Japaner', *Frankfurter Allgemeine Zeitung*, 14 February, p. 31.

Elbing, A. and Gordon, J. (1974) 'Self management in Flexible organizations', *Futures*, 6,326.

Flechsig, K-H. (1987) *Didaktisches Design: Neue Mode oder neues Entwicklungsstadium der Didaktik?* Göttingen: Universität Götingen, Institut für Kommunikationswissenschaften und Unterrichtsforschung.

Fuchs, V. R. (1968) *The Service Economy*, New York: National Bureau of Economic Research.

Galbraith, J. K. (1971) *The New Industrial State*, New York: The American Library/Mentor.

Illich, I. (1973) *Tools for Conviviality*, New York: Harper and Row.

Kahn, H. and Wiener, A. J. (1967) *The Year 2000*, New York: Macmillan.

Norman, A. L. (1975) Informational society', *Futures* 7, 321.

Peters, N. A. (1981) *Arbeits- und Organisationsgestaltung in einer postindustriellen Gesellschaft*, Stuttgart: Haupt.

Peters, O. (1967) *Das Fernstudium an Universitäten und Hochschulen*, Weinheim: Beltz.

—— (1973) *Die didaktische Struktur des Fernunterrichts. Untersuchungen zu einer industrialisierten Form des Lehrens und Lernens*, Weinheim: Beltz.

—— (1983) 'Distance teaching and industrial production. A comparative interpretation in outline', in D. Sewart, D. Keegan and B. Holmberg (eds), *Distance Education: International Perspectives*, London: Croom Helm.

—— (1989) 'The iceberg has not melted: further reflections on the concept of industrialisation and distance teaching', *Open Learning* 6, 3–8.

Siebert, H. (1985) 'Paradigmen der Erwachsenenbildung', in *Zeitschrift für Pädagogik*, 31, 5, 577–96.

Slater, P. E. (1970) *The Pursuit of Loneliness. American Culture at the Breaking Point*, Boston: Beacon.

Toffler, A. (1970) *Future Shock*, New York: Random House.

—— (1980) *The Third Wave*, New York: Morrow.

Williams, F. (1982) *The Communications Revolution*, Beverly Hills: Sage.

Wood, M. R. and Zurcher, L. A. (1988) *The Development of Postmodern Self*, New York: Greenwood Press.

Wurster, J. (1989) *The Future of Media in the Fernuniversität*, Hagen: Fernuniversität, Zentrum für Fernstudienentwicklung.

Yankelovich, D. (1981) *New Rules: Searching for Self-fulfillment in a World Turned Upside Down*, New York: Random House.

# Part II
# Academic underpinnings

# 4 The evolution of theory in distance education

*Cheryl Amundsen*

## INTRODUCTION

Reasoning that the emergence of a new set of problems is the necessary precursor to the establishment of a separate discipline, some have proposed that distance education should be considered a discipline in its own right (Sparkes 1983, Gough 1984, Holmberg 1986). Others might hesitate to speak of a 'discipline' *per se*, but rather view distance education as a 'coherent and distinct field of educational endeavour' (Keegan 1986: 6). Still others choose to refer to simply the 'field' of distance education based on the view that 'there is nothing uniquely associated with distance education in terms of its aims, conduct, students or activities that need affect what we regard as education' (Garrison 1989: 8).

Despite differences in orientation, there is agreement that the definitive characteristic of distance education is the separation between teacher and learner and that this provides a basis for inquiry. Two areas which must be addressed in any effort to distinguish an area of study are theory development and a systematic approach to research.

Over the last two decades, several theoretical frameworks have been proposed which seek to encompass the whole of activity in distance education. Notable contributions have been made by Otto Peters, Michael Moore, Börje Holmberg, Desmond Keegan, D. R. Garrison (and Myra Baynton and Doug Shale), and John Verduin and Thomas Clark. In the following discussion, each of these six contributions will be discussed from the perspective of their possible place in the evolution of theory in distance education. A synthesis of these works will be provided and directions for further theoretical development will be suggested. Detailed explanations of the six frameworks and the background references drawn on in the development of the frameworks will not be provided here. The unfamiliar reader should refer to other sources for a more comprehensive treatment (see, for example, Holmberg 1989 and Keegan 1990).

## A COMPARISON OF DISTANCE EDUCATION AND THE INDUSTRIAL PROCESS

In 1967, Peters (English version revised by the author, 1983) suggested that distance education is a product of the industrial society. To justify his notion, Peters provides a comparison between distance teaching and the industrial production process, identifying mutual characteristics such as division of labour, mechanization, mass production, standardization and centralization. Peters has strongly denied that this comparison constitutes a theory of distance education (Peters 1989), but as it presents a perspective which is considerably different from other contributions discussed here, it cannot be easily excluded from this discussion.

Peters contends that distance education, in its present form, is a product of the industrial society. Distance education as an educational option has been successful because it is compatible with the organization, principles and values of the present industrial society. In his contribution to this book, Peters follows the same reasoning in describing how distance education must now change to match the changes in our industrial society as we enter a postindustrial or postmodern era. This shift is already apparent in many sectors of the society and is reflected in, among other things, the emergence of new, more individualized technology, more decentralized decision-making, and personal values that focus on quality of life, self-realization, self-expression, and interdependence rather than independence.

## A THEORY OF TRANSACTIONAL DISTANCE AND LEARNER AUTONOMY

Over a period of more than ten years, Moore (1972, 1973, 1983, 1986) developed and refined a theory of independent learning and teaching. The theory is composed of two dimensions, transactional distance and learner autonomy. The dimension of transactional distance includes more than geographical distance. Most recently, Moore has described it as:

> The transaction that we call distance education occurs between individuals who are teachers and learners, in an environment that has the special characteristic of separation of one from another,

and a consequent set of special teaching and learning behaviours. It is the physical separation that leads to a psychological and communications gap, a space of potential misunderstanding between inputs of instructor and those of the learner, and this is the transactional distance.

(Moore 1991: 2–3)

Moore maintains that while distance education is education and we can apply much of what we know about theory and practice in conventional education, it is, in effect, the extent of transactional distance that will determine the need for unconventional thinking and practice. The extent of transactional distance is a function of two variables, dialogue and structure. Dialogue describes 'the extent to which, in any educational program, the learner, the program and the educator are able to respond to one another' (Moore 1983: 157). For example, in a programme which offers only printed instructional materials to the learner, no dialogue results. A correspondence programme which provides written feedback or comments on assignments provides varying amounts of (written) dialogue. A programme that combines correspondence and teleconferencing is even more dialogic.

The second variable, structure, is described as 'a measure of an educational program's responsiveness to learners' individual needs' (Moore 1983: 157). More structured programmes set course starts and ends, have established due dates for assignments, use packaged course materials designed for more than one set of students, etc. Less structured programmes allow course registration throughout the year, submission of assignments within a broad time period, and contract individually with students as to course composition.

The other dimension of Moore's theory, autonomous learning, is related to the first in that 'the greater the transactional distance, the more autonomy the learner has to exercise' (Moore 1991: 5). Although the notion of learner autonomy is treated only briefly and without positive or negative value in Moore's (1991) most recent discussion, it is of central importance to his earlier thinking. Moore considers autonomy the ideal towards which each individual will move by virtue of maturation. An autonomous learner will, in his view, seek out a teacher for help in formulating problems and gathering information. He/she will temporarily surrender some autonomy, but Moore believes that a truly autonomous learner will not relinquish overall control of the learning process.

Moore (1976) hypothesized that since distant teaching programmes, by their structure, require more autonomous behaviour from learners, the kinds of people who participate successfully in such programmes will be measurably more autonomous. Additionally, he hypothesized that the more distant the programme, the more autonomous the learners who will choose to participate. These hypotheses were tested and personality-by-treatment interactions were found which tended to at least partially support the first hypothesis. However, others who have sought to test similar hypotheses with various personality measures have obtained mixed results (Thompson 1984, Nelson 1985, Thompson and Knox 1987).

Moore's notions of varying amounts of dialogue, structure and learner autonomy have contributed to further theory development in distance education by serving as the basis for two of the other proposed frameworks discussed here (i.e., that of Garrison and of Verduin and Clark). However, many aspects of Moore's notion of learner autonomy have been criticized as not being well justified (Keegan 1986) and as being too general to explain the differences in learner motivation, ability and learning approaches (Willen 1981, 1984).

## A THEORY OF TEACHING IN DISTANCE EDUCATION

Holmberg's theory of guided didactic conversation, first reported in English in 1983, forms the first part of a theoretical framework which has evolved over a number of years. Unlike Peters and Moore, Holmberg focuses little effort on the analysis of the structure of distance education, but rather concentrates on the interpersonalization of the teaching process at a distance.

Holmberg coined the term 'non-contiguous communication' to describe the communication which takes place when a learner and an instructor/institution are separated in time and place. He maintains that establishing a personal relationship with the learner is a prerequisite to learner motivation and therefore learning. In distance education, this can be accomplished through non-contiguous means of communication.

Equally important to Holmberg's conception of distance education is his reverence for the individual learner and the freedom which he feels should be accorded to each. Like Moore, he considers real learning to be primarily an individual activity which is attained only through a process of internalization. Also like Moore, he considers learner autonomy as the ideal, and maintains that one goal of distance education should be to assist learners to achieve complete autonomy. Holmberg promotes systems which offer open admission, free pacing in the start and finish of study units, no fixed assignment due dates, and no required seminars or activities.

Holmberg used these cornerstone notions of non-contiguous communication, emotional involvement and self-study to develop a teaching theory of guided didactic conversation. He began with the assumption that activities like thinking aloud, elaborative processing of text (i.e., the interaction of the text content with prior knowledge of the reader), private reasoning and silent reading were communication processes. Applying these processes to the development of printed instructional materials resulted in the development of specific principles of guided didactic conversation (Holmberg 1983). Holmberg concluded that if printed materials were developed according to these principles, a simulated conversation would take place between the learner and the author(s) of the materials and between the learner and herself/himself. In turn, if these communication processes were consistently enhanced, then learners would be more motivated and emotionally involved and therefore learn more than they would if given a common textbook format of readings and questions. Several formal hypotheses resulted from this thinking and were tested by Holmberg (1985). Unfortunately, results yielded no conclusive evidence in favour of materials developed according to the theory of guided didactic conversation.

Holmberg (1985) next proposed a more general theory of teaching applicable not only to printed materials, but also to written comments or dialogue, media productions, telephone tutoring and other communication methods. Maintaining an emphasis on personal communication, Holmberg distinguished simulated conversation from real conversation:

> There is constant interaction (conversation) between the supporting organization (authors, tutors, counsellors), simulated through the students' interaction with the preproduced courses and real through the written and/or telephone interaction with their tutors and counsellors.
>
> (Holmberg 1983: 115)

Most recently, Holmberg (1986, 1989) has attempted to provide an even more comprehensive framework:

> These overarching hypotheses, which could be regarded as a theory of teaching for distance education, seem to have explanatory value in relating teaching effectiveness to the impact of feelings of

belonging and co-operation as well as to the actual exchange of questions, answers and arguments in mediated communication.

(Holmberg 1989: 163)

Holmberg's work has served as one basis for a number of studies which have investigated various aspects of personal contact in the distance education process (Rekkedal 1983a, 1983b, 1985; Bååth 1980; Evans 1984; Scales 1984).

## A THEORY OF REINTEGRATION OF THE TEACHING AND LEARNING ACTS

Keegan (1986, 1990) believes that the basis for a theory of distance education is to be found in general education theory, but not within frameworks of group-based, oral instruction. He defends this position by arguing that distance education is not primarily characterized by interpersonal communication, but is instead characterized by the separation of the teaching acts in time and place from the learning acts. In this view he is consistent with Moore, who contrasts distance teaching and learning and contiguous teaching and learning situations. Keegan's basis for the distinction is the nature of the resulting communication.

Initially, Keegan proposed that distance education is also characterized by a more industrial form of education, an incorporation of Peters' perspective. Later, based on mixed reactions to Peters' ideas, Keegan 'moved (the component of industrialization) outside of the definition proper' (Keegan 1990: 43). Keegan reasons that based on the industrial-like character of distance education which emphasizes the separation of the student from the teaching institution, a theoretical justification for distance education is to be found in the reintegration of the teaching and learning acts. In this step, Keegan diverges from both Moore and Holmberg who seem to view separation as both an advantage and a challenge to the autonomous learner. Keegan states:

The intersubjectivity of teacher and learner, in which learning from teaching occurs, has to be artificially recreated. Over space and time a distance system seeks to reconstruct the moment in which the teaching–learning interaction occurs. The linking of learning materials to learning is central to this process.

(Keegan 1986: 120)

Keegan argues that this learning link is a given in traditional education, because the learner is in an environment created to support learning (i.e., the school and/or university). Keegan believes that for the distance student, the recreation of the link between teaching and learning must be accomplished through interpersonal communication which is deliberately planned. The theme of inter-personal communication is similar to Holmberg's thinking, but rather than focus directly on the teaching or the learner, Keegan's focus is on the learning act. Like Holmberg, Keegan also considers that printed instructional materials can be designed to include many of the characteristics of interpersonal communication and he, there-fore, does not limit his notion of interpersonal communication to telephone tutorials, teleconferences, or other similar forms.

Keegan reasons that the more successfully the distance education programme manages reintegration, the lower the drop-out rate, the higher the quality of learning, and the higher the status of the institution. Some support has been found for these hypotheses (Amundsen 1988, Amundsen and Bernard 1989).

## A THEORY OF COMMUNICATION AND LEARNER CONTROL

The starting point for this theory is the educational transaction between teacher and learner. The educational transaction is 'based upon seeking understanding and knowledge through dialogue and debate' (Garrison 1989: 12) and, therefore, necessitates two-way communication between teacher and learner.

Garrison quite literally uses the concepts of teacher and learner and rejects Holmberg's notion of guided didactic conversation as 'no more of a teacher than a textbook' (Garrison 1989: 18). Unlike Moore and Holmberg, who characterize ultimate learning as an individual internal process, Garrison's notion of the learning process requires interaction with a teacher. He reasons that since teacher and learner are separate and two-way communication is necessary, then technology is required to support the educational transaction. Indeed, technology is included as one of three criteria in a proposed definition of distance education (Garrison and Shale 1987, cited in Garrison 1989).

Garrison (1985) has argued that technology and distance education are inseparable and that theory and practice in distance education have evolved based on the increasing sophistication of instructional technology. Like Peters, he has predicted that practice in distance education must change. However, whereas Peters argues that changing societal attitudes and values will require distance education to move away from an earlier industrial format, Garrison suggests that it is the emergence of new and future technologies which will curtail the need to maintain many of the present industrial characteristics. Another prominent notion in this framework, in addition to educational transaction, is the concept of learner control (Garrison and Baynton 1987, Garrison 1989). Learner control is proposed in part to replace the concept of independence or autonomy used by both Holmberg and Moore. Garrison and Baynton believe that these terms have been used with mixed meanings and do not reflect what should be an interdependent relationship between teacher and learner. Learner control is concerned with 'the opportunity and ability to influence and direct a course of events . . . control within the educational setting, however, cannot be established by only one party when the direction of the course of events must inherently be collaborative' (Garrison 1989: 27). They propose that control is based on the interrelationship between independence (as in the self-directed learner), proficiency (as in the ability to learn independently), and support (characterized by the resources available to guide and facilitate the educational transaction). This, in turn, is interpreted within the larger relationship between teacher, learner, and content.

## A THREE-DIMENSIONAL THEORY OF DISTANCE EDUCATION

Verduin and Clark (1991) have proposed a theoretical model that, while retaining the adult education focus of both Moore and Garrison, also attempts to reflect the broader scope of distance education practice. Moore's concepts of dialogue, structure, and learner autonomy and Keegan's defining attributes of two-way communication and his notions of the separation of teacher and learner are the catalysts for Verduin and Clark's framework.

They begin with Moore's concepts of dialogue, structure and learner autonomy as the three dimensions of their framework. However, they broaden and, in some places, significantly change Moore's meanings.

The first dimension of the framework – dialogue/support – reflects the primary purpose of dialogue as support for the learner. This support may range from simply providing directions concerning assignments to substantial motivational or emotional support.

The second dimension – structure/specialized – departs from Moore's definition of structure as the flexibility of due dates, student input into course development, and so on. Verduin and Clark explain:

Some fields of study in distance, adult, and even pre-adult education, in which competence may only be a matter of basic understanding of principles or problems, need only minimal structure. A high level of structure is needed in other fields in which many years of study may be necessary before a learner is competent enough to set objectives and study methods or to take part in evaluation.

(Verduin and Clark 1991: 125)

Thus, the concept of structure is inseparable from the concept of specialized competence. The authors explain:

competence in a field, or specialized competence, is seen as a situational attribute that may occur among adults or children studying at a distance or conventionally, based largely upon the learner's expertise or lack of it, and that is usually a function of the structure of the subject matter.

(Verduin and Clark 1991: 125)

With the inclusion of structure/specialized competence as the second dimension of their model, Verduin and Clark are the first to consider the implications of the nature of the subject matter.

The third dimension – general competence/self-directedness – includes Moore's view of autonomy, but with much qualification. Verduin and Clark pose several questions about the principles of andragogy, including the general applicability of these principles to the individual learner and to various subject matters. The authors suggest:

A better approach to deciding appropriate levels of self-directedness or autonomy might be to determine whether the student is competent in that field at that level, to estimate the student's general competence, and to see if appropriate structure and dialogue have been afforded, given the formality or lack of it in that field.

(Verduin and Clark 1991: 127)

A continuum is proposed based on various combinations of these three dimensions. Twelve points on the continuum are described, each with examples of real educational applications. However, the authors caution that it is probably more useful to think of more than one of these categories applying to an entire course. For example, most courses include at least some high-structure/specialized-competence material and some low-structure/specialized-competence material.

## A SYNTHESIS OF THEORETICAL PERSPECTIVES

The above discussion treats each of the six proposed theoretical frameworks separately. Each is interpreted from the explanations provided by the authors and, in certain cases, the comments and critiques of others. To advance the understanding of each perspective in relationship to the others and to provide an opportunity to reflect more clearly on the evolution of ideas, further comparison is needed. Table 4.1 compares the six frameworks in terms of their central concepts and primary foci, and in terms of the area of inquiry which seems to have most influenced their development. When viewed in this way, two points are immediately noteworthy: the prominent influence of adult education with its primary focus on the learner is evident in four of the six frameworks, and the general theme of communication is evident in five of the six frameworks.

Another way to compare these frameworks is to look at the way each author treats the definitive feature of distance education: the separation of teacher and learner. In the first four frameworks discussed (Peters, Moore, Holmberg, and Keegan), separation or distance is the focal point around which their thinking seems to be organized. Peters' focus is the organization and functioning of the distance education institution or programme itself. However, to Peters, the concept of distance refers to more than geographical distance. He sees distance or separation between people, functions and processes as characteristics of industrial society. For example, the industrial-like standardization of instructional materials focuses on the overall format and product and is distant or separated from considering the individual characteristics of subject matter, courses or learners. In Peters' contribution to this book, he has written about a shift in distance education to reflect the principles and values of a postindustrial society, such as more individualized technology and decentralized decision-making structures. Here he seems to employ the notion of distance or separation in distance education to reflect the degree to which people and processes must come closer together rather than remain separate.

Moore's notion of transactional distance is also meant to represent more than geographical distance, but the focus is primarily on the meaning of separation or distance from the learner's point of view rather than from an institutional or societal point of view. The greater the transactional distance the greater the opportunity for the learner autonomy, which Moore views as positive. Therefore, Moore places a positive value on the notion of distance because it provides the opportunity for more autonomous learning.

Table 4.1 A comparison of theoretical perspectives

| Framework | Central concepts | Primary focus | Apparent influence |
|---|---|---|---|
| Peters | Industrial Post-industrial | Match between societal principles and values | Cultural sociology |
| Moore | Transactional distance (dialogue, structure) Learner autonomy | Perceived needs and desires of the adult learner | Independent study |
| Holmberg | Learner autonomy Non-contiguous communication Guided didactic conversation | Promotion of learning through personal and conversational methods | Humanist approach to education |
| Keegan | Reintegration of teaching and learning acts | Recreation of interpersonal components of face-to-face teaching | Framework of traditional pedagogy |
| Garrison (Shale, Baynton) | Educational transaction Learner control Communication | Facilitation of the educational transaction | Communication Theory Principles of adult education |
| Verduin and Clark | Dialogue/Support Structure/Specialized competence/General competence/Self-directedness | Requirements of both the learning task and learner | Principles of adult education Structures of knowledge |

Holmberg and Keegan both see distance as something that must be bridged through various means of interpersonal communication. Holmberg focuses primarily on the teaching aspects of distance education and places a positive value on both learner autonomy and the possibilities of distance education to enhance learner autonomy. However, Holmberg's emphasis is on the development of teaching that will create the learner interest, motivation and involvement which he maintains will, in turn, stimulate learning. Keegan, however, emphasizes the learning link which he maintains is present in conventional education but severed in distance education. Unlike Moore or Holmberg, Keegan does not place a positive value on distance but rather seems to view it as something which disconnects the teacher and the learner and, therefore, the teaching and the learning. Keegan's choice of the word reintegration suggests that the effects of distance or separation create a situation which must be restored to resemble more closely the interpersonal aspects of traditional teaching and learning.

Verduin and Clark, and Garrison, do not place the notion of distance or separation in a central position in their framework. The background rationales provided both by Garrison and by Verduin and Clark acknowledge the definitive characteristic of distance education as the separation of teacher and learner, but neither begins with the concept of distance and neither seems to place any particular value on the presence or absence of distance.

Garrison's focus is the support of what he terms the educational transaction, which is totally dependent on two-way communication and involves a collaborative experience between a teacher and a learner. He even cautions that distance educators must not become distracted with the idea of distance and overlook the importance 'of the need for the educational transaction between teacher and student' (Garrison 1989: 7). He seems to explore the notion of distance only in terms of the necessity it creates for the presence of technology to facilitate the necessary two-way communication. Verduin and Clark do not treat the notion of distance directly but rather, in their words, they have provided 'a framework by which distance education can be related to adult and conventional education' (Verduin and Clark 1991: 123).

One noteworthy trend that this analysis highlights is the decreasing emphasis placed on the notion of distance. Several individuals have addressed this decreasing reliance on distance as a central notion. Moore notes the overlap with the general goals of conventional education:

when we recognize that distance education *is* education, we can apply much that we know about teaching and learning in both our theory and practice of distance education. In practice, however, we discover that transactional distance in many programs is so great that the teaching we deliver cannot be just like conventional teaching.

(Moore 1991: 3)

Shale insists that if distance education is to evolve beyond 'a sort of correspondence study with bells and whistles' (Shale 1990: 333) we must stop defining it in terms of distance and begin to view it as an educational process. Still others have cited the decreased need to rely on the distinguishing characteristic of distance because of the blending of distance education course development and delivery methods into traditional education (Jevons 1987).

## A PROPOSAL FOR THE FURTHER EVOLUTION OF THEORY IN DISTANCE EDUCATION

Perhaps the next step in the evolution of theory in distance education should be based on a general framework of teaching and learning, with learning, not the learner or the notion of distance, occupying the central position. Distance is a major component, but it is interpreted in terms of its impact on accomplishing the intended learning. This view is represented in Figure 4.1 where the traditional educational relationship of teacher, learner and content is held intact, but the teacher–learner relationship is notably altered by distance or separation in place and time. Learning occupies the central position, and as the connecting lines indicate, the other components are all viewed from the perspective of the intended learning.

It is important to note that the proposed framework shown in Figure 4.1 does not continue the apparent trend to decrease the centrality of distance. Distance is viewed here as having a significant impact on all components of the teaching and learning process: the teacher, the learner, and the subject content. The extent and meaning of that impact is determined by considering the intended learning. In other words, distance education is a field of inquiry that should be well rooted in theories of teaching and learning. The primary contribution of the field could be seen as providing a systematic analysis of the meaning of distance to the teaching and learning process. It is in this sense that the proposed framework is intended to encourage inquiry and instructional thinking which

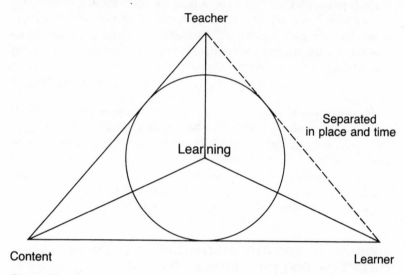

*Figure 4.1* A framework for viewing instructional roles and decisions in distance education

begins with the intended learning and then considers the implications for the content, the learner and the teaching role *within the distance education setting.*

The proposed framework (see Figure 4.1) incorporates many of the central concepts developed in the six frameworks described in Table 4.1. The central emphasis on learning is most closely related to the thinking of Keegan. However, this view does not incorporate his notion of reintegration based on what is missing in comparison to the face-to-face situation. Keegan speaks of the reintegration of the teaching and learning acts in distance education by arguing that the link between them is a given in conventional education but that it is missing in distance education. In fact, this link is not a given in conventional face-to-face education, as the area itself is re-examining current notions and practices about what types of teaching facilitate and support different types of learning. This is one of the primary questions framing contemporary theoretical discussions (Shulman 1986, Resnick 1989) and research (Beder 1985, Shore *et al.* 1990, Amundsen *et al.* 1993) within the context of conventional education.

The importance placed on what Garrison terms the educational transaction is also reflected by the central position given to learning in the proposed framework shown in Figure 4.1. However, while Garrison speaks literally of a teacher and a learner and describes the process as dialogue and debate, the proposed framework does not define the teaching role, the learning role, or the learning process. These are to be determined based on the learning to be accomplished.

The proposed framework does not simply reorganize the concepts of previously proposed frameworks. In fact, one of its attractive features is its ability to incorporate contributions from other teaching and learning paradigms. For example, principles deriving from behavioural, cognitive or andragogical paradigms can be incorporated when they are appropriate to the intended learning. In the distance education literature, Bååth (1982) presents a similar view when he suggests we consider the relationship between teaching and learning theories and learning goals in making decisions about the type of interpersonal communications to use in distance education.

## FURTHER APPLICATION OF THE PROPOSED FRAMEWORK

The remainder of this discussion will be devoted to exploring further the notions presented here. This is organized according to the major components of the proposed framework: teacher, learner, and content. The notion of distance, which affects the way each of these three is perceived, is incorporated into each section.

### Teacher

What is meant by the concept of teacher in distance education? Moore does not use the word 'teacher' and generally speaks about 'programs'. His concept of the teacher is someone who an autonomous learner will seek out to help formulate problems, gather information, and so on. Holmberg also does not speak specifically of a teacher; he concentrates on the teaching process. Keegan speaks of the teaching and learning acts and describes the interpersonal components of face-to-face teaching which are missing in distance education. Garrison is one of the few who speaks literally of a teacher and a student; he describes the teaching role as collaborative and the teaching activity as one of negotiation and dialogue. Verduin and Clark make no direct reference to teaching, but they do address the need for dialogue and support.

Sammons (1990) has criticized those who have proposed the notion of learner independence, autonomy or control for not detailing the teaching role in promoting learner independence. Sammons' point is well taken, and can be applied to more than just those who advocate learner independence. There is a dearth of information on teaching in distance education. A framework which supports questions about the teaching role in relation to various types of learning seems necessary.

## Content

The teaching and learning roles are largely determined by the nature of the subject matter or content. Verduin and Clark call attention to the structure of the subject matter and the resulting implications for the teaching and learning roles. They question the notion of one instructional approach being appropriate for all types and levels of subject matter. In particular, they, like others (Gorham 1985, Beder 1985), have questioned the generalizability of the principles of andragogy to all types of learning. Similarly, the higher education literature is increasingly concerned with effective teaching and is questioning with renewed interest, the ability of university instructors to move from a basic information-giving mode of instruction to other modes of instruction when appropriate (Sherman *et al.* 1987) Distance education would also benefit from a systematic investigation of the match between subject matter, teaching and learning.

## Learner

The learner, and his/her needs to structure and control the learning situation, has received much emphasis in distance education. However, in the simplest view, a learner comes to a distance education situation to learn something. Thus, the learner role may vary depending on the learning to be accomplished. Even the so-called self-directed learners, as Verduin and Clark note, 'may actively seek out a high-structure approach that fits the type of knowledge found in the field and that prepares them for various forms of professional certification (or knowledge)' (Verduin and Clark 1991: 128). A theoretical framework which supports inquiry about the distance learner from the perspective of the intended learning would do much to develop and broaden current directions of inquiry. For example, what affects the way learners approach and carry out a learning task is a relatively recent area of inquiry in face-to-face instruction and is an ideal area of inquiry in which to locate variables specific to distance education.

## CONCLUSION

The focus of this chapter has been the evolution of theory in distance education. The analysis of six theoretical frameworks proposed over the last two decades provided the basis for a proposed framework that can serve as a next step in the evolution of theory and practice. One trend noted here is the decreased emphasis which more recent theoretical proposals have placed on the notion of distance or separation. The view presented here is that the notion of distance must remain central, but that its meaning or importance is in direct relationship to the type of learning desired. In other words, distance education, as a field of inquiry, must focus on the meaning of distance to learning and on the resulting implications for the teaching role, instructional methods and learner expectations. The proposed framework provides a reference point for building new understandings of teaching and learning within the context of distance education.

## REFERENCES

Amundsen, C. (1988) 'An investigation of institutional support for peer contact in distanced education', Unpublished doctoral dissertation, Concordia University, Montreal, in *Dissertation Abstracts International* 49(11).

—— and Bernard, R. (1989) 'Institutional support for peer contact in distance education: an empirical investigation', *Distance Education* 10(1), 7–27.

——, Gryspeerdt, D., and Moxness, K. (1993) 'Practice-centered inquiry: developing perceptions and behaviors toward more effective teaching in higher education', *Review of Higher Education* 16(3), 328–53.

Bååth, J. A. (1980) *Postal Two-way Communication in Correspondence Education*, Lund, Sweden: Gleerup (ERIC Document Reproduction Service No. ED 224 466).

—— (1982) 'Distance students' learning: empirical findings and theoretical deliberations', *Distance Education* 3(1), 6–27.

Beder, H. (1985) 'The relation of knowledge sought to appropriate teaching behavior in adult education', *Lifelong Learning* 9(1), 14–28.

Evans, T. (1984) 'Communicating with students by audiotape', *Teaching at a Distance*, no. 25, 108–10.

Garrison, D. R. (1985) 'Three generations of technological innovations in distance education', *Distance Education* 6(2), 235–41.

—— (1989) *Understanding Distance Education*, New York: Routledge.

—— and Baynton, M. (1987) 'Beyond independence in distance education: the concept of control', *The American Journal of Distance Education* 1(3), 3–15.

Gorham, J. (1985) 'Difference between teaching adults and teaching pre-adults: a closer look', *Adult Education Quarterly* 35(4), 194–209.

Gough, E. (1984) 'Towards a philosophy of distance education', in K. Smith (ed.), *Diversity Down Under in Distance Education*, Australia: Darling Down Institute Press.

Holmberg, B. (1983) 'Guided didactic conversation in distance education', in D. Sewart, D. Keegan, & B. Holmberg (eds), *Distance Education: International Perspectives*, London: Croom Helm.

—— (1985) *Status and Trends of Distance Education*, Sweden: Lector Publishing.

—— (1986) *Growth and Structure of Distance Education*, London: Croom Helm.

—— (1989) *Theory and Practice of Distance Education*, London: Routledge.

Jevons, F. (1987) 'Distance education and campus-based education: parity of esteem', in P. Smith and M. Kelly (eds), *Distance Education and the Mainstream*, Sydney: Croom Helm.

Keegan, D. J. (1986) *The Foundations of Distance Education*, London: Croom Helm.

—— (1990) *Foundations of Distance Education* (2nd edn), London: Routledge.

Moore, M. G. (1972) 'Learner autonomy: the second dimension of independent learning', *Convergence* V(2), 76–88.

—— (1973) 'Toward a theory of independent learning and teaching', *Journal of Higher Education* XLIV(12), 661–79.

—— (1976) 'Investigation of the interaction between the cognitive style of field independence and attitudes to independent study among adult learners who use correspondence independent study and self-directed independent', Unpublished doctoral dissertation, University of Wisconsin, in *Dissertation Abstracts International*, 37/06A, 3344A.

—— (1983) 'The individual adult learner', in M. Tight (ed.), *Education for Adults, Volume I: Adult Learning and Education*, London: Croom Helm.

—— (1986) 'Self-directed learning and distance education', *Journal of Distance Education* 1(1), 7–24.

—— (1991) 'Editorial: distance education theory', *The American Journal of Distance Education* 5(3), 1–6.

Nelson, P. A. (1985) 'The effects of field-independent–dependent cognitive style on achievement in a telecourse', Unpublished doctoral dissertation, Brigham Young University in *Dissertation Abstracts International*, 46/08A, 2239A.

Peters, O. (1983) 'Distance teaching and industrial production: a comparative interpretation in outline', in D. Sewart, D. Keegan and B. Holmberg (eds), *Distance Education: International Perspectives*, London: Croom Helm.

—— (1989) 'The iceberg has not melted: further reflections on the concept of industrialisation and distance teaching', *Open Learning* 4(3), 3–8.

Rekkedal, T. (1983a) 'Research and development activities in the field of distance study at NKI-skolen, Norway', in D. Sewart, D. Keegan and B. Holmberg (eds), *Distance Education: International Perspectives*, London: Croom Helm.

—— (1983b) 'Enhancing student progress in Norway', *Teaching at a Distance*, no. 23, 19–24.

—— (1985) *Introducing the Personal Tutor/Counsellor in the System of Distance Education*, Stabekk, Norway: NKI-skolen.

Resnick, L. B. (1989) 'Instruction', in L. Resnick (ed.), *Knowing, Learning and Instruction*, Hillsdale, N.J.: LEA.

Sammons, M. (1990) 'An epistemological justification for the role of teaching in distance education', in M. Moore (ed.), *Contemporary Issues in American Distance Education*, New York: Pergamon Press.

Scales, K. (1984) 'Ways and means of reducing early student drop-out rates', *Distance Education* 5(2), 268–76.

Shale, D. (1990) 'Toward a reconceptualization of distance education', in M. Moore (ed.), *Contemporary Issues in American Distance Education*, New York: Pergamon Press.

Sherman, T. M., Armistead, L. P., Fowler, F., Barksdale, M. A. and Reif, F. (1987) 'The quest for excellence in university teaching', *Journal of Higher Education* 58(1), 66–84.

Shore, B. M., Pinker, S. and Bates, M. (1990) 'Research as a model for university teaching', *Higher Education* 19(1), 21–35.

Shulman, L. S. (1986) 'Paradigms and research programs in the study of teaching: a contemporary perspective', in M. C Wittrock (ed.), *Handbook on Research on Teaching*, New York: Macmillan.

Sparks, J. J. (1983) 'The problem of creating a discipline of distance education', *Distance Education* 4(2), 179–94.

Thompson, G. (1984) 'The cognitive style of field-dependence as an explanatory construct in distance drop-out', *Distance Education* 5(2), 286–93.

Thompson, G. and Knox, A. (1987) 'Designing for diversity: are field-dependent learners less suited to distance education programs of instruction?', *Contemporary Educational Psychology* 12(1), 17–29.

Willen, B. (1981) Distance Education at Swedish Universities: An Evaluation of the Experimental Progress and Follow-up Study, Stockholm, Sweden: Almqvist & Wiksell International.

—— (1984) *Self-directed Learning and Distance Education* (Uppsala Reports on Education no. 21), Department of Education, University of Uppsala, Sweden.

Verduin, J. R. and Clark, T. A. (1991) *Distance Education: The Foundations of Effective Practice*, San Francisco: Jossey-Bass Publishers.

# 5 Towards a broader conceptualization of distance education

*Chere C. Gibson*

## INTRODUCTION

It has been suggested that it takes more than a family to raise a child; it takes a community. In education we stress the need for involvement beyond the school, teacher and student to include family and community. Both 'truisms' recognize that human development is the result of many overlapping spheres of influence. The purpose of this chapter is to foster discussion on a broader multi-spheric conceptualization of distance education, recognizing that how we conceptualize the distance teaching/learning transaction will influence, for example, instructional design, implementation of distance education programmes and the evaluation of programme and learner success. In addition, this conceptualization drives our research, not only the questions we ask but the models by which we choose to answer them.

## WHY BROADEN THE CONCEPTION OF THE FIELD OF DISTANCE EDUCATION?

To date, research and writings have conceptualized distance teaching and learning in terms of its key elements of teacher, student, communications medium and content (see, for example, Moore 1973, Wedemeyer 1981, Garrison 1989) as a separate sphere unrelated to other life situations and events. More recently an increasing number of researchers have noted the impact of other spheres or systems on the distance teaching and learning transaction (e.g. Billings 1988, Gibson and Graff 1992), assessing the impact of other systems on the learner and his/her learning, albeit in a unidirectional fashion reflecting the impact of other spheres on the learner without recognition or examination of reciprocal effects. Perhaps what we have yet to see is a more transactional model in which a variety of spheres interact, such as an exploration of the impact of having a parent engaged in distance learning on family roles, responsibilities, and values, and the impact of subsequent changes in family values, for example, on that distance learner.

Of particular concern, on reading the literature of the field and reflecting on personal experience as a distance learner and teacher – and especially on those experiences of other distance learners – is the failure duly to consider the environment within which distance education occurs. It is argued elsewhere (Gibson 1990, 1992) that learner behaviour ($B$) is a function ($f$) of the interaction between the person ($P$) and his/her perceived environment ($E$) as posited in Lewin's dynamic theory of personality (Lewin 1936, 1951). With this relationship as a given, our theories of distance education must take into consideration not only the learner, teacher, content, and the communications medium, as duly considered in a number of prevalent distance education theories, but also the content in which the teaching and learning occurs.

As Kasworm concludes in her study of adult students in formal higher education settings: 'adult learning within higher education should be defined by a broader landscape of the adult's life-world of social contexts of higher education, family, work, home and community' (Kasworm 1990a: 19).If we choose to ignore the context in which distance education occurs, our attempts to enhance the teaching–learning transactions in distance education will be of limited success at best.

What follows is an initial attempt at broadening our conception of distance learning. The conceptualization is a dynamic one, one that hopefully will provide a basis for additional thinking, research, and especially critical debate. Towards this end, it seems appropriate to listen to the voices of distance learners as they reflect on their experiences as learners at a distance – reflections which suggest a broader conceptualization; to look to the literature of other disciplines for theoretical insights relative to these new voices with implications for distance teaching and learning; and, lastly, to begin to explore research implications of this proposed reconceptualization.

## LISTENING TO LEARNERS

In an attempt to better understand the relationships among and between the learner and the environment in which the distance teaching–learning transaction occurs, a small longitudinal study has been conducted with adult learners who are pursuing a baccalaureate degree at a distance. The experiences of these sixteen learners at a distance who willingly shared their experiences, hopes, fears, frustrations and successes over the first year of their pursuit of a baccalaureate degree – as well as other distance learners interviewed over the past few years as part of evaluation studies – have led to this broader conception of the field. It was these words that prompted consideration of the applicability of ecological systems theory and its relevance to distance teaching and learning. Let's 'listen' to the words of a number of students learning at a distance as they reflect on their experiences in the first four months of learning at a distance.

At one level, one finds students describing themselves in their distinct and discrete worlds of work, family, community, leisure and school. Jobs are often described with special emphasis on the changes experienced on the job – for example: 'kinda crazy in my department right now. We're trying some new machines, new way of doing things.' Or 'I'm working a part-time mail route now, with the hopes of getting full time, but in 1995 the post system is supposed to be fully automated and that would get rid of about 100,000 jobs nationwide.'

Families of all varieties emerge in vivid terms from standard demographic characteristics of numbers, ages and levels of education, through employment situations, hobbies, athletic prowess, and deaths at all ages.

Community activities continue to play an important role in the lives of our distance learners, with one student noting, as an example, 'I'm treasurer of the council, and I'm still tutoring once a week.' As another noted, 'doing this 4-H thing for kids [organized youth educational activities]. I love it. I thrive on it. It energizes me.'

They also speak of their experiences as students, of victories during their studies,

> I wrote two papers . . . I hadn't written a paper in a hell of a long time. I was really pleased with them, when I got done with them.
> . . . And then I was really extra pleased when I got them back and they were both marked 'A'

and a few failures of sorts 'but I do have some hang-ups like in getting the films I needed when I needed them', or 'my hopes [for completion] are dimming because there's more work to it [degree at a distance] than what I figured'.

And so they describe themselves in their immediate settings of work, family, community, school, and leisure. It is a rich description of our students in a variety of contexts, each with its own set of rules, roles and responsibilities, resources, physical attributes, and casts of characters. But these are not discrete entities and the overlap becomes all too obvious as they speak – overlaps which directly impact on learning at a distance.

As one listens more closely, one hears a wife and mother commenting on the support of her husband who is 'actually working three jobs, helping us along financially' so she can go to school. Another mother, commenting on what would enhance progress in her studies notes, 'I guess if I didn't have kids involved in school activities. . . . Then they also need my help for homework, and that sort of thing too.' But for others, the local school provides more than a distraction, it provides resources. 'And I know a lot of people who know math well and can help me out with this' boasted one student. Another simply described hiring a local college student living in the community as a tutor, once again for mathematics.

Work also provides a resource for some, particularly as an arena to try out new knowledge. Commenting on what she looked forward to in her studies, to any teacher's (or employer's) delight, she said, 'Learning more and relating it to my work!' To others it provided a distraction in terms of needing to work overtime in busy seasons, etc.

On the need for sacrifices when balancing school and leisure, a student suggested that before registering for a degree programme at a distance to: 'Make sure, discuss it with their family first, and make sure they lay it out. Make sure they realize what's going to be, so that you don't get tempted, they don't tempt you so much.'

Sometimes a larger world intervenes (or interferes) with a student's progress. Students pursuing degrees sometimes have limited access to resources at times due to unequal distribution of resources. Sometimes it's money. A student commented, 'Well, we've run out of money, so we're down to one day of daycare a week.' The repercussions are several preschoolers under foot and limited progress with studies as a result. Other times it's the nature of the housing a student can afford as a result of limited employment opportunities in their immediate setting or access to housing-related assistance in the community. Commenting on study facilities, one student noted: 'In the winter we couldn't use the upstairs cause there's no insulation. It's like the temperature outside is inside too.' The larger world of work, including state and federal requirements for credentials for employment, sometimes imposes its own pressures on learning. For example: 'with it [course completed], I can keep my job. 'Cause my promotion was dependent on my finishing this course work. So I have to get it.' Or sometimes advancing one's education is seen as a signal of impending departure, so one student didn't 'Tell a whole lot of people because I'm a little bit concerned about the security of my job' – persons who otherwise might have served as a source of support.

But all of this distance education is taking place within a culture and subculture that permeates the educational, social, economic, legal, political, etc. realms in which the student lives and learns. This cultural milieu colours the student's (and others') conception of education – for example, the student who noted on a visit to the dual mode institution which offered his degree at a distance, 'Oh, it was nice also to get on the campus and just get the feeling of education . . .' Another bemoaned, 'It's like we're not really in school or college . . . because we're not in a structured class setting.' Yet another wonders about the value of a degree that fails to fit the common mould: 'And when you say, well, I'm going through the extended degree, . . . it's not the same status or something.'

But sometimes it's the student not the school which fails to fit the stereotypical mould, as exemplified by the comment, 'I hope my kids see that when they're in their 40s, there's still life and there's still hope, and they're still able to learn.'

What emerges in the words of these distance learners is a rich description of dynamic forces interacting to impact their growth and development and, in turn, their impact on the environment in which they perform their life roles as members of families, the work-force, and the community. But these findings are in no way unique.

Kasworm, in her recent analysis of the literature on adult undergraduates in higher education, notes: 'Undergraduates are expected to focus upon inward intellectual development . . . and to be developed by the unique forces of the collegiate experience. The adult undergraduate is not an easy fit with the inward focus in the academic collegiate experience' (Kasworm 1990b: 366). She continues suggesting that the adult learning experience is more akin to centrifugal growth towards outward roles and experiences. While adult students do experience inward intellectual and personal development, they also have an outward journey of self-efficacy. Knowledge and skills acquired in one domain are applied in another – for example, academic experiences are translated into action at home, at work or in the community. Concluding her analyses, she calls for frameworks and research agendas which recognize the adult's relationship to the undergraduate educational experience. In addition, this agenda should address questions about 'the adult student as learner, adult student as worker/homemaker, and adult student as family/community leader' (Kasworm 1990b: 367) from both organization and ecological perspectives.

Mindful of Evans and Nation's demonstration of how 'apparently disparate theories and concepts from the humanities and social sciences have worked for us' (Evans and Nation 1992: 11), a quest for theories and/or concepts which might begin to help to bring order to the dynamic forces experienced by distance learners described earlier was begun. The quest was pursued remaining mindful of the pitfalls of free borrowing of theories and concepts, i.e., borrowing theories and concepts without regard for the field from which they came, their context, philosophical assumptions, and their ability to set direction for the borrower's field if injected uncritically into the new field, etc. (Gibson 1991). The theory which seemed to best speak to the situation at hand, and in line with Kasworm's call for an ecological perspective on the adult undergraduate educational experience, was ecological systems theory.

## ECOLOGICAL SYSTEMS THEORY

Ecological systems theory, as outlined by Urie Bronfenbrenner (1977) draws heavily on the work of Kurt Lewin and focuses on the multiple contexts in which human development occurs. When published, ecological systems theory was part of a plea for psychologists to attempt to conduct more ecologically and contextually valid experimental research (Way 1991). As Bronfenbrenner argued,

> the understanding of human development demands going beyond the direct observation of behavior on the part of one or two persons in the same place; it requires an examination of multi-person systems of interaction not limited to a single setting and must take into account aspects of the environment beyond the immediate situation containing the subject.
>
> (Bronfenbrenner 1977: 514)

The theory is most correctly described as a transformed and extended version of the preceding Lewin formula: $b = f \ (PE)$. The first transformation yields $D = f \ (PE)$ where $D$ represents development. Bronfenbrenner (1989a) notes that the term development introduces a new parameter not in the earlier formulation: that of time. This seems particularly appropriate as we consider, for example, the cognitive, intellectual, personal, and social development of our dynamic distance learners over time as exemplified by recent research findings of Herrman (1988), Powell *et al.* (1990) and others. The formula, including the time factor, is represented as:

$$D_t = f_{(t-p)} (PE)_{(t-p)}$$

where $t$ refers to the time at which a developmental outcome (e.g. learning) is observed and $t - p$ to the period(s) during which the joint forces *(PE)* were operating over time to produce the outcome existing at the time of operation (Bronfenbrenner 1989a). What this representation allows us to consider is not only the developmental change but also the processes which produce them. In other words, as distance educators we are not only interested in learning, but also in the interaction of those properties of the person and their multiple environments which produce constancy and change in the character-istics of that person over time. Consider, for example, a learner's self-confidence changing over time as a result of the interaction of a growing self-awareness of his/her capabilities, acquiring excellent grades, encouragement of others, independent learning materials which instil confidence, employer rewards of more sophisticated job assignments as a result of new academic pursuits, peers' and family's new-found pride in our learner's success, etc.

Let's look at ecological systems theory more closely, coupled with selected examples relating to distance learners, to better understand the theory and consider its potential contribution to distance educa-tion theory and practice.

In his early writings Bronfenbrenner (1977) suggests that the ecological environment is conceived topologically as a nested arrangement of structures, each contained within the next. He further describes the four systems within the total system. The first of these systems is the Bronfenbrenner *microsystem*, defined as the complex of relationships between the developing person and environ-ment in an immediate setting containing that person (Bronfenbrenner 1977). Place, time, physical features, activity, participant and role constitute the elements of setting in ecological theory. In the 1980s Bronfenbrenner modified his definition of the microsystem to include consideration of the personal characteristics of others in the environ-ment, recognizing the potential impact of another person's tempera-ment, personality and systems of belief. For example, our distance learner may be found at home, at work, and at play at a variety of times engaged in a number of dissimilar activities as learner, parent, worker, coach. etc., interacting with persons who may be more or less supportive of education for adults and, in particular, for women.

Bronfenbrenner's *mesosystem* comprises the interrelations among major settings containing the developing person at a particular point in his/her own life – in essence the mesosystem is a system of micro-systems. For our distance learner the mesosystem encompasses the interactions among the distance learning institution, the family, the work-place, the community, and perhaps a religious institution, and other contexts unmentioned. Many of us have seen the impact of going back to school on our students' job responsibilities. Being assigned to a new or more challenging job is often a 'reward' provided to an employee for taking the initiative to return to personal and professional growth, as well as a recognition of the potential positive impact of additional schooling on job performance. However, the impact of new job responsibilities provides increased challenges in the juggling of home- and school-related tasks some-times adversely impacting both educational progress and family interactions.

Further, Bronfenbrenner suggests that in addition to the micro-systems and mesosystem, one needs to be cognizant of those other social structures, both formal and informal, which, although they may not contain the individual, 'impinge upon or encompass the immediate settings in which that person is found, and thereby influence, delimit or even determine what goes on there' (Bronfenbrenner 1977: 515). Structures which may be considered as part of this *exosystem* include the neighbourhood, the mass media, the world of work, agencies of government at all levels, communications and transporta-tion systems, the distribution of goods and services, and informal social networks. For example, governmental policies regarding financial aid for part-time study, or study at a distance, may require pursuing a second or third job which in turn influences the amount of time available to the learner to devote to studies. As a result, the opportunity for family interaction may be limited and could potentially diminish family support for the continuation of these studies.

Last, one must consider the *macrosystem* which differs in a fundamental way from the preceding systems. Rather than referring to specific contexts which affect the life of the person, the macro-system refers to the 'overarching institutional patterns of the culture or subculture, such as economic, social, educational, legal and political systems of which micro-, meso- and exosystems are the concrete manifestations (Bronfenbrenner 1977: 515). Further, Bronfenbrenner refers to these macrosystems as blueprints that provide patterns. One example he gives is the school classroom, which in any given society looks very much alike school to school. This similarity is found in other settings and institutions as well, both formal and informal. In some cases, laws, regulations, and rules provide the blueprint. In other instances the blueprints are more informal and implicit and manifest in the customs, traditions, and practices of everyday life. The status of distance education specifically, or of adult education in general, needs to be considered as an important aspect in the development of our learner, where dissimilar beliefs about the nature and purpose of education, for example, are held by persons in our learner's social class. As Bronfenbrenner notes, we need to give particular attention to 'the developmentally instigating belief systems, resources, hazards, life styles, opportunity structures, life course options, and patterns of social interaction that are imbedded in each of these systems (micro-, meso- and exosystems)' (Bronfenbrenner 1989a: 228). Throughout we must remain mindful that the context, both proximal and remote can invite, permit or inhibit progressive development over time in interaction with the individual's characteristics (e.g. locus of control), which encourage or discourage interactions with that environment.

Overall, Bronfenbrenner's ecological systems theory helps us go beyond the conception of a decontextualized or single context learner to recognizing the learner in multiple contexts at a specific point in time in sociohistory. In this instance, development is seen as 'a function of the progressive and reciprocal interplay, through the life course, between an active, growing human organism and the changing properties of its environment, both immediate and more remote' (Bronfenbrenner 1989b: 2). Further, Bronfenbrenner reminds us of Vygotsky's thesis (Vygotsky 1978) that individual development is defined and delimited by the possibilities available to it in a given culture or subculture at a given point in time and 'that the context in which cognition takes place is not simply an adjunct to the cognition, but a constituent of it' (Ceci *et al.* 1988: 243).

## RESEARCH EMPLOYING ECOLOGICAL THEORY

Not only does Bronfenbrenner challenge us to see the developing individual in a reciprocal relationship to a larger context, he challenges us to move towards research designs more appropriate to this theoretical position. He returns to Lewin in his discussions of appropriate research to remind us that many research designs have focused on either the $P$ (person) or $E$ (environment), but seldom on both. For example, in distance education, as we look at persistence as an indicator of learning, many of our research studies have focused solely on personal attributes (e.g. learning style, locus of control, grade point average). Other studies which have focused solely on environmental characteristics (e.g. socioeconomic class, rural versus urban, employment status, ethnicity – what Bronfenbrenner terms social address), are less frequent in distance education today although early studies of persistence focused on many aspects of social address. If one counts the raft of media comparison studies in which the learner is placed in one media environment to be compared with the developmental outcomes of a learner in another media-based learning environment, the number of $E$ studies begins to soar.

Most recently, distance education research has begun to focus increasingly on the joint effects of personal attributes and environmental factors, for example determining how certain personal attributes (e.g. gender, age, grade point average) and environment (e.g. ethnic membership, socioeconomic status) affect persistence in college. In one such study of adult undergraduates in traditional higher education, Babler (1992) discovered instances where female Latino students from a lower socioeconomic class immigrant family were more likely to drop out of college than their other Latino counterparts.

Bronfenbrenner would urge us to go one step further in our research designs – to begin to move beyond the 'person–context' design above to what he terms a 'person–process–context' design. He would encourage us to begin to ask what processes, associated with the above characteristics, affect the outcome of persistence in learning. On closer examination of the Babler study, immigrant Latino families questioned the value of education for Latinos in general and Latinas in particular, and thus educational pursuits were often unsupported fiscally and psychologically by families. In addition, given the place of the family in the life of a Latino and the ascribed roles and responsibilities of a young Latina, many family demands interfered with school. Often financial aid was diverted to the family rather than to education. Thus one sees a synergism which existed and produced effects greater than any one variable alone.

The challenge to distance educators is to continue to identify those factors both internal and external to the learner which affect development, and to better understand the nature of the related processes. Reciprocal relationships and new synergisms are not to be forgotten, nor the element of time across which these developmental changes occur. A tall order for qualitative and quantitative researchers alike.

## IN CONCLUSION

At the risk of overgeneralizing, distance education has, for the last approximately 150 years, served to bridge the gap between educational needs and provision (Moore 1990) – to provide both access and success to diverse populations in a wide variety of settings. Some would suggest we have spent an equal amount of time defining and debating. Arguing for a broader conceptualization of our field of practice perhaps adds fuel to the fire of debate towards the end of providing description, explanation, and especially understanding more in keeping with the experience of distance learners.

On reflecting on practical thinking, Scribner noted that

> 'mind in action' . . . is imbedded in the larger purposive activities of daily life and functions to achieve the goals of these activities. The examination of thinking and learning does not need to be evaluated as a performance of isolated mental tasks undertaken as ends in themselves.
>
> (Scribner 1986: 15).

For the most part, distance educators have not wholly ignored the contexts in which the adult lives and learns, but we have perhaps been less than systematic in our consideration of learners, their multiple teaching–learning contexts, the processes by which learning occurs (or fails to occur) within and as a result of these contexts, and the nature of the development which ensues.

Many models utilized by distance education emerge from research on the traditional aged learner in a traditional institution of post-secondary education and thus fail to meet the needs of the distance education researcher and/or practitioner. As Morrison observes, most models of distance education reflect existing theories of learning. Further, 'Given the state of theory and research into human learning, particularly as it relates to learning in live social and cultural contexts outside formal educational settings where most distance learners are located' (Morrison 1989: 13), he suggests that models of distance learning be considered as exploratory, evolutionary in nature.

Ecological systems theory provides yet another valuable perspective on the field of distance education, one that will perhaps broaden our conception of the field as a whole. As Bronfenbrenner noted in his early writings, 'we work from different perspectives in different ways. A variety of approaches are needed if we are to make progress toward the ultimate goal of understanding human development in context' (Bronfenbrenner 1977: 529). If, as Morrison (1989) suggests, the challenge to distance education is to determine how to match the learner, the content, the process, and the context in such a way as to ensure equity of both access to and success in distance learning, ecological systems theory may prove to be a valuable approach to research and practice.

## BIBLIOGRAPHY

Babler, L. (1992) 'The persistence/nonpersistence decision of Latino college students', unpublished doctoral dissertation, Madison, Wis.: University of Wisconsin-Madison.

Billings, D. (1988) 'A conceptual model of correspondence course completion', *The American Journal of Distance Education* 2(2), 23–35.

Bronfenbrenner, U. (1977) 'Toward an experimental ecology of human development', *American Psychologist*, vol. 7, 513–31.

—— (1986) 'Ecology of the family as a context for human development: research perspectives', *Developmental Psychology* 22(6), 723–42.

Bronfenbrenner, U. (1989a) 'Ecological systems theory', *Annals of Child Development*, vol. 6, 187–249.

—— (1989b) 'The developing ecology of human development: paradigm lost or paradigm regained', in Theories of Child Development: Updates and Reformulations, Symposium conducted at the meeting of the Society for Research in Child Development, Kansas City, Missouri, USA, April.

Ceci, S., Bronfenbrenner U. and Baker, J. (1988) 'Memory in context: the case of prospective memory', in F. Weinert and M. Perlmutter (eds), *Universals and Changes in Memory Development*, Hillsdale, N.J.: Erlbaum.

Evans, T. and Nation, D. (1992) 'Theorising open and distance education', *Open Learning* 7(2), 3–13.

Garrison, D. P. (1989) *Understanding Distance Education: A Framework for the Future*, New York: Routledge.

Gibson, C. (1990) 'Learners and learning: discussion of selected research', in M. Moore (ed.), *Contemporary Issues in American Distance Education*, New York: Pergamon Press.

—— (1991) 'One researcher's perspective: questions and research strategies', *American Journal of Distance Education* 4(1), 69–81.

—— (1992) 'Changing perceptions of learners and learning at a distance', in M. Moore (ed.), *Distance Education Symposium Papers – Number 1* (American Center for the Study of Distance Education), Research Monograph Number 4, University Park, Pa.: American Center for the Study of Distance Education.

—— and Graff, A. (1992) 'Impact of adult's preferred learning style and perceptions of barriers on completion of external baccalaureate degree programs', *Journal of Distance Education* VII(1), 39–51.

Herrman, A. (1988) 'A conceptual framework for understanding the transitions in perceptions of external students', *Distance Education* 9(1), 1–26.

Kasworm, C. (1990a) 'Transformative contexts in adult higher education', Revision of a paper presented at the Second International Congress for Research on Activity Theory, Lahti, Finland, May.

Kasworm, C. (1990b) 'Adult undergraduates in higher education: review of past research perspectives', *Review of Educational Research* 60(3), 345–72.

Kember, D., Murphy, D., Siaw, I. and Yuen, K. S. (1991) 'Towards a causal model of student progress in distance education: research in Hong Kong', *The American Journal of Distance Education* 5(2), 3–15.

Lewin, K. (1936) *Problems of Topological Psychology*, New York: McGraw-Hill.

—— (1951) *Field Theory in Social Sciences*, New York: Harper.

Moore, M. (1973) 'Toward a theory of independent learning and teaching', *Journal of Higher Education* 44, 661–79.

—— (ed.) (1990) *Contemporary Issues in American Distance Education*, New York: Pergamon Press.

Morrison, T. R. (1989) 'Beyond legitimacy: facing the future of distance education', *International Journal of Lifelong Education* 8(1), 3–24.

Powell, R., Conway, C. and Ross, L. (1990) 'Effects of students' predisposing characteristics on students' success', *Journal of Distance Education* V(1), 5–19.

Scribner, S. (1986) 'Thinking in action: some characteristics of practical thought', in R. Sternberg and R. Wagner, *Practical Intelligence: Nature and Origins of Competence in the Everyday World*, Cambridge: Cambridge University Press.

Vygotsky, L. (1978) *Mind in Society*, Cambridge, Mass.: Harvard University Press.

Way, W. (1991) 'Frameworks for examining work–family relationships within the context of home economics education', in G. Feltstehausen and J. R. Schultz (eds), *Work and Family: Educational Implications*, New York: Macmillan McGraw-Hill.

Wedemeyer, C. (1981) *Learning at the Back Door*, Madison, Wis.: University of Wisconsin Press.

# 6 What's behind the development of a course on the concept of distance education?

*Louise Sauvé*

To learn, is to discover what you know already,
To do, is to demonstrate that you know it.
To teach, is to remind others that they know it as well as you do.
We are all learners, doers and teachers.

Richard Bach, 1978

## INTRODUCTION

To speak of distance education as a concept and a theory is not new. For over twenty years, several theoreticians and researchers have focused on this subject (Peters, Keegan, Rumble, Holmberg, Moore, Perraton, Garrison and Shale, Baker *et al.*, etc.).

In an attempt to deal with this issue personally, we have decided to examine distance education from the teacher's point of view within the framework of an introductory postgraduate course on distance education (EDU 6000 *Systèmes de formation à distance*). How should we approach this question with students who have little or no knowledge of distance education? What authors should be recommended reading? What should the students learn? These are the questions that guided us through the development of this course.

First of all we will present the theoretical strategy used to choose the texts included in the first part of the course called '*La formation à distance, un débat terminologique*'. Second, we will examine the students' perception of the literature suggested. Third, we will present various thoughts surrounding the distance education debate.

## IN SEARCH OF A DEFINITION AND A THEORY OF DISTANCE EDUCATION

Because of our background in educational technology, we asked ourselves: Is the field of distance education related to educational technology? Are these two fields composed of the same elements or are they different? To answer these questions, we examined our definition of educational technology and pointed out the similarities and differences between it and distance education.

**What is educational technology?**

Educational technology is a combination of many disciplines. It began with the visual aids tried in teaching in the 1920s, became audiovisual instruction in the 1940s, and then drew from the communication and learning theories and the trends of learning psychology in the 1950s. In the 1960s it borrowed ideas about design and management from communication systems with educational functions. In the 1980s it incorporated principles of cognitive psychology, particularly memory, problem-solving and thinking, while paying more and more attention to individualized instruction, computer-assisted instruction and optical storage media.

Thus we see that technological evolution and the contribution of different trends have coloured the definition of educational technology. Despite their background and points of view, theoricians and practitioners (AECT 1977; Lachance *et al.* 1978; Becher 1981; Romiszowski 1981; Mitchell 1981; Scholer 1983; Stolovitch and La Rocque 1983; Boyd 1988, 1991; Hawkridge 1991; Koetting and Januszewski 1991; Winn 1991) agree on certain common characteristics of educational technology:

- Human learning is an objective: educational technology is fundamentally preoccupied with learning-related problems and uses a systematic and a systemic approach to solve them.
- Systematic approach (pedagogical design): a systematic approach is a logical and gradual sequence of operations or activities. It is exemplified in the organizational and operational methods of educational technology.
- Systems method: the relationship between the systems approach, as a science and a source of general systems theory, and educational technology has been well established (Bertrand 1990). It supplies a global conceptual framework for educational technology which is both systematic in its procedures and systemic in its approach to problem-solving.
- Use of media: educational technology's basic focus is on educational resources and the use of media in education.

Considering these characteristics, is there a relationship between educational technology and distance education?

## Is there a relationship between the two fields?

Since its beginnings, educational technology has been particularly preoccupied with learning in individualized situations. Programmed learning was the first manifestation of this preoccupation and consisted of elaborating meticulously planned and controlled teaching systems tailored to the individual situation. Yet distance education requires these situations where the student is isolated for the most part, and must work solitarily. It is not therefore surprising that educational technology considers that its underlying principles and methods are necessary for the success of distance education.

Also, several authors have pointed out the direct relationship between distance education and educational technology. To examine them we consulted Keegan (1986) on the characteristics of distance education: the use of media to transmit information; the importance of two-way communication between teacher and student, who are separated throughout the process; the predominance of individualized learning, and an industrialized form of course development and distribution.

Perraton (1981: 14) defined distance education as 'an educational process in which an appreciable part of the teaching is done by a person who is distant in time and/or in space'. He proposed to examine distance education theory by using fourteen propositions that deal with, among others, the use of multi-media in teaching, and the necessity of using the systems approach to manage the complexity of this type of teaching.

Holmberg (1982), in defining distance education and its course design procedure, identified two major contributions made by educational technology to distance education: the use of learning objectives as a technique to structure course content to meet the needs of students, and the use of the systems approach to develop complex teaching systems.

According to Forsythe (1983), who based her arguments on correspondence and multi-media-based models of distance education, educational technology and distance education are directly linked by the following characteristics: the use of a pedagogical design procedure and medias, the emphasis placed on student responsibility for his or her learning and, consequently, the possibility of a situation that provides for noncontiguous communication between student and teacher.

Peters (see Keegan 1986), by examining the industrialization process of distance education, also studied the relationships between distance education and educational technology. Due to the systematic planning and rationalization of educational methods provided by educational technology, distance education has become more efficient both educationally and economically. In 1989, Peters again pointed out educational technology's important role in the industrialization process in education, but also highlighted the dangers of this techno-logical model of distance education.

Butts (1986) proposed several arguments that support distance education as a natural field in which to apply educational technology. According to this author, distance education houses six types of problems that could be easily solved by contributions from educa-tional technology. These problems are:

- the cohesion and quality of produced course material;
- the costs and constraints of using media other than print;
- controlling broadcasting via large television and radio networks which are constricting to the learner;
- restrictions involving pedagogical design;
- difficulties in applying the appropriate management and control to an industrialized production and delivery system;
- difficulties in predicting distance student behaviour.

Finally, Evans and Nation (1989), like Peters (1989), have claimed that educational technology in distance education represents 'instructional industrialism'.

By re-examining these different relationships, we can establish that educational technology and distance education share these common grounds:

- the systematic procedure used to structure, to choose media and to deliver distance education, which can be viewed as the industrialization of distance education;
- the choice of media which is also one of the essential features of distance education: the use of media to re-establish the link between the student and the source of knowledge;
- the systems approach which is the preferred approach for this form of complex teaching;
- the objective to encourage human learning, the common goal of educational technology and of distance education.

Since the literature recognizes the relationship between distance education and educational technology, can we say that these two fields merge?

Peruniak (1983) suggested that distance education uses technology to deliver instruction to geographically dispersed groups while educational technology uses instructional design and development methodologies in distance education as a context within which to operate.

Wagner views both

> educational technology and distance education as components of an even larger system where each function is a point along a continuum of contemporary educational practices. . . . Distance education provides educational technologists with an exceedingly rich research and application environment, while educational technology provides distance educators with methods and means of improving performance.
>
> (Wagner 1990: 65–6)

Keegan (1992: 17) highlights five distinctions between distance education and educational technology:

1 Distance education is a form of education, educational technology is not.
2 In distance education, the technology is a *substitute* for the teacher. In educational technology the technology is a *supplement* to the teacher.
3 Educational technology studies the efficient use of technology for all types of teaching (at a distance and face to face). Distance education does not have this role. Distance education specialists study the use of technology in teaching the 10 million students who chose to study outside of the conventional institutions. These distance education specialists analyse the findings of educational technologists and adapt them to the particular situations of their clients.
4 Distance education studies the problems of students who learn at home or at the office, for whom face-to-face group-based communication is entirely, or to a large extent, absent. Educational technology does not in any way abandon face-to-face group-based communication. It does in fact presume the face-to-face interaction as the basis for information and interpretation of the technology.
5 Educational technology is different from distance education in terms of cost structures. Educational technology often makes teaching more costly than the teacher without the technology (Teacher + Technology > Teacher). In distance education the technology may make teaching either more costly or less costly depending on the choice of the cost-inducing variables and the volume of students in the programme.

From the analysis of these two concepts, we agree with Keegan (1992) and conclude that distance education requires help from educational technology to establish which technologies are the most effective economically and pedagogically, but that educational technology is not limited to the use of technology in distance education systems.

After having come to the conclusion that educational technology and distance education are similar yet different, we asked ourselves if a theory of distance education exists.

## A LOOK AT THE DIFFERENT THEORIES OF DISTANCE EDUCATION

Many authors have tried to lay the foundations on which a theory of distance education could be based:

- Delling's process model of 1966 (Keegan 1986);
- Wedemeyer's liberal, individualizing 'independent study' (1981);
- Sewart's support model, called 'continuity of concern' (1981);
- Bååth's two-way communication (1982);
- Peters's view of distance education as an industrialized form of teaching and learning (1983);
- Holmberg's theory of the guided didactic conversation (1983);
- Smith's student-centred small-scale approach of 1983 (Keegan 1986);
- Holmberg's normative teaching theory for distance education (1985);
- Perraton's three interrelated systems of teaching, administration, and assessment (1987);
- Keegan's theory of the reintegration of the teaching acts (1990);
- Saba's model of the dynamic interrelationship of dialogue and structure (1990);
- Verduin and Clark's three dimensional model included: dialogue/ support, structure/specialized competence, general competence/ self-directedness (1991);
- Moore's theory of transactional distance included the concept of dialogue, structure, and the characteristics of each learner (1990, 1991)

By examining these models, we have found a certain number of themes.

### Theoretical models can be grouped into two large fields of study

We can divide most authors into two categories if we exclude Peters (1983), Perraton (1987) and Keegan (1990). Peters (1983) proposes a model of distance education based on the industrialization process using a division of labour and technology to mass produce a high-quality teaching model. This model has been discussed and challenged, but has not been included, to the best of our knowledge, in any recent theoretical models. Perraton (1987) presents generalizations rather than a theory of distance education when examining the practices of this type of teaching. Finally, Keegan (1990) provides a working hypothesis to be used to establish a theoretical justification for distance education which reintegrated the teaching act in the educational process by two-way distance systems.

## The first group

This includes models that analyse distance education based on the notions of student autonomy and independence. In Delling's 1966 model, the learner is seen to be autonomous and independent and considered to be at the heart of the distance education process. Wedemeyer (1981) reiterates the principles of individualization and open learning and defines the concept of independent study. Moore (1991), based on the learner autonomy, developed a two-dimensional model 'transactional distance' that incorporates both the rigidity or flexibility of the programme's educational objectives, teaching strategies and evaluation methods (structure), and the interaction between teacher and learner when one gives instruction and the other responds (dialogue). Transactional distance 'occurs between individuals who are teachers and learners, in an environment that has the special characteristic of separation of one from another, and a consequent set of special teaching and learning behaviors' (Moore 1991: 2). Saba (1990) adds the notion of 'virtual contiguity' to Moore's model, insisting on the importance of integrated systems that bring teacher and learner together, optimize dialogue between them, and eliminate consequences of being separate in space. Finally, Verduin and Clark (1991) examine the concept of 'transactional distance' and develop a three-dimensional model including three new variables that affect the learner: dialogue/*support*, structure/ *specialized competence*, and *general competence*/self-directedness.

## The second group

This includes models that analyse distance education based on the notions of interaction and communication. These notions emphasize student support offered by the institution in order to reestablish communication and interaction. Accordingly, Bååth (1982) speaks about the need for two-way communication between the student and the tutor/institution where the tutor is the key to the two-way communication concept. Holmberg's (1983) guided didactical communication model describes interaction as: (a) a continuous relationship between the student and the tutor/counsellor/institution and, (b) a simultaneous conversation with the student through the use of carefully prepared learning material. As for Sewart (1981), the role of the mediator is not only necessary but is also the only means available to adapt distance education to the individual needs of the students. According to Smith's 1983 model, distance education must supply students with learning material that allows them to work autonomously, with *compulsory* support to encourage contact between students and staff, and with regular group activities.

### The basis of distance education is the separation of teacher and learner

Whether it be in the name of student autonomy or of student support, every model studied suggests that whenever distance education is examined it should be done in full knowledge of the separation of the learner and the teacher. However, authors view this separation differently and these differences influence the models they develop:

- the physical distance between student and teacher (Delling's 1966 model, see Keegan 1986);
- social, cultural and psychic distance between the educator and the learner (Wedemeyer 1981);
- the teaching acts are separated in time and place from the learning acts (Sewart 1981);
- allows a large number of students to participate in university study simultaneously, regardless of their place of residence and occupation (Peters 1983);
- not under the continuous, immediate supervision of tutors present with their students in lecture rooms or on the same premises (Holmberg 1985);
- mediated, non-contiguous communication between the student and the educator (Verduin and Clark 1991);
- understandings and perception deriving from the geographic separation of learners and teachers (Moore 1991);
- teaching and learning acts (or behaviours) become separated spatially and/or temporally (Keegan 1990, Perraton 1987).

**The study of the underlying principles of distance education has always been done by comparing them with those of conventional teaching**

When developing their models of distance education, these authors have always considered conventional teaching to be the ideal educational relationship between teacher and learner. In consequence, distance education was seen as having to recreate this ideal relationship either through its learning material or by setting a two-way communication between student and tutor/counsellor/institution. Is this always necessary?

According to Shale (1988), current technological developments are narrowing the gap between distance and conventional education. He states that we should not define distance education in terms of distance but rather in terms of education. Bagnall (1989), in his analysis of distance education, questions the comparative approach used by Wedemeyer, Holmberg, Keegan, and Moore. He suggests that we should examine distance education in terms of student autonomy – an element that is equally important in distance education and in conventional education.

**No global theory of distance education exists yet**

It seems clear that there are a number of theories and, more exactly, a number of models relating to the practice of the distance education, but no overarching theory or concept of distance education. Rumble (1988) states that, in the case of distance education, we are still dealing with a level of generalization drawn from practices and that we lack the conceptual structures that are truly independent of general educational theories. However, the study of these different models can supply the reader with conceptual bases from which a global theory of distance education could be built.

After examining the theoretical models of distance education we questioned the relevance of introducing all these models to the students before they had acquired the terminology necessary to understand them. We felt that our students would need to become familiar with the components of distance education before they could understand these models. We therefore opted to analyse the concept of distance education and to investigate what it means to the student.

**DEFINING DISTANCE EDUCATION: NOT A MEAN FEAT**

In order to provide the students with the data needed to define distance education, we examined the literature from various sources:

*The American Journal of Distance Education* (USA), *Open Learning* and *Teaching at a Distance* (Great Britain), *Journal of Distance Education/Revue de l'enseignement à distance* (Canada), and various recent books dealing with this concept. This investigation led us to highlight the following elements:

- There is a wide sphere of definitions of distance education. Each definition is formulated according to the contexts and the authors involved.
- The rapid evolution of applications in distance education has created a certain amount of terminological confusion.
- Despite the divergent views there are some constants: communication, distance (in terms of time and/or space), the use of media or technologies, planning and organization.
- At present, distance education stands as an umbrella concept covering correspondance courses, televised teaching, radio-broadcast teaching, open learning, computer-assisted instruction, telematic, individualized learning and self-learning.
- Distance education is viewed differently by many authors depending on their personal vision of education, of teaching and of learning.
- For the last ten years, distance education has distanced itself from broadcast-type media and has embraced technologies that offer interactive and individualized communication opportunities.
- Finally, the authors cannot agree upon a common definition.

So, what should we do? First of all, when we designed our introductory course, we decided to use only the term 'distance education' throughout. This term covers both teaching at a distance and learning at a distance, representing both halves of the global educational process. Teaching at a distance therefore refers to course design and student support activities, whereas learning at a distance describes learning activities that occur far from the teaching institution or the teacher.

Then we presented the students with the literature dealing with the issue in order that they arrive at a definition of distance education. But which authors should we suggest they read?

Confronted with definitions of distance education that were, for the most part, a reflection of technologies that existed at the time of their creation, we reviewed the literature and grouped the authors in one of these two premises according to how they developed their arguments and their definitions:

- Distance education is individualized teaching with limited teacher–student interaction; the student is separated from the teacher in time and space and therefore learns autonomously. This option includes authors who analysed correspondence study, one-way multi-media courses and two-way student support. We chose the following authors to represent this position: Rumble (1989a), Keegan (1988), Holmberg (1989).

- Technological innovations, especially digitalized technologies (interactive television, telewriters, etc.) have reduced the gap between face-to-face teaching and distance education by providing a wide range of communication possibilities to the institution willing to establish interaction with the distant learner. These technologies include two-way multi-media teaching (interactive television and audiography), and multi-media student support systems (computer-assisted conferences, audioconferences). We chose the following authors to represent this position: Shale (1988), Garrison (1989), Barker *et al.* (1989).

## STUDENT PERCEPTIONS

Once the course was completed, edited and delivered to the students, what did they have to say about the terminological debate surrounding distance education? Here are some extracts:

'Anybody studying distance education for the first time could find himself confused by the multitude of definitions and the variety of vocabulary used to describe it. . . . This terminological debate surrounding distance education is a sign of both the newness of the field and its many applications.' (43-year-old student)

'The development of distance education resembles the formation of the earth's crust. History tells us that distance education was developed in layers. Each layer corresponding to an evolutionary step represented by the evolution of modern communication techniques and by a more complex and fertile awareness of the learning process. One should not be surprised to learn that the definition of distance education has been evolving and it should be perceived as normal that it continue to do so.' (60-year-old student)

'My readings have brought me to the conclusion that the miracle recipe, the standard definition has not yet been produced.' (30-year-old student)

'Researchers have been influenced as much by ideologies and their own personal interests as by the various learning methods in their definition of distance education. However, the authors do agree on certain characteristics.' (52-year-old student)

'We were slightly amused by the current battle we witnessed between the leaders in distance education. It seemed to us that the entire discussion was centred around the loss of relationship and/or power that the teacher seems to experience within this type of educational delivery system.' (41-year-old student)

'Were they battles, or should I say quarrels, resulting from the evolution of this type of study? Or are they simply a consequence of using different premises?.' (43-year-old student)

'I did my best to grasp the content of this debate. However I found that certain authors get bogged down in trivia and stubbornly consider that their definition is the best one.' (39-year-old student)

'The authors' points of view provoke both pertinent comparisons and the creation of a personal definition of distance education.' (45-year-old student)

'Certain definitions are more restrictive, even purist, especially those that are inspired almost entirely by correspondence, the first generation technology. Others enlarge the concept of distance education to include all new applications and technologies.' (32-year-old student)

'In our opinion, the best way to define 'distance education' is to find the greatest common denominator for the phenomenon in the same manner as we would define a horse.' (35-year-old student)

But what did they get out of or understand from this debate where each author presented his own definition of distance education? To delimit a definition of distance education certain students relied on a concept analyses approach (essential characteristics of distance education), others on their own philosophy of education, whereas most relied on common points that unite the authors. The students produced three characteristics of distance education that we agree with:

1 The main characteristic of distance education is distance – in other words, the temporal, spatial or psycho-social separation. This separation does not necessarily imply the lack of personal or direct contact between students and teachers. However this contact is modified; it is through the use of communication techniques that the transmission of information, teaching, and student support is assured.

2 The use of media (whether it's called technical support, delivery methods, technology, or media) is necessary for the delivery of knowledge or to ensure student support.

3 Communication between the student and the teacher (tutor,

counsellor, or institution), whether it be delayed by mail or real time by telephone, through face-to-face meetings, videoconferences, etc., must be present.

What would our theoreticians think? Do these characteristics reflect a 1990s reality? The debate goes on.


## CONCLUSION

We would like to present you with some of our thoughts that we hope will sustain the distance education debate. These thoughts rely both on student input during audioconferences and on our own teaching experience and research in the field.

As we studied the different authors who defined distance education we became aware that their definitions were coloured by the authors' experience and their philosophy of education. *Each definition reflects a precise image of distance education or what the author would like it to be.* For example, if we believe in student autonomy, distance education becomes more liberal, more open. If we believe in efficient correspondence teaching, distance education becomes a mass-production process where individualized learning and structured learning material require a systematic and systemic approach. If we believe in the supremacy of digitalized technologies over other media, we cheerfully reject all other forms of distance education. Distance education is still an evolving field and will probably stay this way for a long time since each technological change (aren't we limited by distance that can only be lessened by media?) forces us to re-examine the practice and the theoretical foundations of distance education.

*Distance is still at the heart of distance education.* This statement puts us at odds with Shale (1988) who questions most of the authors who define distance education by focusing on distance rather than on education. We feel in fact that distance *is* what makes the difference between distance education and other modes of teaching. Without distance the use of media would no longer remain compulsory to establish the relationship between students and teachers.

*Without the use of media, distance education could not exist.* Distance education is above all media-assisted teaching. Even now in distance education, despite technological developments, the essential functions normally assumed by the teacher in a classroom are carried out by technical means that some authors call technology and others, media. However we cannot deny that the advent of digitalized technology leads us to question the concepts of individualized learning to the benefit of group learning. The notion of interactivity in real time in teacher–student communication takes back its place and in fact reduces student isolation by putting students in regular contact with a group.

Nevertheless, experiments conducted on digitalized technologies in distance education sometimes leave us perplexed. It is often very difficult to distinguish, in these experiments, between what is taught using digitalized technology and what results from student support. For example, computer-assisted conferences and electronic mail serve mainly as a support allowing for content-related discussions between students or between students and the teacher; they are rarely used as teaching devices. Teaching, in terms of content transmission, remains entirely one way (print, audiocassettes, television, computers). In this way we find ourselves in the same company as Garrison and Shale (1987) as they explain that the teacher transmits the course's content by using various means of support such as print, videos, and audiotapes that are supplied to the students. However, in order to close the communication loop, this interaction requires an activity that is distinct from the transmission of information and is frequently conducted by a media other than the one that delivers the content. These media that support learning are mostly two-way and are chiefly the telephone, audioconferences, videoconferences, and computer-assisted conferences.

*Distance education offers a variety of teaching modes related to the technology used.* More authors (Shale, Garrison, Barker *et al.*) are defining distance education swear by real-time teaching at a distance to groups of students located in different areas. This type of distance teaching, allowing students/teacher immediate interaction and feedback in real time, brings them to question the value of distance education modes of the 1970s where individual learning and print dominated over interactive media and group teaching. While it is true that this type of group teaching by videoconference and audiography brings distance education closer to conventional face-to-face teaching, it also reduces the students' freedom to study at their own pace and at a time and place of their choice, and thus restricts the individualization of learning. This return to the style and constraints of conventional teaching does favour those students who need to study and to discuss within a group setting. But it also penalizes those students who chose to study at a distance because distance education responded to their particular needs. Distance education's flexible model allows to meet student needs by removing certain barriers (Guillemet 1989):

- professional and personal barriers: problems working in a group, occasional work, alternating between unemployment insurance and work, irregular schedules, family obligations, reduced mobility, age, institutionalization, reduced income, etc.;
- institutional barriers: course schedules, place of study, group forming, availability of services, etc.

This type of distance education that uses digitalized technology should be carefully analysed and be considered along with the other modes of distance education. Each mode of distance education, from correspondence teaching to interactive-multi-media teaching responds to particular needs and should be used according to the context and the needs of the target population. We feel that an ideal mode of distance education does not exist and that technological advances simply allow us to diversify our approach without necessarily finding the one best approach that is all things to all people.

## REFERENCES

AECT (1977) *Educational Technology: Definition and Glossary of Terms*, vol. 1, Washington, DC: Association for Educational Communications and Technology.

Bååth, J. (1982) 'Distance students's learning – empirical findings and theoretical deliberations', *Distance Education* 3(1), 6–27.

Bach, R. (1978) *Illusions*, Paris: Flamamarion.

Bagnall, R. G. (1989) 'Educational distance from the perspective of self-direction: an analysis', *Open Learning* 4(1), 21–6.

Barker, B. O., Frisbie, A. G. and Patrick, K. R. (1989) 'Broadening the definition of distance education in light of the new telecommunications technologies', *The American Journal of Distance Education* 3(1), 20–9.

Becher, T. (1981) 'Evaluation and educational technology', in F. Percival and H. Ellington, *Aspects of Educational Technology: Distance Learning and Evaluation*, London: Kogan Page.

Bertrand, Y. (1990) *Théories contemporaines de l'éducation*, Montréal: Les éditions Agence d'Arc inc.

Boyd, G. (1988) 'The impact of society on educational technology', *British Journal of Educational Technology* 19(2), 114–22.

—— (1991) 'The shaping of educational technology by cultural politics and vice versa', *ETTI* 28(2), 87–95.

Butts, D. (1986) 'Distance learning and broadcasting', in F. Percival and H. Ellington, *Aspects of Educational Technology: Distance Learning and Evaluation*, London: Kogan Page.

Evans, T. and Nation, D. (1989) *Critical Reflections on Distance Education*, London: Falmer Press.

Forsythe, K. (1983) 'The human interface: teachers in the new age', *Programmed Learning and Educational Technology* 20(3), 161–6.

Garrison, D. R. (1989) *Understanding Distance Education*, London: Routledge.
—— and Shale, D. (1987) 'Mapping the boundaries of distance education: problems in defining the field', *The American Journal of Distance Education* 1(1), 7–13.
Guillemet, P. (1989) 'La problématique de la formation à distance', in A. J. Deschênes (ed.), *La formation à distance maintenant*, Thème 1, Québec: Téléuniversité 37–48.
Hawkridge, D. (1991) 'Challenging educational technology', *ETTI* 28(2), 102–10.
Holmberg, B. (1982) *Recent Research into Distance Education*, Hagen: Fernuniversität.
—— (1983) 'Guided didactic conversation in distance education', in D. Sewart, D. Keegan and B. Holmberg (eds), *Distance Education: International Perspectives*, London: Croom Helm.
—— (1985) *The Feasibility of a Theory of Teaching for Distance Education and a Proposed Theory*, ZIFF Papiere 60, Hagen: Fernuniversität.
—— (1989) 'The concepts and applications of distance education and open learning, *Innovative Higher Education* 6(1–2), 24–8.
Keegan, D. (1986) *The Foundations of Distance Education* (1st edn), Beckenham: Croom Helm.
—— (1988) 'Problems in defining the field of distance education' *The American Journal of Distance Education* 2(2), 4–11.
—— (1990) 'A theory for distance education', in M. G. Moore (ed.), *Contemporary Issues in American Distance Education*, Oxford: Pergamon Press.
—— (1991) *The Foundations of Distance Education* (2nd edn), London and New York: Routledge.
—— (1992) 'La technologie éducative et la formation à distance: amies ou rivales?' in L. Sauvé (ed.), *La technologie éducative, d'hier à demain*, Québec: CIPTE et Télé-université.
Koetting, J. R. and Januszewski, A. (1991) 'The notion of theory and educational technology foundations for understanding', *ETTI* 28(2), 96–101.
Lachance, B., Lapointe, J. and Marton, P. (1978) *Le domaine de la technologie éducative*, Quebec: Université Laval, Département de la technologie de l'enseignement.
Mitchell, P. D. (1981) 'La technologie éducative: un mode en voie de disparition ou une nouvelle profession', *Performance* 5(2), 15–18.
Moore, M. (1990) 'Recent contributions to the theory of distance education', *Open Learning* 5(3), 10–15.
—— (1991) 'Editorial: Distance Education Theory', *The American Journal of Distance Education* 5(3), 1–6.
Perraton, H. (1981) 'Une théorie de l'enseignement à distance', *Perspectives* XI(1), 14–27.
—— (1987) 'Theories, generalisation and practice in distance education', *Open Learning* 2(3), 3–12.
Peruniak, G. S. (1983) 'Interactive perspectives in distance education', *Distance Education* 4(1), 63–79.
Peters, O. (1983) 'Distance teaching and industrial production: a comparative interpretation in outline', in D. Sewart, D. Keegan and B. Holmberg (eds), *Distance education: International Perspectives*, London: Croom Helm.

—— (1989) 'The iceberg has not melted: further reflections on the concept of industrialisation and distance teaching', *Open Learning* 4(3), 3–8.

Romiszowski, A. J. (1981) 'Troubleshooting in educational technology', *Programmed Learning and Educational Technology* 1(3), 168–89.

Rumble, G. (1988) 'Animadversions upon the concept of distance education as a discipline', *Journal of Distance Education/Revue de l'enseignement à distance* 3(1), 39–56.

—— (1989a) 'On defining distance education', *The American Journal of Distance Education* 3(2), 8–21.

—— (1989b) 'Open learning, distance learning and the misuse of language', *Open Learning* 4(2), 28–35.

Saba, F. (1990) 'Integrated telecommunications systems and instructional transaction', in M. G. Moore (ed.), *Contemporary Issues in American Distance Education*, Oxford: Pergamon Press.

Saettler, P. (1968) *A History of Instructional Technology*, New York: McGraw-Hill.

Scholer, M. (1983) *La technologie de l'éducation, concept, bases et application*, Montréal: Les presses de l'Université de Montréal, MEQ.

Sewart, D. (1981) 'Distance teaching: a contradiction in terms?', *Teaching at a Distance*, no. 19: 8–18.

Shale, D. (1988) 'Toward a reconceptualization of distance education', *The American Journal of Distance Education* 2(3), 25–35.

Stolovitch, H. D. and La Rocque, G. (1983) *Introduction à la technologie de l'instruction*, Préfontaine Editions St-Jean sur Richelieu.

Verduin, J. R. and Clark, T. A. (1991) *Distance Education. The Foundations of Effective Practice*, San Francisco: Jossey-Bass.

Wagner, E. D. (1990) 'Looking at distance education through an educational technologist's eyes', *The American Journal of Distance Education* 4(1), 53–67.

Wedemeyer, C. (1981) *Learning at the Backdoor: Reflections on Non-traditional Learning in the Lifespan*, Madison, Wis.: University of Wisconsin Press.

Winn, W. (1991) 'Ebauche d'un cadre théorique propre à la technologie éducative', in L. Sauvé (ed.), *La technologie éducative à la croisée des disciplines*, Québec: CIPTE et Télé-université.

# Part III
# Analytic underpinnings

# 7 Reintegration of the teaching acts

*Desmond Keegan*

## INTRODUCTION

Up to 1980 confusion reigned about the concept of distance education. Writers did not make it clear whether they were writing about
or not writing about the use of computers in schools or Schools of
the Air or rural development projects or technology-based training.
The result was discourtesy to the reader and lack of progress in
distance education research.

An attempt was made to reduce the confusion in 1980 in an article
titled 'On defining distance education'. This study applied basic
definition techniques to the concept 'distance education' in an
attempt to clarify what was to be understood by the term and what
was excluded by it. The article was widely cited. The first unit of the
Téléuniversité masters degree in distance education, *Systèmes de
formation à distance* (Sauvé 1990), provides a selection of major
reactions to the article and of writings, which carry the debate
further, by Garrison and Shale (1987), Shale (1988), Keegan (1988),
Henri and Lamy (1989), Rumble (1989) and Barker *et al.* (1989). Of
work published since the Téléuniversité course was developed one
would certainly wish to add Garrison and Shale (1990) and Verduin
and Clark (1991).

Analysis of these writings shows that considerable progress has
been made in the delineation of the concept of distance education
but that a certain fuzziness remains. There is now general agreement
on the field of educational endeavour under discussion and there is
a healthy amount of debate about finer details. Progress in the
formulation of grounded theory for distance education, however,
requires further analysis.

The purpose of this chapter is to provide guidelines for a conceptual and logical analysis of distance education as a prerequisite
for theory formulation.

**How does one improve clarity?**

Clarity is improved by the philosophical technique known as conceptual analysis. Its importance lies in the fact that the meanings we choose to use for things and how we and others conceive of things (in this case 'distance education') subtly but surely direct the actions that we and others take.

The techniques of conceptual analysis are well known and available to all. The system used here is that provided by the School of Philosophical Analysis (P. Hirst, R. Peters, M. Oakeshott and others in the UK; W. Perry, I. Scheffler, J. Soltis and others in the US). The choice of a system does not imply that it is the best or that one accepts other philosophical positions of the group. It implies that the tools provided are judged to be competently developed and relevant to the inquiry.

The group of educational philosophers chosen holds that the distinctive function of philosophy is analysis. They see the analysis functions as referring to both concepts and arguments, emphasizing the value of both linguistic and logical analysis. Members of the group have subjected to analysis a range of concepts that have relevance for distance education: 'education', 'teaching', 'learning', 'communication', 'content', and their texts are widely used in Philosophy of Education departments today. The techniques can be found explained in Hirst and Peters' *The Logic of Education* (1970: 4–41) or Soltis's *An Introduction to the Analysis of Educational Concepts* (1978: 91–109).

**Need**

It is as well to begin with a warning. Contrary to popular opinion, philosophizing can be a very concrete activity. People's heartfelt beliefs and cherished dreams can be damaged.

'The point of doing conceptual analysis', Hirst and Peters (1970: 8) tell us, 'is to get clearer about the types of distinction that words have been developed to designate.' 'The point is', they continue, 'to see *through* the words, to get a better grasp of the similarities and differences that it is possible to pick out. And these are important in the context of *other* questions which we cannot answer without such preliminary analysis.' These may seem small gains to the busy distance educator or the educational manager, especially if people's cherished beliefs are going to be harmed.

Conceptual analysis, then, is justified on theoretical grounds. The object of the analysis is careful and critical thinking about distance education. We will move through a number of complex ideas, examining their logical underpinnings and attempting to gain precision for theoretical formulation. Comforting and reassuring thoughts are not what we are seeking. Rigorous, clear and precise thinking is the standard. Nor will it be possible to be selective with the data: all the available data are to be considered, including the world of elementary/ secondary correspondence education, proprietary and corporate operations, and a variety of other structures omitted from some recent studies.

There are three bases for this approach. The first is the conviction that distance education has come of age. It no longer needs to be promoted and protected by exaggerated claims. It has existed for 150 years and cannot be damaged by analysis. It can face the academic community with its strengths underlined and its weaknesses revealed. It is not going to disappear nor is it going to 'take over' conventional schools, colleges and universities as some of its more fanciful supporters seem to imply. The emergence in the 1990s of taught degrees in distance education at universities will lead to a new professionalism and maturity.

Second, conceptual analysis is required for theoretical work in the field. Calls for progress in the theory of distance education are premature without it. Not only is it a prerequisite, but the acceptance of the results by a cohesive group of scholars is required.

Finally, there are the dangers of not doing it and of living with imprecision. A good illustration is drop-out studies. A number of these studies claim that drop-out is a characteristic of distance education and as a result distance education has been associated with drop-out. Much-needed enrolments for both public and proprietary programmes may be lost as a result. Conceptual lack of clarity has contributed to these conclusions. For 70 years the data are constant from New Zealand, from France, from Australia, from Canada: students do not drop out from children's distance education courses. In the same way the data from the world's largest programme in the 1990s, the 650,000 students enrolled in China's forty open universities, show that studends do not drop out from distance education.

There is, therefore, no linkage between drop-out and distance education *per se*. Studies of persistence in capitalist economies of adults taking on a distance study programme in addition to work and family/social commitments belong properly to the field of part-time studies. Claims and counterclaims about distance education can only harm the field of study. Unless we know the meaning that the terms carry, it is difficult to agree with or to disagree with the statements made about them. It is the job of conceptual and logical analysis to provide this clarification.

## ANALYSIS

### Conceptual analysis

Well-known examples from the education literature of conceptual analysis in action are R. Peters on 'education' (1966: 7–88), Hirst on 'curriculum' (1974: 16–29), Soltis on 'subject matter' (1978: 30–8), and Hirst and R. Peters (1970: 75–87) on 'teaching'. These are general concepts which have occupied educational philosophers for years. Distance education is a much more difficult problem. Its very concreteness limits the theorist. It may not even be a pure educational concept at all, as some have seen it linked to business (Glatter and Wedell 1971), or to service industries (Ljosa 1993), or industrial production (O. Peters 1967).

Soltis presents the technique of conceptual analysis as shown in Table 7.1. In the present instance *X* is 'distance education' and the standard models of the concept are five well-known providers of distance education chosen at random from the thousands available:

*Table 7.1* Conceptual analysis

| | |
|---|---|
| *Nature of the analytic situation* | Undisputed model cases of the concept are available readily, but generic features shared by model species are not clearly spelled out |
| *Prior question* | What feature must it have to be an example of *X*? |
| *Move 1* | Select standard or models cases and clear contrary cases of *X* |
| *Move 2* | Draw potentially *necessary* features from clear standard cases |
| *Move 3* | Test: use examples and counter-examples (contrary cases) to test for necessity and *sufficiency* |
| *Move 4* | Keep, modify, or reject the feature(s) on the basis of the test(s) |
| *Target or intended result* | A clear idea of what is essential to being an *X* |

*Source:* Adapted from J. Soltis, *An Introduction to the Analysis of Educational Concepts*, Reading, Mass.: Addison-Wesley, 1970.

- Le Centre National d'Enseignement à Distance;
- The Open University;
- The Department of Independent Study by Correspondence of the University of Florida;
- Die Fernstudienabteilung der Universität Leipzig to 1990;
- The Distance Education Centre of the University of New England.

These have been chosen to provide difficulties for the theorist. They represent English, French and German systems; autonomous and mixed institutions; capitalist and communist economies; a complex amalgam of differing didactic strategies.

When the analysis makes references to institutions, then the concrete structures at Vanves, Milton Keynes, Gainesville, Leipzig and Armidale will be used. If the theorist wishes to analyse students, then the examples will be taken from the 250,000 students enrolled in the CNED in 1993; the 100,000 at the OU(UK); the 8,000 enrolled in the Independent Study Program in Florida; the 2,000 enrolled in 1990 in *Fernstudium*; the 7,000 enrolled in the DEC in 1993. Should the analysis focus on courses, reference will be made to the CAPES (*anglais*); the BA (Open); the high school graduation program at Gainesville; the *Diplom* in *Fachschulpädagogik* and the Graduate Diploma in Educational Administration at UNE. The analysis will continually be circumscribed by concrete instances so there is no room for ambiguity.

In practice the methodology commences with the question 'What features must an educational process have to be called distance education?', and proceeds through four stages:

- *Stage 1*: Draw from your general knowledge of standard cases of X some potentially necessary features such as $p$, $q$, $r$.
- *Stage 2*: Test for necessity. Can you have X without $q$ or $r$? If yes, it is not a necessary characteristic. Can you remove $q$ or $r$ and still have X?
- *Stage 3*: Test for sufficiency. Can you have an educational process without it being X? Can you find a counter-example that has all the characteristics so far established but clearly is not an instance of X?
- *Stage 4*: On the basis of the tests for necessity and sufficiency, fine tune the concept by keeping or modifying or rejecting the features.

Commencing the analysis one would establish that distance education is an educational process (and the rules for this have been well established by Garrison and Shale 1990: 23–40) and must in addition have the characteristic of 'distance' and not 'non-distance'.

In *Stage 1* the most fundamental necessary feature that emerges is that the students are at home and study at home. Concretely this means in the standard cases chosen at, say, Versailles, Inverness, Orlando, Halle or Bourke and not at Vanves, Milton Keynes, Gainesville, Leipzig or Armidale.

In *Stage 2* the necessity of the feature 'study at home' as an essential characteristic of distance education must be tested. In all the five standard models it is found to be a basic characteristic and, in at least two of the systems, practically the only location. The other three add the possibility of using, in addition, a range of locations which may generally be called 'study centres': seminar locations, *Konsultationszentrums*, summer schools, teleconference locations. Further analysis would add study at work to study at home, as in the Chinese system.

The sufficiency of the feature 'study at home plus other related locations' as an essential characteristic of distance education must be tested in *Stage 3*. It is found immediately to be insufficient. People study a lot at home: from newspapers, from TV, from looking at the sky. This is not distance education. An essential feature is that it is an institutionalized form of educational provision.

'Institutionalized form of study at home' is found to be incomplete when tested for sufficiency. Without a medium of communication the concept 'distance education' would not be an educational process. The medium must be a technology because the learner is at home and the source of the educational content is not. Thus the use of a technical medium is an essential feature.

This, however, is insufficient and the concept of 'distance education' has not been fully analysed because communications media can be synchronous or asynchronous and can provide one-way communication (TV, radio) or two-way communication (correspondence, telephone). Both synchronous and asynchronous media are viable means of communication for distance education providing that they allow two-way communication.

Distance education as a type of education which features study at home, in an institutionalized context, via technology, of a two-way synchronous or asynchronous nature is insufficient. Reference to the five standard cases makes it clear that the role of the learning group must, in addition, be clarified. Groupings of students can be either non-existent, or optional or compulsory.

In *Stage 4* the analyst modifies the features on the basis of the tests for necessity and sufficiency to reach the target of a clearer idea of what is essential to distance education.

The location of the student at home (or some related location) is best conceptualized as the 'quasi-permanent separation of teacher and learner throughout the length of the learning process'. The term 'quasi-permanent' indicates that teacher and learner are totally or substantially separated and that this may be for the length of the learning process, thereby distinguishing distance education even from advanced-level conventional programmes. If there is not total or substantial separation of teacher and learner then it is not distance education and will be studied in some other field of educational research. It may, it is readily acknowledged, be something superior – but that is not the field of the analyst.

Private study, teach-yourself books and self-study programmes are excellent things, but they are not distance education. This dimension is best formulated as 'the influence of an educational organization both in the planning and preparation of learning materials and in the provision of student support services' with the proviso that a totally synchronous course at a distance is theoretically possible, in which all sessions would be held, for instance, by audioconferencing and at such levels that students need no prior preparation nor materials for subsequent reference.

A suitable formula for the technological medium would be 'the use of technical media (print, audio, video, computer) to unite teacher and learner and carry the content of the course'. Some commentators, like Garrison and Shale (1990: 25) wish every variety of present and future technology to be listed 'when we think about what distance education is and what it might become' but such desires for the future are not the concern of the analyst.

The uses of educational technology in schools, colleges and universities throughout the world are excellent and examples are also to be found of the use of instructional television in now-abandoned experiments in Samoa, El Salvador, the Ivory Coast, Sierra Leone, and elsewhere. 'The provision of two-way communication so that the student may benefit from or even initiate dialogue' is a suitable formula for the distinction between distance education and other uses of technology in education.

'The quasi-permanent absence of the learning-group throughout the length of the learning process so that people are usually taught as individuals and not in groups, with the possibility of occasional meetings for both didactic and socialization purposes' is chosen for the meetings of students. For the analyst, meetings can be physical or electronic; non-existent, optional or compulsory; and the study can be either home-based or study-centre-based or a mixture of the two. In this way the absence of the learning group is best described as 'quasi-permanent': many systems have no meetings at all so that students are usually taught as individuals and not in groups, though physical or electronic (audioconferences, videoconferences, computer-assisted conferences) meetings feature in some systems.

Distance education has been analysed as a type of education characterized by the quasi-permanent separation of teacher and learner throughout the length of the learning process; the influence of an educational organization, both in the planning and preparation of learning materials and in the provision of student support services; the use of technical media – print, audio, video, computer – to unite teacher and learner and carry the content of the course; the provision of two-way communication so that the student may benefit from or even initiate dialogue; the quasi-permanent absence of the learning group throughout the length of the learning process so that people are usually taught as individuals and not in groups, with the possibility of occasional meetings for both didactic and socialization purposes.

## Logical analysis

To complete the analysis one needs a tool for dealing with statements about distance education of the type 'S is P', for instance 'all distance education is cost-effective' or 'all distance education is boring'. As in conceptual analysis one has to anticipate opposition from professional philosophers of certain schools, especially anti-essentialists and Critical Theorists who dislike such formulations, as Derrida explains: 'one of the principle things at stake in what is called in my texts "deconstruction", is precisely the delimiting of ontology and above all of the present indicative: S is P' (Derrida 1985: 3). One has to insist that distance education is not an abstract concept and, in the industrialized business world in which both proprietary and tax-payer-funded systems must survive, no ontological dilution whatsoever can be tolerated.

An adequate tool for logical analysis in education is provided by Scheffler (1964). He shows that statements about educational things are either educational definitions, educational slogans or educational metaphors. Definitions can be either scientific, stipulative, descriptive or programmatic, with other scholars using somewhat different terminology like 'persuasive definition' for 'programmatic'. Scheffler gives rules for allocating statements of the type 'distance education is *p*' or 'the aim of distance education is *q*' to each category, and discusses the contexts in which each is used or can be abused. The

Table 7.2 Affirmations S is P about distance education

| Type | Aim | Example | Methods of identification | Methods of evaluation |
|---|---|---|---|---|
| Scientific definition | Theorizing | See page 120 | Constructs a network of theory adequate to all available facts, calling for specialized knowledge | Theoretical adequacy by use of theoretical criteria |
| Stipulative definition | Economizing | Distance education is home study | Exhibits some term and gives notice that it is to be taken as equivalent to some other exhibited term or description | Coherence. Is it well chosen? Helpfulness in communication |
| Descriptive definition | Explaining | Distance education is a type of education that includes correspondence study and modern forms of mediated teaching | Purports to explain the defined term by giving an account of its prior usage | Correct reflection of prior usage. Clarification of the term as most ordinarily and clearly applied |
| Programmatic definition | Advocating | Distance education is liberal | Raises moral or practical issues; intended to embody a programme of action like assigning a term to some new usage, or withholding a term from an object to which it has hitherto applied, or defending the proprietariness of current orientation | Consistency |
| Educational slogans | Rallying; rousing | Distance education is open | Rallies support for the key ideas of educational movements, fosters community spirit and attracts new adherents to political or moral issues | Value as symbol. Value as assertion |
| Metaphorical descriptions | Illustrating | Distance education moulds independence in students | Uses metaphors like 'forming', 'moulding' or 'shaping' to explain the educational process | Adequacy |

*Source:* Adapted from I. Scheffler *The Language of Education*, New York: Wiley, 1964.

literature abounds with declarations that distance education is *p* or
*q* or *r*–declarations which have rarely been submitted to critical
analysis. A presentation of Scheffler's strategies is given in Table 7.2,
along with his 'relevant principles for their critical evaluation'
(Scheffler 1964: 10).

This is not the place to examine many of the statements that have
been made about distance education; only three brief illustrations can
be considered – 'distance education is liberal'; 'distance education is
open'; 'the aim of distance education is access'.

Utterances of the type 'distance education is intrinsically liberal or
independent or free' can be taken as metaphorical descriptions if they
are to be understood as 'distance education moulds liberal minds',
or as programmatic definitions if they are hortatory: 'distance
education should be liberal'. In the standard cases distance education
is neither liberal nor illiberal. The data about distance education are
quite neutral. Some courses are liberal; some are illiberal or boring
because the course developers chose for presentation and study one
of many possible solutions, thereby blocking the independence and
freedom of the student in searching other paths.

'Distance education is intrinsically open' is an educational slogan,
just as McKenzie *et al.* (1975: 21) described openness in conventional
education as 'an inscription to be carried on a banner gathering
adherents and enthusiasms'. Many distance courses from the standard
cases are closed because the course authors close off all other views
or interpretations besides the one chosen for presentation, or because
they have closed enrolment procedures or closed cut-off dates for
assignment submission. Rumble sums it up well by saying that the
values of openness 'have nothing intrinsically to do with distance
education which is morally ambivalent (i.e. it can promote open
learning or closed learning)' (Rumble 1991: 72). Rumble is right:
distance education is just a form of educational provision. It is quite
neutral. Some courses are open, some are closed. *Per se* it is neither.

'The *raison d'être* of distance education is access' is best viewed as
another advocatory or hortatory utterance of the programmatic type.
It describes somebody's programme. In the standard cases, distance
education does not *per se* promote access. It blocks off access to
the poorly educated, to immigrants, to those with poor or no
reading levels, and to those who have not developed the relatively
sophisticated skills of independent research and motivation. If society
wishes to promote access, it puts on extra courses at local colleges,
or new courses or more innovatory courses or courses for students
with poor study skills. It does not turn to distance education. As

Pagney (1983) explained: distance education is complementary to conventional education – it fills its lacunae but has no intrinsic linking to access.

## REINTEGRATION OF THE TEACHING ACTS

The requirement of Hirst and Peters that conceptual analysis and clarification should precede theoretical formulation has been adhered to, and from what has been established it will be taken as axiomatic that distance education theory forms part of general educational theory, perhaps with leanings towards business/industrial research methods. It is also accepted that the theorist should build on prior work and not restart from zero.

The choice of prior work indicates principally that it is considered to provide adequate tools for theoretical formulation. What is needed is an adequate representation of the distance education process that is readily available to readers of this book and analyses of it. The writer has little to quibble with in the diagrams provided for this volume by Garrison (Chapter 1) or Amundsen (Chapter 4), and will use the work of Wedemeyer on the role of the student in distance education, Garrison and Shale on the role of the teacher, and Winn on the communication process.

### Role of the student in distance education

The role of the student in distance education is central to Wedemeyer's writings and he links it to a democratic social ideal which he developed from Rogers and to a model of the education process which was influenced by Gagné. At a very early stage Wedemeyer (1957: 4; 1962: 15–16) promoted this social ideal: 'nobody should be denied the opportunity to learn because he is poor, geographically isolated, socially disadvantaged, in poor health, institutionalized or otherwise unable to place himself within the institution's special environment for learning' (Wedemeyer 1971: 549). As a model of the education process, valid both for the classroom and distance education, he gives: 'In any teaching–learning situation it is generally agreed that there are four essential elements: a teacher, a learner or learners, a communications system or mode, something to be taught/learned' (Wedemeyer 1981: 38). Thus in 1964 he defined correspondence/distance education as 'personal tutoring carried on by mail or other forms of communication because teacher and student are separated' and claimed that 'the system should be capable of operation any place where there are students – or even only one student – whether or not there are teachers at the same place at the same time' (Wedemeyer 1981: 36). To Wedemeyer's credit goes the early recognition that 'learners external to the institution must be reached through a medium' and that 'student and teacher are separated' when dealing with students external to the institution (Wedemeyer 1964, 1971).

These early thoughts of Wedemeyer about learners external to an institution pose immediate problems for the theorist. The analysis showed that we are dealing with students who study institutional courses (not Teach Yourself Books) either totally or substantially at home (or at their factory). Placing the learner at home or, in Wedemeyer's phrase 'external to the institution', runs immediately counter to the analyses of the School of Philosophical Analysis presented by R. Peters, Hirst, Oakeshott and others, which tell us that the teaching–learning relationship is essentially one of interaction and intersubjectivity – basically a group experience and one in which much is learned by being in the presence of those who have the qualities to be learned.

Society has for some hundreds, if not thousands, of years provided itself with locations called 'schools' and higher-level locations called 'universities' at which this teaching–learning interaction takes place. The question for the theorist is whether institutional learning is *per se* linked to the privileged places for institutional learning created by society. In doing this the theorist abstracts from questions of quality: the theorist regards the quality of learning in schools and universities as a given – it has always been of a given quality and will always be so. The theorist will also be cognizant of the enormous sacrifices that normal students make to go to school or college. Students made these sacrifices to obtain an education a hundred years ago just as they do today: children are sent to boarding schools, huge prices are paid for digs in university cities, families are broken up, lovers abandoned.

Distance education students choose to remain in employment, at home, with their families. They expect to be given institutional learning at home and, more and more frequently in the 1990s, university degrees at home. The ideals of von Humboldt or Arnold or Newman that the university is a place where scholars come together for the purposes of learning do not convince them to make the sacrifices required. Why does the distance student refuse to go to school? is the question that confronts the theorist.

The problem of the location of the distance student is a lasting one for the theorist, even though solutions have been realized today which can bring far-distant students together electronically. In the 1980s some (Jeavons 1982) forecast a blurring of the boundaries between distance education students and face-to-face students. Philosophically this is inachievable. The medieval jurists had a maxim for it: *multilocatio absolute repugnat* which might be translated as 'it is metaphysically impossible for a human being to be in multiple locations' or more colloquially 'you can't be in two places at the one time'.

It is to Wedemeyer's credit that thirty years ago he saw the theoretical implications of the location of the distance student. He realized implicitly that the only way to break out of what he called the 'space–time barriers of education' was to separate teaching from learning and to plan each as a separate activity. Some recent commentators (Barker *et al.* 1989) have called an educational formulation based on 'separation from' or 'absence of the teacher' a negative concept. It remains, however it is formulated, one of distance education's great assets and a positive contribution to the solution of educational provision. The location of the student and the concept of an educational structure 'capable of operation any place where there are students' will be central to any theoretical formulation of distance education.

## The role of the teacher in distance education

In a recent study Garrison and Shale analyse the role of the teacher in distance education. They begin by looking for a unifying theme that can provide a sense of what distance education is. They object to the idea of education being 'delivered' because, in this view, instruction reduces to packaging knowledge, reducing teaching to telling. From that it would be an easy step, they claim, to believing that the role of the teacher is a utility, a resource that can be used and then dispensed with (Garrison and Shale 1990: 23–4). This is a prevalent misconception and they do well to dispel it.

Teaching, they continue, has to encourage the development of new perspectives based upon the integration of the student's existing knowledge with the newly acquired knowledge. The student has then to validate the emerging knowledge through collaborative and sustained interaction with a teacher and other students. Education is a process which is characterized by the interaction of the teacher and a student which takes the form of a dialectical exchange which is a negotiation of meaning. In conclusion they affirm:

We maintain that the most important aspect of the educational transaction is what happens after the student has been presented with the content. In distance education this presents a special problem. With teacher and student being separated, greater effort is required to understand the communication process so vital to support the learning activity.

(Garrison and Shale 1990: 37)

The role of the teacher in distance education, as described by Garrison and Shale, corresponds quite well with the presentation of the role of the teacher in conventional education in the Hirst–Oakeshott–R. Peters group, with the proviso that both analyses pertain more to education than training (see Chapter 15). Teaching, Oakeshott explains, is the deliberate and intentional initiation of a pupil into the world of human achievement or into some part of it. A pupil is a learner known to a teacher, and teaching is, properly speaking, impossible in his absence (Oakeshott 1967: 159–60). Hirst (1974: 113) poses the question can teaching-machines properly be said to teach and attempts to map the features that distinguish teaching activities from all others.

In a well-known passage R. Peters (1966: 23–88) establishes that 'education' implies the transmission of what is worth while to those who become committed to it; that 'education' must involve knowledge and understanding and some kind of cognitive perspective, which are not inert; and that 'education' at least rules out some procedures of transmission, on the grounds that they lack wittingness and voluntariness on the part of the learner. He concludes that the teacher is not a detached operator who is bringing about some kind of result in a person who is external to him. The function of the teacher in the early stages, he proposes, is to get the pupil on the inside of the form or thought or awareness with which the teacher is concerned. At the culminating stages of education, R. Peters holds, there is little distinction between teacher and taught. They are both participating in the shared experience of exploring a common world. The teacher is simply more familiar with its contours and more skilled in handling the tools that make the educational transaction possible.

As an illustration of the intersubjectivity of teacher and learner in the educational transaction of R. Peters and of Garrison and Shale's preoccupations that the teacher and learner share control of the two-way communication in distance education, one can refer to Mitchell's reply to those who attempted to buy his Postgraduate Diploma in Distance Education or the Masters Degree in Distance Education from the University of South Australia. 'As teaching staff we are dealing with adult professional students', Mitchell (1993) writes. 'Together we are exploring a field as wide and as comprehensive as distance education: in many aspects it is the student who is the authority.' Thus the course cannot be purchased because the content is negotiated in the exchanges between the teacher and the student and the students' expertise is not available for purchase by another institution.

The problems created by the positions of R. Peters and his group, and the analysis of the distance education transaction in Garrison and Shale, are formidable ones for the theorist. How can one explain the role of the teacher in distance education when the student studies from materials developed one, five or ten years previously? Is it possible to reconstitute at a distance the intersubjectivity and two-way communication of university education or the detailed psycho-motor skills of distance training with the media available to the distance teacher? Is the great strength of distance education (the separation of teacher and learner) an insurmountable barrier?

## Communication of the content in distance education

Central to the analysis of the educational transaction in distance education is the nature of the communication processes. Distance education is characterized by the replacement of interpersonal face-to-face communication in the learning group by an apersonal mode of communication. In two of the standard cases this absence can be total with no verbal communication between teacher and taught; in the others it is substantial.

Recent studies on the communication of the content in education have focused on the findings of cognitive psychology. Winn (1990, 1991) has applied these findings to the fields of educational tech-nology and distance education. He shows that cognitive psychology can undermine the three bases on which both of these fields rest – namely, that learning can be forecast (if a learning strategy works with a selection of students it had been assumed it would work with others); that learning is logical (it had been assumed that one could design a logical sequence of learning activities towards objectives); that the design of instruction can be separated from its realization (if it is impossible to forecast the efficacy of teaching strategies and if the human mind works by intuition, it becomes impossible to design teaching strategies prior to teaching) (Winn 1991: 21–6, Nunan 1983).

Winn acknowledges that, by and large, distance education courses are more carefully and extensively designed than courses delivered face-to-face and that they take longer to prepare. Cognitive theories of learning, however, make it imperative that students are able to interact extensively with the instruction or the instructor. How then can the communication processes of distance education be achieved? Winn (1990: 61) provides two solutions to this problem. The first is electronic attempts to imitate the live classroom as closely as possible (e.g. teleconferencing). Second, technologies that provide the opportunity for students to 'interact with the materials, rather than with an instructor, in their own time and usually in their own home' are suggested (programmed instruction and interactive computer-assisted instruction).

The summary of the problems of communication in distance education provided by Winn is comprehensive, but his solutions are problematic. The problem for the theorist with his electronic groupings of students is that the ability to study at a distance 'in one's own time at one's own pace', as in a correspondence course, is removed. If a two-way video teleconference via compressed video codec technology along 384 kbit or 2 Mbit fibre optic lines is at 11 p.m. at night 40 km away, you may have to do a lot of travelling to get there.

By insisting that home-based technologies must be interactive to achieve the quality of communication required, Winn seems to be running counter to Dubin and Taveggia's First Law of Distance Education 'one cannot claim superiority for any among different teaching methods used to convey subject content to the student' (Dubin and Taveggia 1968, Schramm 1973). Dubin and Taveggia's law was established by the meta-analysis of 91 studies of 7 million students, and the theorist would not want to see it overturned without detailed refutation on the same scale as it is the basis for most practice in distance education. It also holds out so much hope for students in the poorest countries of what used to be called the Third World: a student can learn as well from a Roneoed correspondence course as from a state-of-the-art interactive hypermedia course. The variables of successful learning lie elsewhere. One does not have to be rich to learn.

## Reintegration of the teaching acts

In this chapter education has been characterized as a process in which a teacher and a learner or learners play essential roles and in which a content that is worth while is transferred in a two-way process of communication in which the teacher participates and learns, and in which the learner may benefit from or even initiate dialogue. Education, however, as the representatives of the School of Philosophic Analysis tell us, is more than the transfer of information, however worth while that information may be. What is required in addition to information, says Oakeshott, is knowledge that enables us to interpret it. Interpretation depends on the ability to determine relevance, thus emancipating learners from crude absolutes and allowing them to give assent or dissent in graduate terms. How, then, does a pupil learn intellectual honesty, disinterested curiosity, concentration and doubt? How does the learner come to inherit the disposition to submit to refutation? Besides information, this is what has to be learned – in Oakeshott's view. And this is what the teacher has to impart to the learner together with whatever information it is decided to convey. It cannot be learned separately; it is never explicitly learned; but it may be learned in everything that is learned, in the carpentry lesson as in the literature or chemistry lesson. It cannot be taught separately; it is implanted unobtrusively in the manner in which information is conveyed, in a tone of voice, in a gesture, in asides and by example (Oakeshott 1967: 174–5).

R. Peters gives an example of the process. One has to learn to think historically, he writes, not just learn some historical dates and data. But the only way to think historically is to probe the past with someone who has mastered this form of thought. To conceive of education as imposing a pattern on another person fails to do justice to the shared impersonality of education (Peters 1966: 40).

These concepts of the education process in the classroom, lecture and tutorial from R. Peters, Oakeshott and others, have points of similarity to the distance education process as described by Garrison and Shale and others. But the problems of distance education remain: the students are not there; they choose not to attend the classes at which information plus all the components of the education process reach the learner. Distance teachers have difficulties establishing the 'essential intersubjectivity' which R. Peters took from D. H. Lawrence as his explanation of the magical moment in which learning from teaching occurs. The two-way face-to-face communication characteristic of the class, the lecture, the laboratory practical, the tutorial, the project group, the seminar is missing, even though it has been normative for all education for so long and, in some cultures, for example Islam, is enshrined in religious tradition today.

In a recent contribution O. Peters (1993) has explained how the search for the central characteristic of distance education led him to the Russian concept *zaochny*. This is the Russian word for 'distance' in 'distance education', he explains, and adds that etymologically the word means 'without eye contact'. This implies that the decisive criterion according to which distance education can be distinguished from conventional teaching and learning is the lack of eye contact. Distance education does not take place 'eyeball-to-eyeball' to use an expression coined by Wedemeyer.

The Russian concept contains a remarkable insight and the implications are far-reaching. As the eye is the organ of a person's innermost feelings, its absence in the attempt to educate is significant. The Russian concept brings home vividly that a whole emotional dimension of the interaction between teacher and learner is lacking in distance education. Distance education is defined and characterized in Russian by pointing to a severe deficiency, as if in a law court a verdict was announced without the accused being present. A form of education in which eye-to-eye contact between the learner and the teacher is absent, limps.

Distance education limps because its teaching acts are, by definition, divided in either space or time and frequently both, from the learner's acts. Learning materials are developed one, five or ten years before they are used for teaching, depending on the organization of the system and the shelf-life of its courses. The teacher teaches in his or her location but the students are at home, or – on occasion – at centres spread over hundreds or thousands of locations throughout a nation or overseas. These are the strengths of distance education but they have their consequences. The crux of distance education, therefore, on which theoretical formulation needs to focus, is the linking of learning materials to students' learning. This is shown in Figure 7.1.

A satisfactory resolution for this situation is the concept of the reintegration of the teaching acts by which two-way communication between the distance learners and the distance teacher can be

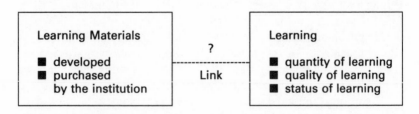

*Figure 7.1*　Linking learning materials to learning

reconstructed and in which learning from learning materials can occur. The focus is on the teaching acts because learning, even institutional learning, can occur anywhere and other chapters of this book (Chapters 13 to 15) show how people learn from machines. A theoretical structure for distance education focusing on the reintegration of the teaching acts by which learning is linked to learning materials may go some way to compensating for the location of the students, causing the lack of eye-to-eye contact which is so important in education.

This is not the place to work out the practical consequences of the reintegration of the teaching acts as the theoretical focus of distance education or to list the many strategies that systems have and will use to ensure that the two-way communication process of teaching at a distance is in reality completed. Some practical guidelines have been given elsewhere (Keegan 1990: 111–12) and are summarized here.

The learning materials, both print and non-print, are designed to achieve as many of the characteristics of interpersonal communication as possible. Various writers suggest the incorporation of easily readable style, anticipation of students' problems, careful structuring of content, self-testing questions, instructional objectives, inserted questions, model answers, typographical considerations: designs, diagrams and drawings. In print, audio-visual, video and computer packages and laboratory kits, authors try to simulate the intersubjectivity of the classroom, tutorial, or lecture.

Second, when the courses are being presented, the reintegration of the teaching acts is attempted through communication by correspondence, telephone tutorials, on-line computer communication, comments on assignments by tutors or computers, teleconferences, videoconferences, and computer conferences.

Attention has also been drawn (Keegan 1990: 152–4) to the work of Kaye and Rumble in demonstrating that distance systems have two characteristic operating subsystems: course development and student support services, and of the importance of integration between the two. Furthermore, indications have been given of the value of Holmberg's intuition of 'guided didactic conversation' as a suitable metaphor for the course development half of a distance education system (Keegan 1990: 88–92) and of Sewart's motto 'continuity of concern for students studying at a distance' for the student support services half (Keegan 1990: 94–7).

## CONCLUSION

The wondrous developments of the Industrial Revolution made it possible for mankind for the first time to teach at a distance. It became possible to provide education 'any place where there are students – or even only one student – whether or not there are teachers at the same place at the same time' even in the remotest and poorest regions of the world. The wondrous electronic telecommunications Revolution of the 1980s, based on an urge to deregulate, the speeding-up of chips and the introduction of broadband technology, made it possible for mankind for the first time to teach face-to-face at a distance. By the end of the 1980s a virtual network of electronic classrooms linked, for instance, by 2Mbit or 384kbit compressed video signals along fibre optic lines restored eye contact to distance education: a student coughing or fidgeting in Stockholm could distract the teacher and the students in Dublin. The next Revolution may provide fibre in the local loop, and the benefits to distance education and the challenges it would pose would again be immense.

In spite of all of this the daily work of the distance educator is still painstakingly to reintegrate the teaching acts, shattered by the benefits of distance education, so that quality education can be achieved year after year by real students. In the same way the responsibility of distance planners is to design systems for quality learning at a distance for even the poorest students on the globe.

## REFERENCES

Barker, B. *et al.* (1989) 'Broadening the definition of distance education in the light of new telecommunications technologies', *The American Journal of Distance Education* 3(1), 20–9.

Derrida, J. (1985) 'Letter to a Japanese friend', in D. Wood (ed.), *Derrida and différence*, University of Warwick: Parousia Press.

Dubin, R. and Taveggia, T. (1968) *The Teaching Learning Paradox. A Comparative Analysis of College Teaching Methods*, Eugene: University of Oregon.

Garrison, D. and Shale, D. (1987) 'Mapping the boundaries of distance education: problems in defining the field', *American Journal of Distance Education* 1(1), 4–13.

—— —— (1990) *Education at a Distance: From Issues to Practice*, Malabar: Krieger.

Glatter, R. and Wedell, E. (1971) *Study by Correspondence*, London: Longman.

Henri, F. and Lamy, T. (1989) 'La formation à distance: des choix technologiques et des valeurs', in R. Sweet (ed.), *Post-secondary Distance Education in Canada*, Edmonton: Athabasca University/CSSE.

Hirst, P. (1974) *Knowledge and the Curriculum*, London: Routledge & Kegan Paul.

—— and Peters, R. (1970) *The Logic of Education*, London: Routledge & Kegan Paul.

Jeavons, F. (1982) 'How different is the distance student?', in J. Daniel, *et al. Learning at a Distance*, Edmonton: Athabasca University.

Kaye, A. and Rumble, G. (1981) *Distance Teaching for Higher and Adult Education*, London: Croom Helm.

Keegan, D. (1980) 'On defining distance education', *Distance Education* 1(1), 13–36.

—— (1988) 'Problems in defining the field of distance education', *American Journal of Distance Education* 2(2), 4–11.

—— (1990) *Foundations of Distance Education* (2nd edn), London: Routledge.

Ljoså, E. (1993) 'Distance education in the society of the future: from partial understanding to conceptual frameworks', in K. Harry, M. John and D. Keegan (eds), *Distance Education: New Perspectives*, London: Routledge.

McKenzie, O. *et al.* (eds) (1975) *Open Learning*, Paris: Unesco.

Mitchell, I. (1993) 'Academic education of distance educators', in K. Harry, M. John and D. Keegan (eds), *Distance Education: New Perspectives*, London: Routledge.

Nunan, T. (1983) *Countering Educational Design*, New York: Routledge.

Oakeshott, M. (1967) 'Learning and teaching', in R. Peters (ed.), *The Concept of Education*, London: Routledge & Kegan Paul.

Pagney, B. (1983) 'What advantages can conventional education derive from correspondence education?' in D. Sewart, D. Keegan and B. Holmberg, *Distance Education: International Perspectives*, London: Routledge.

Peters, O. (1967) 'Distance teaching and industrial productions: a cooperative interpretation in outline', in D. Sewart, D. Keegan and B. Holmberg (1983) *Distance Education: International Perspectives*, London: Routledge.

—— (1993) 'Understanding distance education', in K. Harry, M. John and D. Keegan (eds), *Distance Education: New Perspectives*, London: Routledge.

Peters, R. (1966) *Ethics and Education*, London: Allen & Unwin.

Rumble, G. (1989) 'On defining distance education', *American Journal of Distance Education* 3(2), 8–21.

—— (1991) 'Book review', *Open Learning*, February, pp. 71–2.

Sauvé, L. (ed.) (1990) *Systèmes de formation à distance: EDU 6000*, Québec: Téléuniversité.

Scheffler, I. (1964) *The Language of Education*, New York: Wiley.

Schramm, W. (1973) *Big Media, Little Media*, London: Sage.

Shale, D. (1988) 'Toward a reconceptionalization of distance education', *American Journal of Distance Education* 2(3), 25–35.

Soltis, J. (1978) *An Introduction to the Analysis of Educational Concepts*, Reading, Mass.: Addison-Wesley.

Verduin, J. and Clark, T. (1991) *Distance Education: The Foundations of Effective Practice*, San Francisco: Jossey-Bass.

Wedemeyer, C. (1957) 'Learning by mail', *Writers Digest*, September, pp. 15–16.

—— (1964) 'Correspondence instruction', *General Educational Development* (US Armed Forces Institute), October, pp. 1–2.

—— (1971) 'Independent study', in L. Deighton (ed.), *The Encyclopaedia of Education*, New York: Macmillan.

—— (1981) *Learning at the Backdoor*, Madison: University of Wisconsin.

Winn, W. (1990) 'Media and instructional methods', in R. Garrison and D. Shale (eds), *Educational at a Distance*, Malabar: Krieger.

—— (1991) 'Ebauche d'un cadre theorique propre a la technologie educative', in L. Sauvé (ed.), *La technologie educative a la croisse des disciplines*, Québec: Téléuniversité/CIPTE.

# 8 Matching teaching methods to educational aims in distance education

*John J. Sparkes*

## INTRODUCTION

In distance education the range of possible educational methods differs considerably from those normally used in face-to-face teaching; but in either case the aim must be to provide 'quality education'. Although the importance of this concept is now widely acknowledged, and methods of 'quality assurance' (i.e. procedures for sustaining and improving quality) are widely canvassed, few attempts are made to state what 'quality' actually means. In this chapter I shall be regarding 'quality in higher education' as meaning: 'Defining worthwhile goals and enabling students to achieve them.'

In determining what is 'worth while', academic standards, the demands of employers and professions, the aspirations of students, the expectations of society and the government all need to be taken into account to a greater or lesser degree, so there are many valid interpretations of what is worth while. In any educational provision, therefore, the aims of the activity must first be specified so that everyone involved knows what they are. Enabling students to achieve these goals involves creating an effective learning environment appropriate to these aims, by choosing and using different media and methods effectively, by building on successful experience, and by applying the results of some excellent recent research into 'how students learn'.

This chapter concentrates on translating the results of this research into practical educational strategies and distance-teaching methods aimed at achieving specified learning goals. The words 'education' and 'teaching' are interpreted to mean 'creating environments in which students can learn successfully', so teaching-at-a-distance can involve the effective use of many media, including printed texts, videotapes, audiotapes, practical work, projects, computers and telephones as well as occasional lecturing, classroom teaching and tutoring.

It is, of course, implicit in the title of this chapter that it is possible to distinguish between different kinds of learning, and that there are significant differences in the way they should be taught and learnt. The detailed taxonomies of Bloom *et al.* (1956), Gagné and Briggs (1979) and others are not appropriate here, partly because the hierarchical arrangement of their elements cannot be sustained (e.g. it is possible to 'synthesize' before 'analysis', and to 'evaluate' without 'synthesis' etc.) (Rowntree 1977) and partly because their emphasis is on student performance rather than on teaching and learning. The work of Marton and Säljö (1976) brought into focus the concept of the 'deep approach' to learning, with its emphasis on the 'intention to understand' rather than simply to try to memorize information and practise skills. From this idea there follows the implication that the concept of 'understanding' is an important educational parameter, not previously explicitly isolated in educational taxonomies.

The taxonomy adopted and in this chapter therefore comprises *knowledge, skills* and *understanding* in the cognitive domain, and *attitudes* and *values* in the affective domain. These are simply different kinds of learning, with no implied hierarchy. They not only have different inherent properties, but also need to be taught, assessed and learnt differently, though not necessarily in separate courses.

Only the 'cognitive' domain of learning is considered here in detail, although the motivation to learn, which is part of the 'affective' domain, is a crucial aspect of effective learning. Distance students have to be highly motivated even to start their studies, so it is usually only necessary to sustain their enthusiasm. Ensuring that they can see that they are making good progress towards their chosen goals is enough motivation for many adult students, which is one of the main reasons for ensuring that effective teaching methods appropriate to these aims are used.

## KNOWLEDGE, SKILLS AND UNDERSTANDING

Unfortunately, the terms: 'knowledge', 'skills' and 'understanding', as used in everyday discourse, do not have precise enough meanings for use in educational analysis, so it is first necessary to specify clear meanings for them. (A similar problem was faced in science, where everyday terms like 'force', 'work', 'energy', etc., were given precise scientific meanings, without apparently causing confusion in their everyday usage.) It is as important in designing effective courses to be clear about the meanings of key educational concepts, as it is in science and engineering to be clear about the relevant scientific concepts.

For the kind of analysis presented here, the elements of this three-component taxonomy are defined and explained as follows. Other definitions are possible, but these map on to teaching, learning and assessment methods better than most:

- *Knowledge* is here defined as 'information that has been memorized and can be recalled in answer to a question'. So the 'information' in books etc. only becomes 'knowledge' once it is well remembered. The quizzes on radio and TV, for example, are concerned only with knowledge in this sense. Knowledge (i.e. memorized information) can be acquired very rapidly by interested students.
- *Skills* are here defined as 'the ability to do specific things without thinking too much about how to do them'. Examples include many of our everyday activities, such as speaking, writing, designing, doing elementary mathematics, playing tennis, operating computers, making friends, etc. Although such skills are clearly learned at some stage, they cannot be acquired rapidly, or 'recalled', in the same way that knowledge can be. Manual skills are not distinguished here from intellectual ones (as they are in Bloom's taxonomy), because their learning is no less a mental activity than the learning of intellectual skills. The amount of knowledge and understanding needed to be deployed in skills varies considerably, from very little in speaking and walking, to a great deal in science and engineering design, for example. (Note that it is often a great deal easier to *know how* to do things than to be *able to do things well* oneself, so a good deal of self-monitoring of performance is possible.)
- *Understanding* is defined as 'the capacity to use explanatory concepts creatively' in such activities as explaining new phenomena, designing new artefacts or systems and predicting their performance, diagnosing causes of failure or error and correcting them, asking searching questions, making good decisions based on incomplete data and knowledge, and so on. Understanding is the basis of thinking, especially logical thinking.

There are many levels or degrees of understanding. At its most elementary level it simply involves comprehending the meanings of everyday words such as 'table' or 'red'. At its most advanced level, understanding involves internalizing abstract academic concepts such as 'entropy' or 'status'. At all levels the educational requirement is for a 'rich learning environment'. For small children, guided exploration of an everyday environment is enough. In higher education however, the key concepts cannot normally be inferred from individual exploration since they are not directly revealed by experience. Thousands of years of human experience of 'moving objects' elapsed before geniuses like Newton and Galileo created the concept of 'inertia'. So special attention needs to be paid to the teaching of understanding, as explained later (see pp. 141-9).

It turns out that there is a need to distinguish understanding from *know-how*. Know-how is an alternative problem-solving capability which is acquired through extensive experience of dealing with particular kinds of problems. It is very valuable for tackling familiar kinds of problems. It usually comprises a mixture of knowledge and skills but rarely also involves grasping the underlying explanatory concepts upon which understanding depends, so it cannot reliably deal with new and unfamiliar problems. Courses, whether at a distance or face to face, usually have to concentrate on teaching understanding rather than developing know-how because of time limitations. Apprenticeship is one of the ways of acquiring know-how.

This simple taxonomy is useful not only as a means of distinguishing between different kinds of teaching and learning but also as a means of distinguishing between different kinds of courses, especially in practical or vocational areas such as science, engineering, medicine, education, etc. For example,

- *training courses* are mostly concerned with developing skills;
- *general interest courses* are mostly concerned with non-specialist knowledge;
- *up-dating courses* are mostly concerned with specialist knowledge – the necessary prior understanding being assumed;
- *awareness courses* are concerned with knowledge and understanding at a fairly superficial level (but no skills);
- *degree courses* and *up-dating courses* develop knowledge, skills as well as understanding – usually for the purpose of gaining a qualification.

In continuing education in particular, these distinctions provide a simple way of ensuring that students register for the kind of course they want; the course title alone can be quite misleading.

The three basic kinds of learning defined above are not normally taught in separate courses. Indeed, just as some prior comprehension is needed in order to acquire knowledge and skills, so too advances in knowledge and skills can provide the context for further advances in conceptual development and understanding. So, for example in degree courses, educational progress is often a kind of upwards spiral involving a cyclic development of knowledge, skills and understanding and perhaps know-how too. Hence course design involves interleaving different kinds of teaching to form a well-structured whole.

Following the terminology introduced by Marton and Säljö (1976), it is usual to refer to understanding together with any relevant knowledge and skills, as 'deep' or 'conceptual' learning. Then memorization and the straightforward practising of skills is referred to as 'surface learning'. Note that deep and surface *learning* are *outcomes* and are not the same as the deep surface *approaches* to learning which describe processes. In general, the deep approach is necessary for achieving deep learning, but it can also be more effective for certain kinds of surface learning.

## STUDENTS' PREFERRED LEARNING STYLES

Another factor to be borne in mind in designing effective courses is the fact that students differ in their preferred learning styles – at least where conceptual development is concerned. Memorizing information and practising skills are relatively straightforward activities, even if they may be difficult or tiresome, and the appropriate teaching techniques are not very student-dependent. But where deep learning is concerned, students seem to differ significantly.

For example, some students tend to be 'holist' learners whilst others tend to be 'serialist' (Daniel 1976, Pask 1976). That is, 'holist' students prefer to take an overview of a complex subject before filling in the details in their own way, whilst 'serialist' ones prefer a logical step-by-step progression through a subject. Pask showed that matching the teaching to students' learning styles can result in almost a doubling of their performance. Printed texts, for example, are usually 'serialist' in character, so when dealing with concepts, they need a structure, as explained later, to enable holist learners more easily to find their own way through the printed material. On the other hand, projects – especially design projects – are naturally 'holist' in character, so serialist students may need guidance in the normally iterative process of design or problem-solving.

Similarly, it is clear that some students are primarily 'verbalizers', and find it preferable to hear or read about concepts and discuss them; whilst others may be 'visualizers' or 'doers' and may prefer visual information or practical activities to support their learning.

Since it is evidently not practicable to select students according to their learning styles, it follows that conceptually difficult material should be taught in more than one way, rather than solely in the most convenient way or in the way that the teacher perceives as the most appropriate – as is often the case in distance education. Similarly, there is little doubt that some students prefer private study to tutorials, whilst for others the reverse is true; so, where possible, opportunities for either should be created. The current enthusiasm for learning-by-doing, whilst often good for motivation, may well be inappropriate for the brightest students intellectually. It is important to realize therefore that, since course evaluation rarely takes such differences of learning style into account, students' responses to questionnaires are likely to reveal more about the learning characteristics of the individual students than about the courses being evaluated!

Gibbs (1981) and others have pointed out that it is important that students 'learn how to learn'. Many books have been published on study skills of one kind or another (e.g. Buzan 1974), but these are mainly concerned with support skills such as note-taking techniques, ways of organizing one's time, or methods of improving one's ability to memorize – all of which are important but are more to do with surface learning than with deep learning. For deep learning students also need to discover their own preferred learning styles and to distinguish between the different kinds of learning expected of them. Just appreciating the difference between 'memorising a fact and grasping a concept' can lead to a big improvement in students' learning abilities (Downs and Perry 1982).

## ASSESSMENT METHODS

Assessment methods have a profound effect on students' approaches to learning and on the kinds of learning they achieve, so it is as important to match assessment methods to aims as it is to match teaching methods to them.

Knowledge is tested by questions which demand recall. It therefore presents few problems. Multiple choice tests and descriptive essays usually provide valid and effective forms of assessment. Skills are tested by performance at particular activities. Complex skills, such as communication or interpersonal skills, are not as easy to assess reliably as are measurable skills, such as doing mathematics, spelling and grammar and many practical skills, but the task to be done is clear enough.

By contrast there are no direct indications of the level of the understanding achieved; it has to be inferred from students' performance in response to the kinds of challenges which are difficult to deal with solely on the basis of recall, know-how or well-practised skills. Only inputs and outputs to students can be observed, so to test for understanding it is first necessary to provide appropriately challenging inputs and then require outputs of a kind which require thought and insight. Research has shown that, despite most teachers' intention to set such questions in typical exams, students often find that they can answer them more successfully by relying on well-remembered model answers of previous questions and well-practised skills (Black 1962, Prosser 1987, Ramsden 1986, Ramsden *et al.* 1987). Indeed the Open University in the UK even broadcasts programmes aimed at helping students to rely mostly on memory in the exam room!

Oral examinations, in the hands of experienced examiners, are particularly effective at the testing of understanding, but are rarely practical in distance teaching situations. Exams which ask students to discuss unfamiliar complex issues; or which ask how they *would* tackle problems rather than ask them actually to solve them; or which require students to detect and correct errors of principle or inference or logic in passages of text, can be very effective. These types of questions not only challenge students' understanding quite severely, but also widen the range of possible questions to such an extent that remembering model answers is unlikely to be of much help.

## METHODS OF TEACHING AT A DISTANCE

In order to design a distance-teaching course to match a range of educational aims it is often necessary to intermix various teaching methods. If understanding a subject (such as electromagnetism or microeconomics or cognitive psychology) and complex skills are included in the aims, they have to be given priority since they are the most demanding and take the most time to learn. The teaching of knowledge and specialist skills can then be fitted in where appropriate.

There are a number of methods available for teaching knowledge (i.e. conveying information) at a distance: principally printed texts and audio and videotapes and computer-aided learning. To convert this information into knowledge the tedious task of memorization can be made more palatable by showing the 'relevance' of the information through case-studies, by 'discovery' methods and by frequent testing at a rate of progress which ensures good scores.

Skills are taught by instruction and demonstration and are learnt by practice, with error-correction where needed. The instruction and demonstration aspects of this can easily be achieved at a distance. Videotapes are very effective, even for intellectual skills, and are often better than real demonstrations because they can be replayed, stopped, played in slow-motion, and can show world experts in action. The provision, at-a-distance, of opportunities for practice can, however, present real problems. Paper-and-pencil skills, or those that can be handled by computers, can be exercised through assignments. For more practical skills, summer schools, day schools, or home kits are necessary. Monitored peer assessment is worth while for many skills since much can be learned from marking another's work according to clear guidelines. But students' motivation must be the main driving force of skill development.

The teaching of understanding involves providing a variety of experiences of the kind which engage the relevant concepts. The aim is to illuminate from a variety of directions the concepts forming in students' minds, so that they become as 'real' and useful as the everyday concepts they use all the time. The concepts need not only to be defined, described, used and analysed in the distance-teaching materials, but they also need to be discussed, exercised, applied, read about, written about, asked about, etc. by the students if they are to be properly internalized. Even multi-media methods of giving 'information' are only likely to be successful at developing understanding if they make repeated use of the concepts which underpin it.

The following paragraphs indicate how different distance-teaching methods can be adapted to different educational aims and to different learning styles. Special attention is given to achieving conceptual development in students. To quote Ramsden (1988): 'Quality education is conceptual-change learning.'

**Printed texts**

Printed texts are likely to remain the backbone of distance teaching for some time to come. But it is only fairly recently that textbooks have begun to include features aimed at improving their teaching effectiveness. Texts are naturally 'serialist' in character so, in order to help holist learners, as well as develop conceptual learning, a number of features are now often included. These include: in-text exercises on the application of basic principles; explanations of difficult concepts expressed in different words, symbols and illustrations; the use of audiotapes in conjunction with texts (i.e. 'audio-vision') since spoken explanations of diagrams, etc., are very different from written ones; the inclusion of statements of 'aims' (i.e. the teachers' general intentions) and 'behavioural objectives' (the specific performances expected of students); the addition of summaries at the end of each chapter; 'signposts' and notes referring to related topics; diagrams and pictures with full explanatory captions, etc. All these techniques help to remove the need to study the texts sequentially, and so help with independent study, especially that of the holist students. To maintain motivation the material obviously needs to be attractively presented, clearly written with no unexplained jargon, and related wherever appropriate, through explicit modelling procedures, to real problems or issues.

## Lectures

For the purpose of helping students with their understanding the almost total absence of lectures in distance teaching need not be a serious loss. It is never to be expected that students will leave a lecture with any significant internalization of the concepts described and used by the lecturer. Most of the conceptual development has to take place in other learning activities. (Note that 'understanding a lecturer' is very different from 'understanding the subject being explained'.) Similarly students are unlikely to leave a lecture with any significant advance of the intellectual or communication skills which the lecturer might have demonstrated. However, lectures can perform some important functions at day schools or summer schools as part of a distance-teaching package. They can demonstrate a variety of important skills, they can enthuse and entertain students, they can provide a sense of 'belonging' to a course and they open doors to communication between students and between students and teachers. So, provided they do these things, even though they don't help much with deep learning, they can contribute significantly to learning in the affective domain and they remain popular with students and lecturers alike.

**Small group tutorials**

Small group tutorials, like lectures, are usually few and far between in distance-teaching courses, but because they can be very effective it is important that the best use is made of them. Abercrombie (1979) distinguishes between three kinds of small group activities:

- they may be remedial in nature, concentrating on students' questions and correcting their errors or misconceptions;
- they may be strongly tutor-directed, as in a school classroom, with the tutors instructing and explaining and helping individual students who get stuck on the tasks they have been set;
- they may become a kind of forum in which students can express and compare their own understandings of the issues presented to them.

The first two kinds of tutorial are good for developing knowledge and skills and can be made quite effective at developing understanding by giving students, in pairs, the opportunity of explaining their problem-solutions to each other. This is because to develop understanding it is important to ensure that students actively participate, not by asking questions for the tutor to answer but by expressing their own views and explanations. As any teacher knows, explaining difficult ideas is a severe challenge to one's own understanding, so it is usually better for students to try to talk about what they believe they *do* understand, than for them to listen to the tutor explaining yet again the latest thing that they *don't* understand! When lack of understanding is the problem, it is better for tutors to help students sort out their own misunderstandings than to try to sort them out for them.

Stimulating students to participate in an educationally rewarding way is not easy in the sciences and engineering. This is mainly because the aim in these subjects is to help students to master *accepted* concepts and apply them (so it is easy to be 'wrong'), rather than to help them formulate a well-thought-out personal viewpoint, as is the case in a number of other subjects (where disagreements are more common than mistakes). One effective way is to provide an immediate, challenging, common experience for students to concentrate their thoughts on, as when students are tackling the same problems and explaining their methods to each other, or as in 'Tutored Video Instruction' (Gibbons *et al.* 1977). Here, the tutors' role is to interrupt a videotaped lecture and facilitate discussion of the difficult ideas it contains. Tutors should resist correcting students as long as possible.

Nowadays face-to-face tutorials can be augmented or replaced by distance-teaching versions, such as one-to-one telephone tutorials, telephone conferencing or computer-conferencing (Hiltz *et al.* 1990, Mason and Kaye 1989). Live tutorials, whether face to face or in a telephone conference can be rather daunting, not only for shy students but also for students who don't think very rapidly during a discussion of new subjects or who have difficulty expressing themselves orally. For such students computer conferencing can have positive advantages. Since the 'computer conversations' do not take place in real time, students can prepare their comments and questions at their own pace before entering them on the 'bulletin board' for others to read and comment upon. They also improve the clarity of their use of language. Oral communication can follow later as confidence grows.

## TV, radio and tape recordings

Well-made educational TV programmes are good for publicity. They are also excellent for providing information and demonstrating skills because they can show actions and places that cannot be seen in any other way. To support deep learning, the aim of producers of educational TV is generally to enable students 'to observe evidence; to analyse it; to develop an argument from it; and to draw conclusions from it' (Coe 1990). Unfortunately these aims, of presenting information and developing the skills of analysis and argument, fall far short of conceptual development. This is mainly because the kinds of concepts of importance in higher education do not readily emerge from observation, as explained earlier. Videotapes are much better educationally than broadcast TV because they can be stopped and replayed allowing time, too, for students to think and take notes, but they still suffer from the simple fact that abstract concepts cannot be photographed. Provided conceptual teaching has preceded them, video programmes can put concepts in context, explain them or illustrate them by analogy and animation and show how to solve problems using them, but the spoken word has to be allowed to dominate. It is impossible, for example, without a good deal of explanation, to 'see' such concepts as 'energy' or 'efficiency' or 'profit' in pictures of a power-station or of solar cells, even though they are crucial aspects of their existence. Because of the importance of verbal explanations where deep learning is the aim, audio-vision (i.e. audiotapes linked to printed diagrams, pictures, tables, poems, etc.) is often a better system, and is certainly much cheaper and more convenient.

Radio is relatively cheap and is equivalent to good lecturing, but without a visual focus it is very easy for students to be distracted unless they take notes. The 'chalk and talk' of a lecture, or the combination of sound and vision which characterizes audio-vision or video is therefore usually more successful.

A valuable additional use of audiotapes at-a-distance is sometimes referred to as 'dial access'. This consists of providing access by telephone to three- to five-minute recordings of information. These have been found to be particularly useful for updating purposes in continuing education (e.g. of doctors), but can also be used for providing students with generalized help on assignments, etc.

**Practical work**

Practical activities are difficult to organize in distance education, so it is again important that they are well used. In general they are confined to home kits, day schools and summer schools. They can be used for a variety of educational purposes, such as:

- exercising practical skills;
- verifying information and theories given in lectures;
- 'discovering' facts or laws of behaviour,
- helping students to design experiments and choose appropriate apparatus;
- enabling students to tackle projects, especially design projects;
- helping students grasp difficult concepts, etc.

The actual purpose(s) chosen must depend on the educational aims of the course of which the practical work forms a part.

If practical activities are to be used to develop understanding, the kinds of experiments which, like many scientific ones, require students to follow instructions, obtain data, plot curves and draw conclusions in well specified ways, are not challenging enough. They need to be more than experiments. As well as a teaching phase, they need also to include a mini-project, or an open-ended problem-solving task, so that the principles demonstrated in the teaching phase of the activity have to be applied immediately in a challenging way. This tends to make them more motivating and students' individual contributions provide worthwhile topics around which students can develop their communication skills.

For other purposes, of course, practical activities should be designed differently. 'Discovery learning', involving the collection of information which is new to the students, aids memorization.

Practical exercises are obviously important for developing practical skills, such as, in science, those of measurement, error estimation, etc.

## The use of microcomputers

Free-standing micro-computers in the home can nowadays be used in a variety of ways for educational purposes. They have long been used successfully for 'drill-and-practice' to help with the teaching of certain skills; as spread sheets for repeated calculations; as word-processors, for communication skills; as databases to support design activities and for computer-aided instruction. Interactive video is especially effective at skills training. These uses are however focused mainly on knowledge acquisition and the developing of certain skills; they only indirectly assist with conceptual development. Except as word processors in support of effective writing, such uses of computers don't usually provide the kind of challenge that deep learning requires. Even multi-media work stations, including hyper-media, do no more than allow students efficiently to explore an information store; they cannot yet handle the open-ended output of students, which is so important an aspect of conceptual development.

Simulation, especially in design, can however provide a sufficiently rich form of interchange between student and computer to promote conceptual learning. Simulation enables students to try out different designs or solutions to problems – the computer doing the analysis of each proposed solution. If students just explore all the possibilities by trial-and-error in the hope of arriving at a good solution, their understanding is unlikely to be much improved. But if they accept the challenge of trying to arrive rapidly at good solutions through the intelligent use of the new concepts they are trying to grasp, their understanding can be significantly advanced. (The numbers of times students run the computer simulations before arriving at good designs can act as an inverse measure of the students' levels of understanding!)

## Projects

Projects and problem-based learning (Boud and Feletti 1991) are now popular for several reasons, especially for sustaining motivation. That students enjoy them is often regarded as a key factor, even if they 'don't learn much'! The depth of understanding which projects demand varies considerably, from very little in simple information collection, to a great deal in complex problem-solving. Only the latter are likely significantly to advance students' conceptual development. In general, then, the main function of projects is to develop various personal skills, such as integrative thinking, confidence, attention to detail, initiative, persistence, independent learning, etc. It is these factors which Higher Education for Enterprise emphasizes (Stephenson and Weil 1992). Group projects also encourage interpersonal and communication skills. Project work at-a-distance usually needs a local supervisor as well as a central organizer.

## Assignments

'Computer-marked assignments', consisting of multiple-choice questions for example, are usually thought to have little to do with deep learning, their main function being a simple and efficient way of testing certain kinds of knowledge and skills. But the CADE system developed in Sweden (Bååth and Månsson 1977) has shown how computer-marked assignments can contribute to conceptual learning in much the same way that good tutors do when they write comments on students' written assignments. In CADE the computer-generated responses to students' mistakes in answering multiple-choice assignments do not contain the correct answers; instead they are friendly, personalized, encouraging letters suggesting in a general way (i.e. not specific to the kind of mistakes made) how the students might correct their own errors. It is found possible in this way to persuade students to think further about the problems they have been set, and so begin to overcome their own misunderstandings.

## Independent study

In all the above activities it is, of course, possible for students to adopt a surface approach and be purely passive learners. Indeed if students know that the examinations will require only knowledge and skills, it is tempting, even for motivated students, to do no more than look up the answers to assignments in their distance-teaching materials. A number of actions are therefore necessary if students are to be persuaded to adopt a 'deep approach' to learning. These include: using educational strategies, such as active or problem-based learning; designing assignments and examinations that demand understanding for their solution; explaining to students the different kinds of learning expected of them; not overloading the course with information which can be acquired at other times; structuring educational material to match different learning styles, etc.

Once students have embraced the 'deep approach' and know what they are trying to achieve, active learning is no longer so important and they can become effective independent learners. Deep learning can then be achieved even through passive modes of study like reading and attending lectures. It is often said that interaction with a tutor or a group of fellow students is essential for conceptual development, and for some students this may well be so. For others – perhaps even the majority, if attendance at voluntary tutorials is a valid measure – independent study may well be more effective.

## CONCLUSION

Any complex activity can be analysed in a variety of ways depending on the purpose of the analysis, and education is no exception. The simple taxonomy of the cognitive domain used in this chapter is valuable because it relates well to the three fundamental aspects of the educational process: learning, teaching, and assessment methods. So, by ensuring that educational aims in the cognitive domain are expressed in terms of the knowledge, skills, know-how and understanding expected of students, the teaching provided can be matched to these aims without much difficulty or ambiguity. Since the teaching of understanding is much the most difficult to achieve, it is essential, for courses in which understanding is an educational aim, to design the learning materials with conceptual development primarily in mind. The teaching of the relevant knowledge and skills can then be added where appropriate and relevant. Most importantly, if understanding is an aim, the assessment methods used must make deep learning essential, otherwise students will continue to follow the easier route of relying on their memory and well-practised skills.

Finally, it must not be forgotten that most real-world problems are normally complex, and therefore need a mixture of *knowledge, skills, know-how, values* and *understanding* for their satisfactory solution. Problem-based learning demands the integrative thinking needed for such problem-solving, but it rarely, on its own, provides sufficient depth of conceptual development in all aspects of a subject. Well-designed courses, for which understanding is a specified aim, therefore require a balance between the more formal educational methods described earlier aimed at conceptual development and the less formal project-based activities. This is true whether the subject is religion, science, philosophy, education, technology or any other conceptually rich subject.

## REFERENCES

Abercrombie, M. L. J. (1979) *Aims and Techniques of Group Teaching*, Society for Research into Higher Education, University of Surrey, Guildford.

Bååth, J. A. and Månsson, N.-O. (1977) *CADE – A System for Computer-Assisted Distance Education*, Malmö, Sweden: Hermods Skola.

Black, P. J. (1962) 'University examinations', *Physics Education* 3(2), 93.

Bloom, B. S. *et al.* (1956) *Taxonomy of Educational Objectives, Handbook 1: Cognitive Domain*, New York: Longman Green.

Boud, D. and Feletti, G. (eds) (1991) *The Challenge of Problem-based Education*, London: Kogan Page.

Buzan, T. (1974) *Use Your Head*, London: BBC.

Coe, T. (1990) 'What's hard about teaching easy things?: television in social science, educational studies, continuing education and the humanities', in A. Bates, *Media and Technology in European Distance Education*, Milton Keynes: The Open University.

Daniel, J. (1976) 'The work of Gordon Pask', in N. J. Entwistle and D. Hounsell, *How Students Learn*, University of Lancaster.

Downs, S. and Perry, P. (1982) 'Research report: how do I learn', *Journal of European Industrial Training* 6(6), 27–32.

Gagné, R. M. and Briggs, L. J. (1979) *Principles of Instructional Design*, New York: Holt, Reinholt & Wilson.

Gibbons, J. F., Kincheloe, W. R. and Down, S. K. (1977) 'Tutored videotape instruction: a new use of electronics media in education', *Science* 195, 1136–49.

Gibbs, G. (1981) *Teaching Students to Learn: A Student-Centred Approach*, Milton Keynes: The Open University.

Hiltz, R., Shapiro, H. and Ringsted, M. (1990) 'Collaborative teaching in a virtual classroom (R)', *Proc. of Third Guelph Symposium on Computer Mediated Communication*, University of Guelph, Ontario, pp. 37–55.

Marton, F. and Säljö R. (1976) 'On qualitative differences in learning: outcomes and processes', *British Journal of Educational Psychology* 46, 4–11.

Mason, R. and Kaye, A. (eds) (1989) *Mindweave: Communication, Computers and Distance Education*, Oxford: Pergamon Press.

Pask, G. (1976) 'Styles and strategies of learning', *British Journal of Educational Psychology* 46, 128–48.

Prosser, M. (1987) 'The effects of cognitive structure and learning strategy on student achievement', in J. T. E. Richardson, M. W. Eysenck and D. W. Piper (eds), *Student Learning*, Milton Keynes: SRHE and the Open University Press.

Ramsden, P. (1986) 'Students and quality', in G. C. Moodie (ed.), *Standards and Criteria in Higher Education*, Guildford: SRHE and NFER-Nelson.

—— (ed.) (1988) 'Preface', *Improving Learning: New Perspectives*, London: Kogan Page.

—— Beswick, D. and Bowden, J. (1987) 'Learning processes and learning skills', in J. T. E. Richardson, M. W. Eysenck and D. W. Piper (eds), *Student Learning*, Milton Keynes: SRHE and the Open University Press.

Rowntree, D. (1977) *Assessing Students: How Should We Know Them*, London: Harper and Row.

Stephenson, J. and Weil, S. (eds) (1992) *Quality in Learning*, London: Kogan Page.

# 9 Structural analysis of distance education

*Benedetto Vertecchi*

## AN ERA IS ENDING

In the industrialized countries schooling has been developed to a level that probably cannot be further extended in a meaningful way. I am referring to 'schooling' as a service primarily addressed to the education of children and adolescents in specialized structures which are organized in a rather uniform way from the temporal and spatial point of view – a definition which can be applied to schooling as it has been practised since the sixteenth century in Europe. Nowadays, almost the whole population is involved in sequential schooling for a substantial number of years. Compulsory schooling, which used to be limited to primary education and to some years of secondary, is now being extended to the completion of secondary education for an increasing number of youngsters, and it is possible to note the same trend in higher education too.

Even though the characteristics of schooling do not show complete uniformity everywhere because of social, economical and political influences, our century can none the less be considered a turning point in the history of education. To go to school is no longer considered a privilege for the happy few, but everybody's need. A basic grounding of knowledge is today a condition for existence.

In complex societies people who do not have a proper education can play but a reduced role because they do not have the tools for understanding processes and situations and therefore are unable to participate in political life and productive activities. It can even be said that a new marginality is developing, involving people who are marginalized not because of the lack of physical goods but yet live in a condition of marginality because they are not culturally prepared to interpret change and, therefore, can be easily manipulated through mass media.

Each individual now spends the first part of life going to school. Nevertheless, children used to work in the fields and in factories only a few decades ago, and it was not unusual to see young persons worn out by toil and deprivation. The result of the development of schooling is a transformation in standards of living: the protected age has extended its boundaries so that children have better opportunities to develop physically, to understand their interests and to express their abilities.

The elements I have mentioned describe a situation in progress. They show, nevertheless, that some dangers are involved in the development of sequential schooling. It is not possible to imagine young people who are indefinitely dependent on adults for the satisfaction of their needs, mature from a physical point of view but still lacking autonomy. It is already possible to observe that young people are often uneasy that the number of years they spend in school is not completely justified by the acquisition of the knowledge they actually need, but also corresponds to the necessity of 'parking' them to minimize the contradictions which are characteristics of adult society.

Finally, the historical period of the extension of schooling is coming to an end. Clearly it is still necessary to remedy certain situations and to secure for everybody, whatever their social or personal disadvantage may be, a period of schooling of adequate quality and sufficient length, but one has to conclude that a continuous lengthening of schooling would probably create more problems than it can solve.

## THE NEW DEMAND FOR EDUCATION

We have examined above why a further expansion of sequential schooling is becoming impossible from the social point of view. There is another reason which results from an analysis of the relationship between the period of schooling and the speed of the transformation of knowledge in contemporary society. In traditional European thought the time of schooling (the time required for transmitting knowledge from one generation to the other) was a small proportion of the time of knowledge (the time required for establishing the knowledge which had to be transmitted). This relationship between the time of schooling and the time of knowledge contributed to the simplification of school organization and even more to the social application of the knowledge acquired. There were two main reasons for this:

- school culture was stable because it was possible to define the educational curriculum before a cohort of students began to be trained;
- the knowledge acquired at school could be applied during all the working life.

Each worker used to carry on the same activities in the same way during all of his or her working life: the turner used a lathe, the miller used a cutter, the accountant kept the books until the day of retirement. Those engaged in professional activities knew that university training secured for them stable knowledge which provided a solid basis for future professional activity.

Education cannot rely on the stability of the knowledge to be acquired anymore. The twelve or thirteen years (depending on the country) needed to complete primary and secondary schooling is a very long time during which changes in knowledge can be profound. When competencies are based on formal abilities they have, it is true, a longer life but there is a high and increasing turnover for all competencies which refer directly to professional profiles. This trend has two main consequences at school level:

- elements which contribute to cultural stability (linguistic, historical, mathematical abilities) need emphasis;
- professional training acquired at school cannot be considered complete but must be modified, reviewed, and, in some cases, replaced during the working life.

This is the reason for an increasing demand for education (often of an advanced level) from adults who already work. In many cases people do not want to study again to improve their economic and professional position but wish to study because they want to understand what is changing in their contemporary world, especially in their professional field.

In other cases the demand for education is coming for other and differing reasons: people are not happy anymore with the cultural level they reached at school; they want to change their professional profile or they change their minds about what they want to do. In all these cases the demand for education comes from adults and it would be rather difficult to satisfy the demand for education in a traditional education system.

In many countries distance education has been seen as the correct solution to the problem.

## THE IDEA OF SCHOOLING

Distance education breaks the temporal and spatial restraints that are typical of face-to-face education. Other functions, however, which are characteristic of traditional schooling are still present in distance education: above all clear distinction between the teacher and the learner. More particularly, there is a social delegation (at least of a part of society) that legitimates the teacher's educational activity. No less important is the intent that all the students receive the same educational content. Finally, the teacher (it does not matter whether it is a person or a structure) has the moral or legal authority to award certification for completed study.

Summarizing, we can distinguish seven elements in a classical educational theory:

- temporal unity;
- spatial unity;
- uniformity of the educational content;
- definition of the teacher's role;
- social delegation for education;
- definition of the learner's role;
- authorization of certification.

Initially distance education had no strong formal characteristics but now it has acquired an institutional role: distance education courses interest more and more people and complement traditional education; certificates may be awarded and so on. Therefore distance education presents all the seven characteristics of traditional face-to-face education, except the first two. It is thus possible to formulate two different hypotheses depending on whether one considers all the seven elements as essential for the definition of schooling or one considers that temporal and spatial unity are historical characteristics of the idea of schooling but not structural elements of its definition. In the first hypothesis distance education represents a new form of education. In the second, distance education contributes one of a great number of modes in which historically education is achieved.

In the rest of this chapter I will try to demonstrate that the second hypothesis is the right one; in my interpretation 'space' and 'time' are not essential characteristics for defining an educational system but generalizations relating to a specific period in the history of education. In contemporary society communication systems are available which are capable of breaking the narrow spatial boundaries defined by the sensory possibilities of the learner. Those communications media allow educational messages to be stored and their transmission to be graduated. These show how false it would be to continue to consider as essential the generalizations about space and time: to be considered an educational activity it has only to fulfil the remaining five conditions.

## CREATING A 'SCHOOL'

If one accepts the hypothesis that distance education is an educational mode, it is relevant to apply to it the problems that usually arise in forms of education in which teachers and students are co-present in a determined place and space. In this way the themes of didactic research have to be reconsidered in the specific situation of distance education.

The most important contribution of research on the teaching/ learning processes in recent decades has been the establishment of the need to support the work of each student by the activation of individualized procedures which are capable of compensating for possible learning difficulties. In distance education the same problem has to be solved by designing a strategy tailored to the main characteristic of distance education: the (almost) total absence of direct interaction between teachers and learners.

Distance education students should not consider that they have to study in a second-class way. On the contrary, it is important to emphasize its possibilities: didactic flexibility (each learner studies when he/she has the time) and compatibility with other commitments (work, family, social duties). But it is also necessary that the students realize the continuity of the didactic support at their disposal: distance teaching cannot be based on educational anonymity in which an undifferentiated educational offering is addressed to a public whose characteristics and needs are unknown. If distance education was reduced to the dispatch of study materials, it would be possible to avoid the complications of formal structures (enrolments, assignments, certificates, etc.) and to issue the materials directly to the booksellers. On the contrary, teaching at a distance requires the existence of a 'school'. The school's responsibility is to organize the teaching activity and to control so that each learner achieves the course objectives.

When we emphasize the idea of distance education as a 'school' we underline two consequences. First, in general terms one places the discussion in the perspective of the continuous evaluation of educational systems in the contemporary world. Distance education is an answer to educational needs that have been growing in modern society, but it cannot offer an alternative to face-to-face education. In other words, the development of the field of distance education does not mean the acceptance, even in an implicit way, of the idea that the institutional education system is out-of-date and has to be replaced by information distribution networks (this is the 'deschooling' thesis). On the contrary, distance education is a means of diversifying and specializing the face-to-face educational offering in response to the evolution of educational needs, its extension to people of all ages, the dynamics of the developments of science, and changes in the world of work.

Second, from the educational point of view it means that distance education is not a modern version of isolated self-study. It is only in the vaguest sense that one could consider that the only necessary condition for teaching at a distance is the existence of a public who can read written communication. If one were to accept such a vague definition the history of distance education would coincide with the history of writing. Whoever writes a text about anything has the purpose of 'teaching' something to somebody (at least to himself or herself in the case of a private text such as a diary). It is clear that this intent is not always explicit and from time to time the intention is expressed as 'to communicate', 'to discuss', 'to reflect' or 'to suggest'. Nevertheless, each text is written by an author who knows (or believes he or she knows) something that somebody else wants to know. Therefore one can hold that anybody who writes a text 'teaches' something and anybody who reads the same text 'learns' at a distance.

This approach is too general to identify the central problem of distance education. Distance education presupposes the existence of a 'school'–that is, an organization whose explicit purpose is to teach to a public who wants to learn. The idea of a 'school' justifies the use of the term *distance education*: 'distance' implies the idea of spatial and temporal separateness between teacher and learner and the necessity of bridging the gap by a technical medium.

Equally restrictive are interpretations of distance education which place the emphasis on the possibilities offered by the developments of technology to overcome 'distance'. It is not the technical solution in itself that can qualify as education but the educational structure and the didactic use of each medium. A television broadcast or a computer connection does not 'teach' better than a written text. If one identifies distance education with the technical solution adopted to overcome distance, one only modernizes the situation of the self-taught learner.

## THE LONELINESS OF THE STUDENTS (WHO DO NOT STUDY AT A DISTANCE)

Educational innovation, both with regard to distance education and other sectors of didactic renewal, often encounters criticism that should more suitably be addressed to traditional education. An objection that is often raised about distance education is the isolation of distance students and the impossibility for them of building a positive interaction with their teachers. One would be led to think that traditional educational organization was distinguished by the constant attention it offers to students and the intensity of the interaction it establishes between them and their teachers.

Anyone who is familiar with university teaching knows well that that is the exception rather than the rule. On the contrary, it often happens that students are completely neglected as individuals. In fact the examinations are often their only personal contact with their lecturers. Each student's loneliness is not minimized by being co-present in a physical space thronged with other students: the solitude we are talking about is defined by the circumstances in which study takes place and not by a general need of personal interaction that can probably be better satisfied in other contexts.

The need of interaction is here referred specifically to the pattern of a learning activity: it is an educational interaction. Students who attend lectures regularly probably have a rather precise idea of their lecturers' personalities, can appreciate the clarity of their explanations, their ability in presenting the subject, and can sometimes have some verbal exchanges with them. But it is almost certain that the student will be alone at the time of study, that there will be no real contact when the attempt is made to translate what has been listened to into genuine learning.

If this happens to students who attend lectures regularly, we can imagine the situation of the student who only goes on and off to the lectures or does not attend them at all. There is a strange and widespread prejudice in the academic world: nobody wants to admit that most face-to-face university students study as if they were 'at a distance', without being supported by a distance education system. A traditional model of instruction that does not exist any more (if only for numerical reasons) is being used to criticize systems that organize distance education in a correct way.

## ORGANIZATIONAL STRUCTURE

When educational research aims to harmonize different technical and cognitive elements of the educational process, especially when there is question of a 'technological' idea of the educational process, it is indispensable to disassemble the learning task into its different functions. This necessity is particularly important in the case of distance education.

In traditional education the different functions of the learning task overlapped because they were accomplished, more or less efficiently, by a single teacher who organized his or her own work, planned the educational methodology, communicated the different elements of the educational content to the students, and assessed their learning results. During the lessons the teacher had the opportunity to develop other dimensions of the teaching process. For instance, as the teaching progressed the teacher got an idea of the students' characteristics, realized what their interests were from individual contacts, could modify the content from analysing the students' reactions. As the process was not based on explicit planning, teachers had to rely on their personal ability and gifts to identify students' needs and give them appropriate interaction.

The development of educational research has emphasized the role of analytical processes as a preliminary condition for optimizing teaching. Different teaching functions have been separated out and specialized to make them more effective. This process of specialization has made it improbable that an individual teacher can provide all the didactic functions. In this interpretation the unity of the educational process, which formerly was guaranteed by the role of the teacher, is now the result of the logical design of the educational project. If the project is effectively designed its characteristics do not depend on the choice of the teachers to implement it. The success of the project can depend on intrinsic conditions of validity that are only marginally dependent on the personal gifts of the people who implement its different parts.

In distance education this specialization of functions has to be very precise to ensure a satisfactory degree of interaction with students. The structural organization involves three different fields, with differing needs and competencies corresponding to each of them:

- *Design*: outlining the general features of the educational offering, defining the target public, deciding the didactic strategy, selecting the technical choices and the communication system, deciding on student support.
- *Development*: preparing all the study materials needed. Those involved in this phase need to have two kinds of skills: in distance education strategies and in the content of the subject to be taught.

- *Implementation*: many activities are required to ensure regular communication with the students once they have begun to study: dispatch of study materials, correction of assignments, processing of data, preparation of correcting and compensatory communications to be sent to the students. In addition and at the same time the whole of the operations have to be controlled; student profiles have to be developed to monitor the progress of each student, information has to be collected to allow for the evaluation of the didactic quality of the learning materials, periodical reports on the progress of the system have to be produced.

## CONTINUOUS CONTROL ACTIVITY

As in any other educational activity, distance education requires continuous control of the progress of the operation from the point of view of the students considered as a whole and as individuals.

In face-to-face education the physical presence of students is a source of information in itself. In distance education, on the other hand, the control structure provides, if not the only, certainly by far the most important source of information on the students. Therefore it is vital for the control system to be based on explicit structures which can collect information that can be stored and processed, which will elicit the students' collaboration in data collection and which will give an overview of all teaching and learning activities.

When a control system is functional to the needs of an educational structure it provides information on the following:

- *Initial analysis of student characteristics.* Before the educational activity begins it is necessary to have detailed information about the students enrolled, particularly about their previous study experience and professional profile and about the reasons why they enrolled in a distance course, etc.
- *Intermediate evaluation of the students' learning activity.* This is the most important aspect of the control system because the intermediate evaluation allows the implementation of compensatory procedures and the provision to each student of the help needed in overcoming difficulties in the learning task. After each intermediate assessment the control system should redefine the individual profile of each student and as a result redefine, at least in part, the course objectives. The intermediate assignments have in addition the function of evaluating the progress of the whole course, the problems met by the students, the success of the learning materials, and the effectiveness of the assignment itself.

- *Final evaluation*. Its purpose is to evaluate the quality of the results obtained from the distance education course.

In the educational framework we are describing most of the control procedures have the characteristics of formative evaluation. The main purpose is not to assess the level of learning of each student but to gather data on the process of learning so that timely intervention may be made when needed.

# Part IV
# Philosophical underpinnings

# 10 The education of adults and distance education in late modernity

*Peter Jarvis*

In precisely the same way that Peters (1983) has argued that distance education can be analysed from the perspective of industrial production, it is possible to interpret it as being symbolic of late modernity. This chapter explores this thesis in relation to the education of adults. Prior to presenting the argument, however, it is necessary to discuss the three component concepts of the title of this chapter since each is, at least, contentious. Consequently, the first part undertakes this, whilst the latter ones introduce the argument under consideration.

## LAYING THE CONCEPTUAL FOUNDATIONS

The three concepts in the title all need some elaboration since there is no general agreement about any of them, and so they are each discussed in turn.

### The education of adults

A multitude of concepts have arisen in recent years that approximate to this idea: adult education, continuing education, lifelong education, recurrent education, etc. Each carries its own connotations and nuances, so that it is necessary to explain precisely how this term is being employed here.

The term 'adult education' has tended to be restricted to the provision of the traditional, liberal education for adults that they might pursue as a leisure time activity. However, the development of continuing professional education, human resource development, vocational education, etc. has meant that education is now being offered to adults on a much wider scale than ever before. For some, more traditional theorists (e.g. Paterson 1979), liberal adult education is the purest form of education while other types of teaching and learning are less educational and more like training. However, this distinction is rather difficult to maintain within this broader context of teaching and learning and, consequently, all institutionalized processes of teaching and learning are treated here as differing forms of education. The concept of 'adult' is also problematic, although one which is not explored here, apart from noting that it refers to those individuals who are regarded as adults within their own society. Hence it is suggested that the education of adults is a more exact term to describe the ideas being presented here, since it does not carry specific orientations towards one form of education or another. The expression which approximates most closely to this is 'continuing education', which refers to all education which occurs after initial education has been completed.

**Distance education**

Perhaps the most complete discussion of the meaning of the term is to be found in Keegan (1990: 28–47). He (1990: 44) characterizes distance education in the following manner: it has a semi-permanent separation of teacher and learner; it is influenced by the educational organization in both the preparation of the teaching materials and the support of the students; it uses technical media; it is a two-way process; it has a semi-permanent absence of a learning group. Naturally, these characteristics are open to certain criticisms: for instance, it may well be true that in certain forms of distance education there is a two-way relationship between teachers and taught so that the learners may also initiate teaching and learning situations, but this is by no means universal. Consequently, this characteristic appears superfluous to any definition of the concept. Distance education is, therefore, defined here as those forms of education in which organized learning opportunities are usually provided through a technical medium to learners who normally study individually, and removed from the teacher in both time and space. Naturally, each educational institution has its own procedures and provides its own facilities and so this definition endeavours to be narrow enough to be meaningful but not so wide as to include almost any form of learning. Nevertheless, it is possible for the teaching and learning to occur simultaneously, although this is increasingly rare.

**Late modernity**

Modern society has emerged as a result of a variety of causes and one of the current debates is the extent to which the modernity project is over and a new post-modern era dawning (Lyotard 1986). Whether or not there has been such a dramatic change in society is beyond the scope of this study: suffice it to note that it is maintained here that this is a period of late modernity rather than post-modernity. Late modernity is an advanced stage in the historical and cultural process which had its beginnings in the west at the time of the Renaissance; it is now about societies which are industrial and capitalistic, and is characterized by a number of specific features which are discussed fully by Giddens (1990, 1991), among other writers.

Giddens (1990: 53) suggests that among the hallmarks of late modernity are: the separation of time and space; the development of disembedded mechanisms; the reflexive appropriation of knowledge. He argues that in pre-modern societies 'space and place largely coincide, since the spatial dimensions of social life are, for most of the population, and in most respects, dominated by "presence"–by localised activities' (Giddens 1990: 18). However, in late modernity locality is influenced by social considerations quite distant from them. Disembedded mechanisms refer to the removal of social relations 'from local contexts of interaction' (Giddens 1990: 21) which restructure them across time and space so that globalization occurs. This results in what was once local, perhaps personal, social interaction being replaced by impersonal expert systems which demand a form of trust from those who use them. Finally, the reflexivity of late modernity is characterized by constant change as every element in society seeks to respond to the forces of change.

Another feature of late modernity significant for the following argument is that as society has become more complex and so much information is transmitted to people, so there has emerged a contrasting emphasis upon individualization. In late modernity, social ties are weakened which results in more freedom of choice to the individual. Emphasis is now placed upon individuality and personal identity. There is a sense in which society has moved from the traditional community through a period of association to individuation. Now it appears to be more an agglomeration of individuals than a community and individual biography and self-identity are assuming more significance. At the same time it must be recognized that the social and cultural institutions still determine the parameters within which individual responsibility operates.

Having outlined the three basic concepts upon which this chapter is based it is now possible to proceed with the argument under consideration. It will be suggested in the following section that distance education is the educational symbol of late modernity and that adult individuals will increasingly utilize this expert system.

## DISTANCE EDUCATION AS A SYMBOL OF LATE MODERNITY

Distance education contains a number of features which underlie the typification of contemporary society as being one of late modernity: industrial–capitalistic; space–time distanciation; disembedded mechanisms and expert systems; reflexivity; individual responsibility. Each of these are now discussed in the order that they appear here.

### Industrial capitalistism

Peters has shown how thoroughly the production of distance education materials epitomizes industrial production, although he does not demonstrate its relation to the capitalist market in quite the same manner. However, inherent in capitalism are three features that can also now be discovered in distance education – namely, commoditization, competition, and globalization.

Once any commodity is technologically produced it becomes an object, and within a capitalist economy it is a commodity which can be sold. A distance education package, or a course, or an interactive video compact disc is a marketable commodity and one which educational institutions have been encouraged to sell. Now they have marketing managers committed to selling educational courses and, of course, the market is limited if the commodity is a course offered only at a local college or university. However, if the programme is contained within an object that can be carried away from the vendor, or even mailed or transmitted electronically to the purchaser, then it becomes a more attractive marketable commodity.

Even so, the capitalistic market is one of competition. The rhetoric of the market is that only the best quality commodities will survive, but its reality is that only the strongest and largest organizations survive irrespective of the quality of the product which they sell. Distance education now advertises its wares and buyers wish to know not only about the nature of the course being studied but also the length of time that it will take, the qualification that will be awarded on successful completion, the number of assignments that have to be submitted, and the fee that they will have to pay. Purchasers can then decide for themselves which is their 'best buy' according to their own instrumental concerns. One of the obvious outcomes of this process is that those unsuccessful institutions, irrespective of the quality of their product or of their potentiality, will lose out and may be forced to close. Hence, the large get larger at the expense of the small, unless the small discover a gap in the market etc., but the consequences of this are self-evident.

But the market cannot be limited to the local area of the producing institution. The market is bounded only by the size of the globe! Hence, globalization has entered into distance education – many universities are running their courses internationally, the British Open University is opening offices throughout the world, the University of Surrey organizes a Masters Degree programme in post-compulsory education which can be studied anywhere in the world, etc. so that it is becoming possible to study for a British university degree, for instance, in the farthest reaches of the world. Naturally, there are tremendous advantages to this – but it might also be wondered about the effect that this will have upon small indigenous universities of poor Third World countries and once again it might lead to accusations of cultural imperialism. However, it might be much more a matter for some of trade or, as others would argue, aid rather than anything else.

### Space–time distanciation

Giddens (1990: 18) indicates that in 'pre-modern societies, space and place largely coincide, since the spatial dimensions of social life are, for most of the population, and in most respects, dominated by "presence" – by localised activities'. In other words, students had to be in the presence of the teachers to hear their profound words. The history of the university is of students travelling to places where teachers expounded; in order to gain a degree from certain universities, residence qualifications were imposed, and so on. Now it is possible to study for, and to be awarded, even higher degrees from some universities without ever being physically present, not only at the university itself but even in the country in which the university is located. Now the teachers record their lessons and they can be studied in the students' own time and place. The learning experience is no longer immediate and face-to-face, but mediated and secondary. Distance education, by definition, symbolizes the process of space–time distanciation.

**Disembedded mechanisms and expert systems**

Disembedding implies a process of extracting the specific localized social relations and re-implanting them within a global context of space and time. Consequently, the distance-teaching institutions can be experienced, not as a place to which learners travel for study with a teacher but as the mechanisms through which the pursuit of their studies is facilitated wherever they study and at whatever time they choose to undertake their work. The distance-teaching institution is disembedded and needs have no campus and no geographical location.

In other words, the academy is now no longer a place but is a disembedded process and a system – its educational offering is now a product guaranteed to provide specific learning for the purchasers; now it is not only the teachers who are important, it is the whole system – producing, packaging, marketing, processing, support services for clients, and so on. The system is removed from its localized context and now the clients and learners have to be persuaded to trust in the efficiency and expertise of the whole system.

**Reflexivity**

The reflexivity of modernity, according to Giddens (1990: 38), involves a constant examination and re-examination of social practices which are 'reformed in the light of incoming information about those very practices'. Consequently, the traditional mode of doing things is no longer sufficient justification for continuing a practice. Indeed, change in the mode of production and distribution of distance education materials will alter as new technologies initiate different ways of doing things. For instance, the interactive compact videodisc, and the interactive computer program, will no doubt replace the traditional correspondence material when the market makes it a worthwhile financial investment. However, in seeking a world-wide sale such hi-tech productions will limit the size of the market able to purchase costly commodities and so many educational materials will remain in traditional, and cheaper, written form for a few more years to come.

**Individuation**

As the functioning of many elements of society has become organized and distanced from everyday life, there has been a new emphasis upon the individual. Emphasis is placed upon the existential questions of humankind – upon the self and upon self-identity. People do not always feel so constrained by the demands of organizations because they do not always have to attend them to be part of them, although they are actually controlled by their procedures in precisely the same way! Consequently, individuals feel able to follow their own pursuits, at their own time and in their own way and, to some extent; be self-determining individuals. Distance education, therefore, provides the opportunity for people to continue their education individually in their own space and at their own time and pace and have it serviced by a disembedded educational institution, an expert system.

Distance education may, therefore, be seen to fit many of the characteristics of late modernity and it may be regarded as being a symbol of this form of society. It is now necessary to relate this discussion to the education of adults.

## THE EDUCATION OF ADULTS AND DISTANCE EDUCATION IN LATE MODERNITY

The education of adults is also adapting to late modernity and, therefore, it becomes apparent that some of its forms can easily be changed into the distance mode. There are two ways in which this may be seen: from the development of the field itself and from the emphases being placed within its own theoretical development.

### The development of the education of adults

It is perhaps significant that adult education was one of the earliest forms of education to adopt the distance education mode. In the 1870s the Chautauqua Institution in the USA popularized the correspondence course. Chautauqua was formed as a summer school for Sunday School teachers in 1874 but within a very few years it had grown into a nation-wide system of home study (Knowles 1980b).

Home study was the beginning of distance education in the education of adults. It was the first stage of space–time distanciation and it has subsequently developed forms which can be more easily mailed and, indeed, marketed. Now the emphasis is not upon the study of a whole academic discipline or sub-discipline, it is upon the study of a module of learning devised to be studied over a specific period of time. Time is one of the predominant symbols of modernity and the current emphasis on modularization of courses in the education of adults makes study both more flexible and much more easily marketable.

Both the fact that the subject of study is specific and that it can be studied in the home as a leisure time pursuit also makes it a most attractive area of growth for continuing professional education. Employers are more likely to purchase a module for their employees to study at home than they are to send them on paid educational leave!

Indeed, the education of adults is sufficiently flexible to respond to the demands of the market. There is a plethora of educational courses and qualifications offered to all potential students throughout the world, with First World universities offering their courses throughout the world. Individuals are now able to study at a distance at any level, including undertaking research doctorates at a distance. Centres of excellence are now providing educational material through a variety of media world-wide to whoever wishes to purchase them. Indeed, in the USA a Commission of Non-Traditional Study was formed in 1971 (Knowles 1980b: 30) to investigate the variety of new forms of education for adults which were emerging. In a similar manner there has been a growth in non-traditional courses and qualifications in the United Kingdom, which has resulted in an endeavour to standardize the wide variety of qualifications through the National Council for Vocational Qualifications.

Adult education as a field has also changed quite dramatically over the past few years. There was always a slight international dimension to the study of the field, but in the past decade the field has internationalized, reflecting the whole process of globalization. The formation of the International Council of Adult Education, while not the beginning of the process, was one of the first symbols of the global concern. More recently, such organizations as the Highlander Center have endeavoured to respond to the types of environmental and human problem caused by large industrial concerns – with Highlander adult educators, for instance, working with the people in the communities of Appalachia (in the USA) and Bophal (in India) in response to the same problems caused to the people by the same industrial concern. Responding to similar concerns throughout the world makes it even more probable that adult education will continue to adopt modes of delivery which enable the same disquiets to be addressed wherever they appear.

The education of adults is, then, a flexible phenomenon able to respond to learning need wherever they occur in the world. It has used a variety of methods to respond to the demands and has been at the forefront of distance education.

**Theoretical developments**

From the above discussion it is clear that a number of characteristics prevail and some of these are also to be discovered in the emerging body of knowledge in the education of adults. They include being learner-centred; emhasizing individual responsibility in adulthood; emphasizing reflective learning; and needs-meeting approaches to programme planning. Each of these are in accord with the above thesis.

Traditionally, education has relied on the expertise of the teacher and has been teacher-centred, but more recently the place of the teacher has been played down. It has been commonplace to claim that the teacher is not the fount of all wisdom and that teaching 'is a vastly overrated function' (Rogers 1983: 119). Knowles, rather like Rogers, has sought to place the responsibility for learning on the adult; indeed, he regards adulthood as a self-directing phenomenon (Knowles 1980a: 45–6). Self-directed learning (Candy 1991) has become a major area of study and concern as a result of early studies, such as that by Houle (1961). However, most forms of self-directed learning are actually teaching techniques in which the learner has a certain autonomy within the constraints of the system rather than totally autonomous learning projects. Candy (1991) makes the distinction between autodidaxy, which is totally autonomous and outside the system, and self-directed which occurs within it. It is this latter form which is most appropriate in distance education.

In addition, the emphasis on reflective learning (Mezirow 1990, 1991; Jarvis 1987, 1992) has mirrored the reflexivity of late modernity. Indeed, the emphasis on and research into learning rather than teaching also reflects the fact that the system has tended to take precedence over teaching in recent years.

Adult education has traditionally used the vocabulary of welfare – it has regarded itself as needs meeting. However, it has never been predominantly a welfare provision but rather it has provided a leisure time programme for whoever wished to enrol. Indeed, one of its main claims has been that is has been flexible and responsive to whatever learning needs arise. Consequently, its emphasis on 'needs' has reflected its concern to be responsive to the educational market as much as its altruistic orientations, and it is this flexibility which has enabled it to be reflexive to the changes that are currently occurring within late modernity.

From both the development of the education of adults and from its theoretical emphases, it may be seen that it reflects certain of the characteristics of late modernity in precisely the same way as does distance education and so it is not surprising that distance education should have developed primarily for adults. However, the market does target its sales and prepare commodities to sell to different groups and, therefore, distance education will no doubt expand its market to young people studying for examinations etc. and then they grow even more.

## CONCLUSION

It could be argued that it is only through the reflexivity of late modernity that change has become so endemic as to create learning needs throughout the lifespan. Hence, the education of adults is itself a symbol of the period. In precisely the same way, distance education is symbolic of the era. Hence, it is not surprising that distance education has grown simultaneously with the development of the education of adults – for both are signs of the times.

## REFERENCES

Candy, P. (1991) *Self-Direction for Lifelong Learning*, San Francisco: Jossey-Bass.
Giddens, A. (1990) *The Consequences of Modernity*, Cambridge: Polity Press.
—— (1991) *Modernity and Self-Identity*, Cambridge: Polity Press.
Houle, C. O. (1961) *The Inquiring Mind*, Wisconsin: University of Wisconsin Press.
Jarvis, P. (1987) *Adult Learning in the Social Context*, London: Croom Helm.
—— (1992) *Paradoxes of Learning*, San Francisco: Jossey-Bass.
Keegan, D. (1990) *Foundations of Distance Education* (2nd edn), London: Routledge.
Knowles, M. S. (1980a) *The Modern Practice of Adult Education: From Pedagogy to Andragogy* (revised and updated), Chicago: Association Press.
—— (1980b) 'The growth and development of adult education', in J. Peters and Associates, *Building an Effective Adult Education Enterprise*, San Francisco: Jossey-Bass.
Lyotard, J-F. (1986) *The Postmodern Condition: A Report on Knowledge*, Manchester: Manchester University Press.
Mezirow, J. (1991) *Transformative Dimensions of Adult Learning*, San Francisco: Jossey-Bass.
—— and Associates (1990) *Fostering Critical Reflection in Adulthood*, San Francisco: Jossey-Bass.
Paterson, R. K. N. (1979) *Values, Education and the Adult*, London: Routledge & Kegan Paul.
Peters, O. (1983) 'Distance teaching and industrial production: a comparative interpretation in outline', in D. Sewart, D. Keegan and B. Holmberg (eds), *Distance Education: International Perspectives*, London: Routledge.
Rogers, C. (1983) *Freedom to Learn for the 80's*, New York: Merrill.

# 11 Understanding distance education

*Erling Ljoså*

## THE COMPLEXITY

What exactly is it we are trying to understand when we talk about understanding distance education?

Somewhere out there is a student. The student has a wife, or a husband, perhaps a child or two. They like to come together with friends now and then, and with relatives at other occasions. Probably the student also is working and has an employer and some colleagues. These are just examples indicating that a student lives in a social context characterized by numerous relations with other individuals and groups of people.

Being a student means that this person also has a relationship with an educational institution, in this case at a distance. Somebody has prepared the study materials the student is dealing with when he manages to set apart some time for his studies. The student sends assignments to his teacher, and gets them back with correction, comments and a grade. He may have other contacts as well with staff from the institution. In some cases it is possible to follow local classes or to get advice from somebody by telephone or by personal visit to a study centre. We could say that distance education is a process going on over some time, with relations between a number of persons, who are more or less involved in the process or have some impact on it.

Usually, there is more than one student on the course. All the relations I have pointed at are duplicated, although with considerable variation, each time we enrol a new student. Consequently, distance education is not a single process but an aggregation of such processes. And this aggregation goes further to comprise all the processes in other courses and programmes within the institution teaching at a distance. In my institution, NKS, we have about 70,000 distance education processes going on at the same time. And they are all different.

Although Norway is a small country, there are several other distance teaching institutions, with other students, other courses, other technologies, other administrative systems and procedures. There are small correspondence schools run by religious organizations, there are training departments of branches of industry and the armed forces, there are universities and colleges experimenting with satellite transmission or computer conferencing. To cover what is meant by distance education we must continue the aggregation of processes to include all these institutions in Norway. And we must add other countries, other cultures, other educational systems and traditions. There is an almost overwhelming complexity and variation involved when we are trying to understand distance education.

## LEVELS OF UNDERSTANDING

I believe it is useful to distinguish three levels of understanding (see Figure 11.1):

- the intuitive, common-sense understanding we have as participants in or as observers of distance education activities;
- reflective analysis based on experience, communication and comparison;
- systematic research and theory building.

An individual's intuitive understanding of what is going on in distance education is of course dependent on the individual's own role in the process or processes. But it also depends on his or her previous experience of similar situations. Any event needs interpretation, and individuals derive meaning for events from their everyday understanding of the world, the persons and situations involved.

The next level implies the development of concepts and expression of relations between concepts. The intuitive interpretation of events is confirmed, refined, corrected and expanded through the accumulation of experience and through communication with other people. The concepts and the way you use the concepts express your personal 'picture' of what distance education is all about.

At the third level, researchers work even more systematically and according to accepted methods and rules to derive meaning for their data from concepts, models and theories. But these research activities are also dependent on the understanding achieved at the

*Figure 11.1* Levels of understanding

two other levels to establish concepts and theories which they can confront with the data available.

Although I have described these three levels of understanding as belonging to an individual, they also have a collective dimension. Development of understanding and use of concepts depend on language and culture, which are social phenomena. The individual derives meaning and understanding not only from individual experience but also from the way other people tend to use words and interpret situations.

The three levels of understanding are interrelated and depend on each other. Our concepts are developed both from our own and from other people's experience and intuitive understanding of events and situations. The theories and models which we develop, give new insight and help us understand the everyday situations better. Therefore, concepts and theories influence what is going on in the everyday world at the same time as they are picturing and explaining it. The struggle about words and definitions is not only a theoretical battlefield.

This is easy to see when we consider the discussions provoked by Otto Peters' description of distance education as an industrialized form of education. It is also an important aspect when D. R. Garrison (1989) describes the 'three generations' of distance education, referring to systems based on communication by mail, by telecommunication and by computer communication. In many cases, concepts and descriptions serve a purpose. They promote and advocate something, or they are used for such a purpose. They may even have a moral aspect, and try to tell us how things ought to be and how distance education should develop. It is an illusion to believe that understanding is neutral. Understanding usually has a purpose.

## PARTIAL UNDERSTANDING AND COMPLEMENTARITY

Since our understanding of distance education is rooted in experience and interpretations of this experience, it is always a partial understanding. St Paul, by some historians presented as the first distance educator, realized that knowledge and understanding is partial, and never absolute: 'Now we see only puzzling reflections in a mirror, but then we shall see face to face. My knowledge now is partial; then it will be whole, like God's knowledge of me' (1 Cor 13,12). The student's experience is different from the teacher's experience, and both the administrator's and the researcher's experience reflect their particular perspectives which are again different from the perspectives of the student or the teacher.

This situation is, in my opinion, of epistemological significance. The Danish physicist, Niels Bohr, has put a label on it, known as the principle of complementarity. In quantum physics, different explanations of phenomena, explanations which are derived from different observation situations, seem to be mutually exclusive but are nevertheless necessary to cater for all the experimental observations. The famous example is the complementary explanations of quantum phenomena in terms of models from classical physics – on the one hand waves, on the other hand particles.

The principle of complementarity, which meant a fundamental shift of paradigm in physical science, was influenced by Bohr's study of the American psychologist William James. In his book, *The Principles of Psychology*, William James described the paradox of self-observation – of analysing one's own stream of thoughts. Niels Bohr often referred to this as 'the paradox of being at the same time an observer and a participant on the scene of life'. These complementary roles may also be described as on the one hand analysis and the search for causal explanations, and on the other hand immediacy and feeling of finality and purpose.

Bohr's idea of complementarity has been made use of by sociologists and anthropologists reflecting on the methodological aspects of participative observation in the study of cultures and social relations.

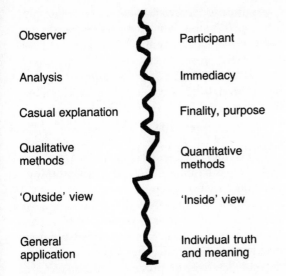

| | |
|---|---|
| Observer | Participant |
| Analysis | Immediacy |
| Casual explanation | Finality, purpose |
| Qualitative methods | Quantitative methods |
| 'Outside' view | 'Inside' view |
| General application | Individual truth and meaning |

*Figure 11.2*   Characteristics of complementary approaches

J. Peter Rothe (1985) has discussed complementarity as a link between quantitive and qualitative research in distance education, or between an 'inside' and an 'outside' viewpoint on individuals and situations – where the 'inside' view represents experiential knowledge of the everyday world, and the 'outside' view represents accepted generalized understanding of human actions. These two complementary approaches should, according to Rothe, be combined to form a holistic, representative picture of educational phenomena (see Figure 11.2).

## THE PROBLEM AND POTENTIAL OF GENERALIZATION

A similar problem reveals itself when we consider that research, be it based on qualitative or quantitative methods, aims at generalization. It looks for common aspects and structures shared by individual events and situations. The Danish philosopher Søren Kierkegaard coined the expression: 'Subjectivity is the truth', which became a basic principle in existentialist thinking. Although I will not argue against objectivity (or inter-subjectivity) in research, we should consider that generalization is in a way complementary to the search for individual truth and meaning. One could therefore be tempted to ask to what extent research is possible in social science, or better: What do we lose and what do we win when we look for generalization?

Is the authenticity of the individual event maintained when we concentrate on what it has in common with other events, or do we leave important things out of our understanding? This is not only a theoretical issue. It has something to do with the way we meet individual participants in our distance education systems.

The knowledge acquired through research can never be complete knowledge. It is partial in perspective, it is subjective in conceptualization, and it is incomplete as a result of generalization. However, the loss of completeness is compensated by the number of cases where the knowledge can be applied, and that is the reason why systematic research, in spite of its limitation, is such a powerful tool in our endeavour to understand reality.

The search for understanding is firmly based in the nature of human existence, and the value of research may be derived from this general search for understanding. However, I believe that the case for research in distance education is even stronger when its power of generalization is used to optimize existing processes and systems of distance education at any level of aggregation

## UNDERSTANDING DISTANCE EDUCATION FROM DIFFERENT PERSPECTIVES

I started by asking what we mean by distance education, referring to the complexity of the processes and relations involved. We may look at these processes from a range of different perspectives. One perspective is the student's perspective. To the student, the distance learning process represents a unique set of activities and relations with a particular distance education system, the persons involved in that system and the impacts of his study on his own everyday life and personal context. The student's focus is on the object of study – or its representation in the form of course material – on his individual strategies of learning, on the interaction with the teacher and the institution, and on the outcomes of what he is putting so much effort into. This perspective offers several topics for analysis and research, drawing on knowledge and methods from educational psychology, learning and motivation theory, communication theory, etc.

The teacher is, of course, also an individual participating in the process with a particular perspective. But to the teacher, the relationship with the student is far from unique. The student is one among a number, and the teacher may tend to perceive the student as just one more case and not as a distinct individual. Together with other teachers, a teacher will perform a defined role within the particularly designed distance education system, with a limited freedom of action. In most cases, the teacher will not be among the persons who developed the course material, but may influence a revision, either of the whole course or of the assignments for submission. The teacher's focus will be more on the product and outcome of the student's efforts than on the student as a person, but will also be on the feed-back that is adequate from the teacher to the student in order to support the student's learning process. Theories, models and methods of teaching at a distance would be a major concern for the teacher, but the information would not be found in general education textbooks.

Such textbooks would be more useful, however, to tutors in local classes and to lecturers in teleconferences. The danger is that they may find their role so similar to the role they play in conventional education that they don't actually realize that the situation of the students may be quite different.

Other perspectives are those of the curriculum planner's, the course writer's or the instructional designer's. They are often working in a team, and they may or may not be in direct contact with students. They have to know the subject and how to teach it, and particularly how to design study material (text or other) for effective self-study.

My own perspective as head of a distance teaching institution is different from all the others mentioned so far. My focus is on the system design and organization to take care of all the different functions and elements involved in distance education as this particuar institution offers it. I am interested in the optimal operation of the system, in the people involved in running it, in financing and cost effectiveness, in its external contacts and alliances, in its visions for the future and in its development in order to serve future students.

The last perspective I will mention is that of a politician concerned with the role of distance education in the education system and how it should develop in the future. The politician will look at target groups, labour market effects, distribution forms, range of programmes and institutions, co-ordination of resources, costs, financing, budgets, pressure groups, etc.

## DISTANCE EDUCATION AS A FIELD OF STUDY

Distance education is not only complex. It is also in a stage of fast development, particularly because the development of information and communication technologies is going on with considerable speed. This development has a direct influence on the methods and techniques available in what we call distance education.

I agree with Desmond Keegan (1991) that there is sufficient consensus on the definition of distance education, both in theory and practice, to consider distance education as a distinctive field of study. Although it has to be placed within the general discipline of education, general education theory has been developed to describe conventional education, with students and teachers in direct inter-action in a classroom. Therefore, it is difficult just to apply general education theories as they are for understanding distance education. It is similar to the situation when the inventors of the automobile tried to imagine the car as a sort of carriage with something in front of it which was not a horse. Distance education is also very often conceived from what it is similar to, but still is not like.

On the other hand, I do not believe that distance education theory could, or should, be developed in isolation from other fields of study. Distance education is quite often mixed with other forms of study and it has many elements common with other forms. When we look at how people learn from textbooks and course material there are no fundamental differences between distance education and conven-tional university education. But teaching and communication processes may be quite different. Group-based learning processes may also be quite different in a classroom, as compared with an audio conference or a computer conference. But it also varies with types of learning activities and with the communication styles of people involved.

Distance education is only one possible delineation of a field of study. I believe it is useful to develop general theories of distance education. Some of them, like Otto Peters' industrialization theory (1973), have already proved to be useful paradigms, contrasting distance education with conventional types of education. But it may be of equal relevance to study particular types and sub-sets of distance education, and to look at them together with other forms which may have similar elements. Distance education seems to me to be a field of study with obvious characteristics of interdisciplinarity. It remains to be shown exactly how useful the general criterion of distance actually is from a theoretical viewpoint. Distance is only one factor in most distance education processes.

I don't agree with those who sometimes tell us that distance education as a term will become obsolete as distance education merges into the so-called 'mainstream' of educational systems that is supposed to open up and incorporate the use of modern communica-tion technologies (see, for instance, Foks 1988). I believe in this merger if it means that distance education should be conceived as part of education, and will be used increasingly by conventional educational institutions in combination and coexistence with other methods. But I also believe that distance education will continue to be both a distinct and meaningful term and a particular field of study and practice.

Neither do I agree with another popular notion, namely the tendency to look at the development of distance education as a succession of 'generations' of technologies and forms (see, for instance, Garrison 1989). I notice that this analogy is often used by people who propagate the use of a certain type of technology, and the very notion implies that other forms ('generations') of distance education are obsolete and will not survive. I think of the field of distance education more as a set of different system structures available for learning and teaching at a distance, structures made possible through the availability and successive refinement of different technologies which at least partly overcome the problem of physical distance between learners and between learners and teachers. Some technologies become obsolete, and the structures associated with them vanish. But I can see no reason why postal communication, printed materials or broadcasting should become obsolete in the foreseeable future. What will happen, and it is happening already, is that 'old' and 'new' technologies are combined in new ways to form hybrids from different 'species' – if we stick to biology for analogies.

## DISTANCE EDUCATION SYSTEMS AS VALUE-ORIENTED SERVICE SYSTEMS

I believe that Garrison and Shale (1990) are right in stressing that the 'transaction between teacher and student is at the heart of the educational process and distance education must address this reality when attempting to overcome the constraints of distance'. This quotation is taken from a discussion in the *ICDE Bulletin* between the authors and Holmberg based on Garrison's book from 1989. They were discussing whether there is a 'paradigm shift' going on in distance education at the moment. Although Holmberg actually would undersign their statements about the central role of two-way communication, there seems to be a significant difference in perspective between them. Holmberg is also concerned with the role of the pre-produced study material, and has written extensively on how one may put parts of the 'guided didactic conversation' in simulated form into the study material. He also seems more concerned with the individual student and with student autonomy, while Garrison and

Shale are primarily concerned with the groups of students that can be addressed through electronic communication.

Are these different perspectives contradictory? I have revealed my opinion by calling them perspectives. Perspectives usually are not contradictory but complementary. That does not always mean that you are free to choose between them. The choice of perspective may depend both on what your object of consideration or study actually is, and on your personal views and values.

Garrison (1989) almost neglects what could be called the organizational context of the teacher. Maybe that is one of the reasons why he and Shale oppose the 'paradigm' based upon Peters' theory of distance education as an industrialized form of teaching and learning. There may be examples of teachers who operate without an educational institution, but in distance education they are rare exceptions. The organizational perspective on distance education therefore is an important one, and in my opinion Peters' analysis is still one of the few fundamental contributions to the theory of distance education – even if (or perhaps because?) the main categories of the theory are drawn from areas outside education.

I think that people working in dedicated distance education institutions should understand that the way of functioning of these institutions is different from and more complex than that of most institutions of conventional education, and that there is an interrelationship between, for instance, logistics, organization, costs, and educational issues. This means that we need to analyse our institutions as we analyse companies and similar organizations, and that theories of management and organization are needed to understand some important aspects of distance education.

Otto Peters' industrialization theory is not the only example of such an approach. It was quite fashionable, particularly during the 1970s, to apply what was called 'the systems approach' or system theory to distance education. This approach was often applied to education in general, and as a result of this way of analysing educational processes we still have the field of educational technology. In distance education, its main influence was on the development of study material. The systems approach as such, however, is equally relevant to other aspects of the organization of distance education.

Since manufacturing industries now constitute a less dominant part of modern society, it is only natural that we also look for new insights from schools of thought where provision of services has a distinctive role. After all, education is not a manufacturing industry. Although distance education as a rule also comprises the production and delivery of study material, the overall classification of the activities involved in distance education would rather be provision of services, or service industry. Most of the criteria of services are fulfilled by any education system or organization:

- Service is intangible. So is education. You cannot touch it or put the whole of it into a store-house.
- Service is activities. So is education.
- Production and consumption of services are connected. You cannot produce education without students being involved in what is going on.
- The customer participates in the production process. Some would put it even stronger: learning takes place within students, and the teacher can only try to help them.

According to service management theory, the delivery of service takes place in a series of decisive moments, when the customer experiences the service and decides what it is worth. These moments are often called 'moments of truth'. They may be moments when the individual customer is confronted with a service carrier, one of the 'front-line staff', in person, by telephone or in writing. But there may also be moments when nobody else is there, when the customer experiences the value of what is delivered to him. The decisive impression of service and quality comes from such moments – for instance, when a student phones the institution, or receives the corrected assignment from the teacher, or attends a tutorial seminar. This aspect of service theory does right to what I previously called the authenticity of the individual event. Service theory is therefore extremely user-oriented – or student-oriented – when applied to distance education.

The fundamental problem of the service industries is to combine the two words:

- *service*, which means taking care of an individual with his individual goals and needs, and
- *industry*, which means standardization, division of labour, and mass production.

In order to deliver good service, the front-line staff needs efficient back-up systems. Only when the back-up systems run smoothly will the service carriers be able to add the personal touch that is a characteristic of high-quality service.

Service management has to do with people. The success of the whole operation depends on people delivering internal or external service. In distance education interaction with students is fundamental. The value of the service will become evident when the students interact with the course material and with the various categories of staff of the institution. It is therefore of vital importance that everybody involved has a clear understanding of what the student wants, what the institution's 'service package' (another key term) and service philosophy is. The institution should be aware of the main values of its product, and all the service carriers should not only know, but also share the values and the philosophy of delivery. A service industry needs what Ross Paul calls 'a value-driven leadership approach' (Paul 1990).

But service management has not only to do with people. An equally important aspect is back-up systems: production systems, procurement systems, logistics and delivery systems, marketing systems, information and administration systems. The back-up systems have to be adapted to the values and qualities we want to offer our customers. That is not always the case. There is often a struggle between efficiency and flexibility, between decentralization of decisions and central control. And when we perceive changes in market demands and opportunities, the existing systems are often barriers to the development of our service.

Service management theories offer some tools for analysing services, systems and organizations from a particular perspective. Murgatroyd, Woudstra and Powell have in a couple of articles described a more general approach, based on Michael Porter's thinking of competitive forces and value chains in business and industry. The important aspect of both these approaches is that they put the emphasis not on the inherent efficiency of the system as a goal in itself, but on the values and services offered to the students.

Woudstra and Powell (1989) describe in a very illuminating way how Porter's ideas were adapted to the strategic thinking of Athabasca University in a combined effort to control costs and achieve strategic organizational objectives. They analysed competitive forces outside the institution, value-generating activities and cost drivers within the institution, value chains across departments and value systems across the borders between the institution and its surroundings. One of the main benefits of value chain analysis as described by Woudstra and Powell seems to be the increased awareness of interrelationships both within the organization and between it and its external partners: suppliers, delivery channels and competitors.

Private distance teaching institutions have always been aware that they are operating in an education market. I also believe that public institutions in the future will have to look more to market needs and demands, to develop consistent strategies, and to establish criteria of quality of operation and services. There have always been people opposing the mixture of educational and industrial concepts and theories. Quite often they have been right, arguing that tools and theories from industry cannot easily be applied to strictly educational processes. But we are in a 'business' with both characteristics. This is one example of the interdisciplinarity of the whole field of distance education. And the two characteristics do not have their separate existence in separate departments. In distance education, educational and organizational aspects are interwoven in every part of the system. Therefore, the perspectives of management and organization have to be included in any comprehensive theoretical description of distance education.

## BIBLIOGRAPHY

Bohr, N. (1957) *Atomfysik og menneskelig erkendelse*, København: Schultz.

Foks, J. (1988) 'Distance education – a developing concept', in D. Sewart and J. S. Daniel (eds), *Developing Distance Education. Papers Submitted to the 14th ICDE World Conference in Oslo 9–16 August 1988*, Olso: ICDE.

Garrison, D. R. (1989) *Understanding Distance Education. Frameworks for the Future*, London: Routledge.

—— and Shale, D. G. (1990) 'Tilting at windmills? Destroying mythology in distance education', *ICDE Bulletin*, vol. 24, 42–6.

Gjessing, G. (1968) *Complementarity, Value and Socio-Cultural Field*, Oslo: Universitetsforlaget.

Holmberg, B. (1990a) 'A paradigm shift in distance education? Mythology in the making', *ICDE Bulletin*, no. 22, 51–5.

—— (1990b) *On the Rationale, Typology and Methodology of Research and Scholarship. A Practitioner's Understanding of Epistemology*, Hagen: Fern Universität.

—— (1991) 'Windmills and paradigm shifts – a continued discussion of the character of distance education', *ICDE Bulletin*, no. 26, 23–5.

James, W. (1890) *The Principles of Psychology I–II*, London: Longman.

Jammer, M. (1966) *The Conceptual Development of Quantum Mechanics*, New York:

Keegan, D. (1990) *Foundations of Distance Education* (2nd edn), London: Routledge.

—— (1991) 'The study of distance education: terminology, definition and the field of study,' in B. Holmberg and G. E. Ortner (eds), *Research into Distance Education/Fernlehre und Fernlehrforschung*, Frankfurt am Main: Peter Lang.

Kierkegaard, S. (1846) *Afsluttende uvidenskabelig Efterskrift*, København: Gyldendal.

Ljoså, E. (1986) 'Service managment in distance education', *Epistolodidaktika*, 1986/1 27–50.

—— (1991) 'Distance education in the society of the future: from partial understanding to conceptional frameworks', in B. Holmberg and G. E. Ortner (eds), *Research into Distance Education/Fernlehre und Fernlehrforschung*, Frankfurt am Main: Peter Lang.

Murgatroyd, S. and Woudstra, A. (1989) 'Issues in the management of distance education', *American Journal of Distance Education* 3(1).

Paul, R. (1990) *Open Learning and Open Management. Leadership and Integrity in Distance Education*, London: Kogan Page.

Peters, O. (1973) *Die didaktische Struktur des Fernunterrichts. Untersuchungen zu einer industrialisierten Form des Lehrens und Lernens*, Weinheim: Beltz.

Petersen, A. (1968) *Quantum Physics and the Philosophical Tradition*, New York: Yeshira University.

Rothe, J. P. (1985) 'Linking quantitive and qualitative distance education research through complementarity', *ZIFF Papiere* 56, Hagen: Fernuniversität.

Woudstra, A. and Powell, R. (1989) 'Value chain analysis: a framework for management of distance education', *The American Journal of Distance Education* 3(3), 7–21.

# 12 Distance education: what is it and can it have an educational future?

*Ted Nunan*

## INTRODUCTION

Attempts to describe and explain the nature of distance education are yet to arrive at a series of organizing ideas, theories or values which receive universal support of both practitioners of the specialist area and those engaged in more general educational endeavour. It has been argued that description and prescription in the field will result from developing a theory of distance education. To this end, various authorities have analysed the concept of distance education in an attempt to identify the types of knowledge which ought to seek legitimation through connection to a theory of distance education. This knowledge, it is argued, will identify the essential nature of distance education.

Holmberg (1989a) begins *Theory and Practice of Distance Education* with an analysis of the concept of distance education. In the absence of legitimated knowledge it makes sense to clarify what should be theorized about. However, Holmberg provides but one view and others attach different meanings to the term 'distance education'. Their competing ideas often present contradictory faces. The range of ideas, concepts and values they advance are yet to coalesce into some sort of coherent framework which guides explanation and predicts the activities which constitute distance education. In short, attempts to arrive at a theory of distance education and thereby develop an understanding of its nature are as difficult as attempts to arrive at a general theory of education.

Juler (1991a), in summarizing the literature of the field for a Masters in Distance Education, provides an excellent analysis of theorizing in distance education. He employs as a pedagogic device the three criteria proposed by Garrison and Shale (communicating non-contiguously, two way communication, the use of technology to mediate two-way communication) and relates these to other theorists and their constructs (Moore's transactional distance, Holmberg's guided didactic conversation, Peters' industrialized form of teaching and learning) as starting points for further theorizing. He also notes that:

> If I discount the third criterion as necessarily entailed by the first two I am left with Moore's work on 'distance', which is helpful in elaborating some of its complexities, and with Holmberg's emphasis on 'conversation' which suggests a whole range of tactics for dealing with distance.
>
> (Juler 1991a: 143)

Juler moves well beyond these starting points and illustrates the impact of 'critical theorising' through an analysis of the usefulness of the concepts of interaction and interaction networks for distance education and, in so doing, develops new ways to describe and explain events within distance education.

However, Juler's analysis is the exception rather than the rule. The majority of theorists have sought to identify particular characteristics of the enterprise which are thought to define and distinguish distance education from other forms of educational activity. As Moore (1990: 14) comments of these approaches, 'We do not need any more repetition of naive descriptions of the variables that distinguish the field. Those who make such repetitions, especially by merely changing the labels attached to these variables do a disservice by the confusion they cause.'

According to Moore, distance education is, in essence, a set of interrelationships about dialogue, structure and autonomy. To advance knowledge about distance education requires the empirical testing of variables which describe and explain these interrelationships. This empiricist framework would produce theories in much the same way that theories are generated in the natural sciences. Holmberg, in particular, places a strong emphasis upon this form of methodology, citing Karl Popper's work as providing guidance on theory formation.

The problem of theory within distance education, along with whether distance education has 'discipline status', has engaged various authorities. Rumble (1988: 39), for example, notes that 'while distance education shares many of the extrinsic characteristics of disciplines, it lacks autonomy and independence from education, and an independent disciplinary culture, and hence cannot be regarded as a discipline in its own right'. Devlin (1989: 56) likewise offers the notion that 'distance education is a derivative field of adult education which itself is not a discipline'. Holmberg, while qualifying his initial views with the statement that 'whether distance education is a discipline or not is a matter of definition', returns to the position that, according to his criteria for disciplinary status 'distance education as a well defined area of research and academic teaching is to be described as a discipline' (Holmberg 1989b: 64).

The authority of Holmberg and Keegan led the debate towards the ideal of a tradition for distance education forged from an empiricist position – Holmberg (1989a: 162) recommends the attempted falsification of some ten testable hypotheses as a way to establish a prototype distance learning theory. Selman (1989: 86) is one of the few writers to challenge this by pointing to the 'long recognised contradiction which has plagued positivist approaches to human understanding' noting that 'many of the ways in which we care most about advancing the field of distance education involve practical reasoning and wise arbitration between competing values'. The question of what distance education is good for is and will always remain central to the field. Before the debate can be advanced Selman believes we need to jettison some of the intellectual baggage of empiricism and focus upon answers to questions of value.

Juler also takes up this theme, noting that this older tradition of empiricism requires humanizing. It's supplementation and modification is necessary and will occur by the process of critical theorizing. This theorizing involves plurality (not theory, but theories), is different in kind from scientific theorizing (it acknowledges and embraces commitment, relativity and subjectivity), is emancipatory (it claims to provide guidance as to what to do), and links the personal with the institutional and structural within its explanations (Gibson 1986).

## DECONSTRUCTING DISTANCE EDUCATION

Critical theorizing is a complex activity which has many starting points. For some, it begins with exploring the value-laden nature of social facts; for others, an analysis of self and vested interests and power relations initiates theorizing; a focus upon personal practice and how and who this emancipates is a central issue for some; others may choose to clarify their taken-for-granted assumptions through challenging them from the viewpoints of alternative theories of activity. Where theory formation is at an early stage and the debates about the activity are in their infancy, a simpler entry point to critical theorizing is through the interrogation of the language that we use to portray distance education. Margaret Haughey (1991), for example, offers an analysis of three metaphors in an attempt to generate discussion about 'how distance education is perceived'. Discussion of values portrayed through metaphors of distance education as production (or an industrial system), as student growth, and as travel, relies heavily upon illustrating these well worn educational metaphors through characteristics of distance education.

The use of metaphors extends and creates 'coherences' which give value to particular features of educational activity. The use of such techniques to explore the nature of distance education is welcome as it opens possibilities for analysis which are not confined by empiricist methodology. Indeed, a focus upon language to analyse the way that it is loaded can reveal key features of the enterprise.

Garry Gillard (1991a, 1991b) has taken this deconstruction approach in a series of articles which explore the way that distance education is framed within educational discourse. He notes that,

> Distance Education is, however, defined formally by people working in the field, and it is commonly – though not always – defined in oppositional terms. Following the principle of dualism, the process of definition is frequently carried out in a dialectical way. An entity – particularly an abstraction – is named and defined in terms of its opposite, with this other term being assigned the positive value. Q is defined as not-p, where p means possessing a particular group of characteristics.
>
> 'Distance Education' as such is commonly defined or named as non-contiguous, external, off campus, extramural (Keegan, 1980). It is 'a form of indirect instruction' (Peters, 1973, p 16). It is 'not under the continuous, immediate supervision of tutors present' (Holmberg, 1977, p 17).
>
> It is done by correspondence, at home, with the implication that people only study at home – or in the situation in which they spend their days – when they are forced to. In fact, this is commonly turned into a defence of the existence of distance education, and therefore an argument for funding it, that it is unfortunately a necessity. We must presume, we are told 'the existence of two forms of education which are strictly separable: traditional education based on personal communication and distance education based on industrialised and technological communication' (Keegan, 1980, p 17). And distance education is done, above all, by reading.
>
> (Gillard 1991a: 2)

A further example supporting Gillard's contention is provided by Burge and Lenskyj, where they note:

Distance education is now better defined in terms of what it is not – that is, one physically defined visual space holding all course members – than what it is – that is, any version of a wide range of delivery formats planned and implemented by an institution.

(Burge and Lenskyj 1990: 21)

This work on analysing metaphors and deconstructing common assumptions regarding distance education is interesting in that it has brought into sharper focus the ways in which the hierarchy between distance teaching and contiguous teaching operates to privilege contiguous teaching. However we are yet to identify a set of organizing ideas or metaphors which project the field of distance education forward on its own terms. This sentiment has perhaps been captured, if not somewhat overstated, by Foks (1988) when he contends that distance education is a concept which has developed itself out of existence. Likewise, Gawthorne provocatively writes that the:

segregation of 'distance education' into a special category for policy development has outlived its usefulness. Distance education is outmoded in the sense that something may be outflanked, or outclassed. There are so many different 'modes' of study that distance education is no longer the only alternative to face-to-face 'internal mode' instruction. It is not suggested that the activity of educating at a distance is outmoded. On the contrary, it is anticipated that the pedagogy of distance education will pervade other 'modes'.

(Gawthorne 1990: 1)

Taking a lead from Gawthorne (1990), this chapter is an attempt to highlight values about teaching and learning which have their roots in distance education but are increasingly being translated and re-worked within 'other modes'. That is, this chapter wishes to discuss the nature of distance education by analysing key values held by those who identify themselves as distance educators. It seeks to identify educational (that is, social and political) values which are taken to characterize the field of distance education. The following analysis is not about testable theories coming together to form a discipline. Instead it is an attempt to answer a sociological question: can we characterize the educational sub-culture of distance educators through their acceptance and support for particular educational value positions? If this is in any way possible we shall have arrived at one way of identifying the nature of distance education – it becomes those values and beliefs which are held in common by this group.

## WHAT VALUES ARE CENTRAL TO THE BELIEF SYSTEM HELD BY THOSE ENGAGED IN DISTANCE TEACHING AND LEARNING?

Educators employ various sets of values to convey their beliefs and direct their practices. They come to different understandings and explanations of educational activity and have different prescriptions about good practice according to the set of values they use as their base for reference.

A set which has a limited number of well rehearsed and powerful values can provide the essential core which identifies members of a sub-culture. These core values exist both in the theories and practices of the activity. They identify and name events as part of the activity of distance education. Because of their central importance such values are subject to re-interpretation as a field of practice develops. Where tenets and values are not subject to use and re-interpretation they move from the centre of the stage to the wings. Of lesser importance, they may eventually disappear from the discourse of the area.

It is important that we focus upon values and not facts. For example, one might note the fact that a learner may be geographically distant from an institution and its teachers. However, the more interesting use of the term 'distance' involves such contentious and value laden constructs such as 'institutional distance', 'psychological distance' and 'social distance' (Evans 1989a). Our search for core values is a way of identifying essential concepts or constructs which occur within discourse about distance education.

There appear to be four key statements containing value positions which are central to distance education. These core values are:

- Education by distance mode serves a political end. That is, in addition to the purposes inherent in the curriculum that it conveys, its very existence is directed towards increasing access to education. Distance education is unavoidably connected to issues of social justice, involving equity for groups and personal liberation for individuals.
- The processes and power relations of the interactions between learners and teachers at a distance are valuable in their own right. Mediated and structured interactions, directed towards helping individuals to learn are desirable components of any educational activity.
- Planning approaches for distance education are educationally valuable for their focus upon student learning and their openness

to critical scrutiny. Design for learning is conducted 'with students in mind'. There is a strong connection between a concept of teaching-at-a-distance and the design process which anticipates learning activity through its analysis of the intentions embedded within course materials.

- Distance education, like other forms of education, values communicative competence between participants. While distance learning strategies are usually encapsulated in mass-produced learning materials, such materials are not sufficient in themselves and must be accompanied by communication processes which link individuals or groups with a teacher.

When educationists explore a particular area of concern there is usually the need to develop concepts which enable greater definition and refinement in addressing the area. Thus particular patterns of language become identified with the fundamentals of the debate in the area concerned. This situation can lead to the identification of a 'discourse' which typifies the ways in which the activity is portrayed. A discourse, according to Gottlieb, is a

> regular, recurrent pattern of language which is trans-individual (i.e. not an idiosyncratic style) and trans-situational (i.e. not a technical, occupational or professional register or situation bound variety) and which both shapes and reflects the users' (often unconscious) basic intellectual commitments.
>
> (Gottlieb 1989: 132)

Can we claim that patterns of language used to justify, explain and describe educational situations involving the four values introduced above is a discourse of distance education? Or is it the case that distance educators simply borrow from the language of other, broader debates?

Within the first value area, distance education has largely borrowed from the language of social justice and equity; access, equity, educational opportunity, situational disadvantagement and gender-related barriers are all taken from the general discourse of education. There has been some work to create special concepts. Distance educationists have developed an interest in constructs such as 'openness' and 'closure' as these terms can be applied in an integrative fashion to account for characteristics of institutions and their teaching and learning processes in relation to external students. In addition, there have been research studies which attempt to address equity issues. These include disproportionate use of educational resources by identifiable social groups and the related role that distance education can play in achieving more equitable outcomes in resource use.

In the second value area of valuing the types of interactions employed within distance education and the power relationships embedded within them a specialist discourse may be emerging. Juler (1990) analyses the nature of discourse and proposes a 'discourse model' as a way of conceptualizing the relationship between interaction and independence in distance education. In a recent paper (1991b: 2) he looks at the nature of discourse and what it might reveal about the role of various voices within textual materials.

In relation to the third core value, it is clear what many distance educators dislike. They eschew the language and intellectual commitments of systems approaches to instructional design. There is, however, little consensus about how to describe and think about designing for learning at a distance – for some the text-related concept of 'transformer' is useful as 'distance teaching is often thought of as text' (Evans 1989b).

The fourth core value, communicative competence, borrows from the general language of communications studies and education.

It is a contention of this chapter that distance education is yet to develop and sustain its own form of discourse that can shape and reflect the users' basic intellectual commitments and values. For distance education to have an educational future, distance educators will need to focus their policy initiatives, research and practices to articulate and apply core values within educational systems. Without a focus upon the four core values previously described, distance education can be readily subsumed within education in general and portrayed as technique. The next section of this chapter looks at the ways in which these core values currently operate within distance education.

## EDUCATION AT A DISTANCE AND EQUITY

This first value, that distance education should be seen as a means of providing access to education, is linked with the social value that access to education should be a right of citizens of a state. Distance education, like all forms of education, will always be subject to social valuation. Its purposes are linked, in part, to the curriculum it conveys – thus, as a mode it can promote instrumentalist, liberal or learner-centred views of education. And, if as Sharma (1987) contends, 'learning rather than schooling has become the driving force of human capital formation', then distance education may be used as a means of promoting, cheaply and economically to the masses, learnings which serve the economic and technological imperatives of social systems, be they democratic of repressive. Arger (1987: 48) in an extensive review of the literature of distance education in the Third World, notes that the promise of distance education was portrayed as its ability to offer mass, quality, cost-efficient education which could effect social equality and that evidence 'does not indicate that in reality this has been, or will be, achieved'. In summary he concludes that 'manipulation of distance education by the dominant group is widespread' and that it is 'used by the elite in much the same way they use any other educational process'.

This first core value asserts that distance education, although often characterized as a mode of study or form of pedagogy, is useful as an educational concept only where it stands for liberatory ideals. It should threaten the educational 'priesthood' officiating within current systems of education. It should challenge conventional face-to-face educational systems both at the personal level of how it treats individuals as students and at a social level to attempt to lessen the way that educational systems in general produce and reproduce social inequalities.

Adding distance to the term education begs the question of what, if anything, about what we understand by the concept 'education' has changed. If education refers to sets of techniques for imparting knowledge skills and attitudes, theories which set out to explain or justify such techniques, and sets of values which lie behind who constructs particular types of knowledge skills and attitudes and who participate in the process, then distance education must have some or all of these qualities. The first core value is central to our understanding of what is meant by education within the term 'distance education'. Distance education is a loose connection between technique and a value position (which may be incorporated in a larger set of values which identifies an educational position). While adding distance to education can mean technique it should not be disconnected from its capacity to provide access and equity.

Stephen Fox reminds educationists that post-modern developments challenge such values. He writes:

On the one hand open and distance learning represents 'freedom to learn', 'learner centreness' and 'open access', all of which are species of rhetoric belonging to the emancipatory narrative of legitimation which arose within humanism through the events of the French Revolution, and which Snell has identified with the rhetoric of some kind of 'Marxist Utopia'. On the other hand, open and distance learning represents 'self-help', 'self-development' 'lifeskills' and the opportunity to equip (or re-equip) oneself with the knowledge, skills and competencies with which to flexibly navigate the vagaries of the labour market. In this sense open and distance learning adopts the legitimating narrative of performativity, by which learning is valued for its pragmatic effects in enhancing the efficiency of the social machine as managed by the decision makers.

(Fox 1989: 275)

Open and distance learning, according to this view, have inherent ideological contradictions. Distance educators will need to grapple with value contradictions by interpreting what the first core value means in particular circumstances. For example, distance educators may be thrust into the role of managers and producers of educational products which are to be offered on the free market. Unless educationists take the effort to appraise such a situation against the first core value and decide upon a way of responding, then the field is destined to be dismissed by other educationists as a sometimes clever technology for distribution and dissemination.

The impact of what Fox terms 'performativity' (i.e. knowledge legitimation by its effects and the efficiency of those effects) can be linked to human capital approaches to education and, in particular, distance education. Nunan (1991), for example, examines structural changes within Australian higher education provision of distance education noting the linking of distance education with work-place productivity, for providing vocational 'retreads,' and industry restructuring.

## DISTANCE EDUCATION AS A CATEGORY OF VALUABLE EDUCATIONAL INTERACTIONS

The second value position derives from a perceived relationship between distance education and adult learning theory. The latter embodies certain ideals which are consonant with many distance education practices. In particular, the expansion of distance education into post-secondary fields of training and higher education has led to a focus upon designing and employing interactions which employ personal experience, are self-directed, located in a context which employs 'real life', and appeal to intrinsic, rather than extrinsic, motivations (Robinson 1992). Devlin (1989: 56) sees this perceived relationship as one where 'distance education is a derivative field of adult education'. However, it is useful to note that there are differences in andragogy and feminist principles of teaching and learning (Burge and Lenskyj 1990: 23) (as examples of 'adult learning') and practices which identify distance education – that is, there is a relationship between ideals and techniques of 'adult learning' and education at a distance, but not an identity.

A number of factors become obvious when the learning milieux of distance students are analysed. These include learners being largely removed from the social constraints and dynamics of group-based learning, experiencing greater dependence upon the starting points of learning contained in course materials, and the possibilities for learners to take greater responsibility for the unfolding of their learning arrangements within the course. However, the impact of this second value goes beyond such factors to focus upon the quality of educational interactions that are employed – central concepts for valuing interactions are the notions of autonomy and control.

Not surprisingly, there are considerable disagreements about the values inherent in the process and power relations embedded in the possible interactions employed within distance education. As we have noted learners at a distance can have unique opportunities to shape their learning milieux without direct and continuing intervention from teachers or fellow students – their situation releases them from institutional arrangements, constraints and opportunities of face-to-face teaching and learning. Yet the course materials, through their mass production and through their structure which necessarily anticipates the unfolding of a particular (or limited number) of teaching and learning sequence(s), exert control over students. The balance between these competing influences of autonomy and control is at the heart of this value. Gillard, for example, describes this balance when he writes 'learning in distance education is supervised but not invigilated, organised but not controlled, student centred but not anarchic' (Gillard 1991b: 6).

Clearly, other forms of education face exactly the same issue of balancing autonomy and control. What is important with distance education is that the balance is evident and open to scrutiny in its portrayal within course materials, it is influenced by the design of materials and technology used, and it is influenced by the learning mode and situation of adults. Indeed, this balance has importance for pre-tertiary situations especially where students reject learning because of their questioning and resistance to power relationships lived out within the social systems of schools. Distance education, with a potential for realizing more student autonomy and less overt control may provide the necessary 'space' for such students.

It is possible to negotiate a qualitatively different balance than that employed in contiguous styles of teaching. Further, because the mix of interactions is qualitatively different from those normally employed in group-based teaching there is a direct challenge to the 'primacy' of voice within educational interactions. Distance teaching and learning does not seek to devalue interactions of group-based teaching – instead, it seeks acknowledgement that a range of interactions are employed within all forms of education and that different mixes of interactions can equally, but differently, meet the sum of course objectives.

Another aspect of this value is that it reminds distance educators that interactions which are facilitated through technology can equally be analysed in terms of the balance between autonomy and control. Mediation is not a neutral process and it can introduce, both in structural terms and within the ambience of interactions, particular constraints and possibilities for learning. For example, Walker (1991) notes that 'Fordist' approaches to distance education carry assumptions about the way that learning is best packaged and systems for learning are organized.

## DISTANCE EDUCATION AND DESIGN FOR STUDENT LEARNING

The third value asserts that the processes used to design approaches to learning at a distance are distinctive and are educationally desirable because of their focus upon student learning and their openness to critical scrutiny.

The field of distance education has long been concerned with the role of instructional design and instructional designers within distance teaching and learning. This is to be expected as the distance learning environment is initially shaped by intentions expressed through course materials. The planning process, in its attempts to foreshadow approaches which suit the range of learners, the logistics of delivery and communication with learners, and the interventions and interactions appropriate to the area under consideration, involves a level of analysis beyond that of other teaching and learning arrangements. In effect, planning becomes an exercise of balancing constraints and opportunities in terms of a range of likely outcomes which both flow from, and determine, decisions about design. Distance teaching and learning is, in part, about constructing futures within which teaching and learning processes can operate – this can be quite different from contiguous styles which rejoice in the unplanned immediacy of the moment and where events unfold to create an ever-changing teaching and learning situation. This is not to say that distance teaching and learning is not responsive – instead, it simply records that in planning for distance teaching and learning the distance educator is delineating an interlocking range of outcomes on a scale of complexity which involves the whole course and considers detail which anticipates a variety of specific options within the microstructure of the content.

While some of the literature of the area is borrowed from educational technology there are attemts to clarify what development and design mean for the field of distance education (Parer 1989). However, the field is loosely defined with a range of competing models and metaphors. For example those engaged in instructional design or educational development perceive their function as involving a multiplicity of roles such as innovators, managers, teachers, counsellors, and even the educational equivalent of an amicable guerilla!

In short, fundamental matters remain contested. Gupta (1989), for example, claims that literature from luminaries such as Reigeluth, Bååth, Lewis, and Jenkins have led to a notion of instructional design which

> involves the fine-grained analysis of the structure of the subject matter; the assessment of the critical learning attributes of the learners; the specification of the clearly defined learning outcomes; the selection of appropriate learning experiences in a planned sequence; the design of appropriate assessment techniques and instruments based on the principles of self-instruction; the design of relevant diagnostic, remedial and feedback systems; and the design and development of learner support systems/ services.
>
> (Gupta 1989: 171)

Judith Riley (1984), on the other hand, describes the events of planning, writing, and evaluating distance teaching and learning materials which avoid the language and metaphors of the systems approach such as those employed in the above characterization of instructional design.

Nevertheless, the problem of how to construct appropriate teaching and learning 'futures' remains – and, significantly, its resolution is a part of what we mean by distance teaching. What is at issue here is that, whatever the processes of design, there is a concept of teaching which only makes sense in terms of the design of the whole course. Teaching, under these terms, does not recognize the 'primacy of voice' or the pressing demand of the moment of interaction – instead, it becomes intertwined with constructed futures for 'students in mind', it loses its single locus within the teacher and comes connected to learning in a variety of holistic ways. The artefacts of the education process – the teaching and learning materials – show how this has arisen through the processes and procedures of design. What is valued is the central place of design in its linking to a concept of teaching. It is recognized by the ways in which detailed planning connects with learning and how this planning is continually evaluated through its embodiment within course materials.

Further, since the meaning of design for teaching and learning is a function of its application within particular teaching and learning situations, it does not make sense to adhere to any inappropriately 'constructed future' where it is patently being reconstructed by the participants of the teaching and learning process. Thus a focus upon design may be valued for the way in which it orients processes towards the learning of students and enables the communication of these processes to learners who are about to undertake studies. Learners are empowered by knowing the total framework of the 'constructed future' that they are being enticed to participate in – their knowledge of intentions of the teacher enables them to inter- vene, to make teaching a more responsive activity.

## COMMUNICATION PROCESSES AND EDUCATING AT A DISTANCE

The fourth value asserts that the transmission of information is considered a necessary but not sufficient condition for educative processes to occur. To be termed educative, the process must address changes which occur in individual learners and teachers.

Clearly, this value has the potential to sit uneasily with the preceding second and third values. For example, the concept of design for learning inevitably involves predicting educational processes and outcomes thereby reducing the impact of communicative processes and the means of generating the 'curriculum in action'.

Mass producing course materials which contain these predictions leads to charges of depersonalization, constraint of learning through prestructuring which is deemed irrelevant to learner needs, and unwarranted control by the designer over the learning process. This value asserts the need to incorporate within our concept of teaching, processes which cannot reside within the course materials or even be anticipated by them.

Consequently, the concept of teaching-at-a-distance, when viewed from this fourth value, contains elements of 'communicative competence' which occur within any concept of teaching. When combined with the third value there is the need carefully to delineate ways in which the term 'teaching' might be used.

This valuing of communicative competence as a factor influencing the educative value of the processes comprising distance education is hardly surprising and occurs with all forms of education. Its inclusion amongst the core values for distance education is to balance the influence of the way that the third value can focus upon the generation of course materials as distance education. Ultimately, what is valued here is the quality of communicative processes where factors such as access to communicative technologies, the impact of the technology itself upon the communication process, the interactions and dialogue established between teacher and student, the availability of both parties to participate, and the roles and power relations revealed through interactions all influence judgements about the quality of interactions.

## WHAT WOULD BE THE CONCERNS OF DISTANCE EDUCATION FROM INTERPRETING AND APPLYING THESE VALUES? AN EXAMPLE

We have already noted from Gillard that distance education is often defined in oppositional terms. This is both expected and unexpected: expected, in that if we accept that predominant ideology for teaching and learning is 'simultaneity of communication and instantaneous experience of the meeting of minds' (Gillard 1991a) then distance education provides a challenge; unexpected, if we accept Terry Evans's proposition that 'many of its concepts and ideas are ones shared with or taken from education' and that 'broadly the discourses of education and distance education overlap to such an extent that one might have expected distance education to be a child of education as it matured as a discipline itself (Evans 1991: 11).

During the 1980s the oppositional approach attempted to differentiate distance education from other forms of education. As Bagnall (1989: 21) notes '[the] exclusive focus on educational distance as a quality that is recognised against the standard of conventional education situations is all-pervasive in distance education scholarship'. However, by the end of this decade some writers were pointing to the futility of holding 'distance' as a point of differentiation (Shale 1988: 25). Thus, for such writers, 'there are no special characteristics of distance education which logically lead to conceptions of "teaching" or "learning" which would differ from the way we use those terms in relation to education generally' (King 1991: 27).

Interpreting and applying the values that were previously outlined would relocate the debates of distance education within general discourses of education. While the preceding section outlined four key values which are frequently applied within distance education it also pointed to a situation where these values are applied within other modes of education. In short, these values, either separately or collectively, do not define a new entity – while they may be helpful in directing attention to key areas of concern, such concerns are not uniquely identified with distance education.

Given this situation, debate which was centred around such values would fold into the mainstream of educational debate – the fads and fashions, ideological influences, metaphors and jargon of mainstream issues would rub against the particular circumstances presented by distance teaching and learning.

Interestingly, Otto Peters (1991) has returned to look at 'designations' of distance education and the lay theories contained within them. In explicating 'designations' he provides an analysis of some of the key terms used within discourses of distance education – Fernunterricht, Ferstudium, correspondence study, open learning, home study, guided self-study, *zaochny* (without eye contact), study without leaving producting all capture elements of the enterprise while guided didactic conversation, two-way communication, 'continuity of concern', independent study, and industrialized form of instruction are seen as containing the most important elements of the enterprise. He concludes that,

> each of them [the catchwords] was coined to characterize distance education by emphasizing its most important aspect. Four of them have something in common: the intention of improving distance education. They do not depict it as it is but rather as it should be. They are prescriptive. Accordingly, distance education is to be developed after the pattern of a 'guided didactic conversation', must be 'continuously concerned' about the learner's progress, and emancipate the learner from traditional restrictions of time, place and persons by developing a truly 'independent study' which is open enough to allow for a 'degree of autonomy and self direction'. The fifth catchword is basically descriptive. It

characterizes distance education as a form of study which, because of its typical features, is the product of a particular period in the development of culture: industrialisation. It is useful in discerning and understanding particular features in which it does differ from face to face education.

(Peters 1991: 56)

In focusing on the normative, Peters has drawn attention to those aspects of the enterprise of distance education which are, or should be, valued. However, what remains unclear is whether these 'designations' can come together with ways which advance the debate about the field. As Peters notes, the lay theories represented through catchwords are 'incoherent and inconsistent and can, consequently, contradict themselves' (Peters 1991: 49). To advance the field there is a need to identify a 'critical mass' of agreed values which have a degree of coherence – that, is, while not totally consistent, the positions have enough consistency to be used by a group of practitioners to guide their collective practice.

Ideally, the sort of discourse which would emerge from interpreting and applying the values already discussed would be grounded within general educational debate. For example, if we can accept Ramsden's (1992) view that 'one of the most influential concepts to have emerged from research into teaching and learning in higher education during the last 15 years . . . [is] the concept of "approach to learning"', then we could expect to see the context of distance learning analysed in relation to deep and surface approaches to learning. Because approaches to learning are not something that the student has, but, instead, what the learning is for the student, we could expect a strong focus upon researching students' perceptions of their learning and teaching. Ramsden remarks, 'Good teaching and good learning are linked through the students' experiences of what we do. It follows that we cannot teach better unless we are able to see what we are doing from their point of view (Ramsden 1992: 86). Interestingly, he continues by outlining six key principles of effective teaching (in higher education) which represents 'effectiveness' from a student's point of view. A consequence of incorporating distance education within such general educational debate would have led to the expectation that such principles of effective teaching could apply to teaching-at-a-distance and that part of the discourse of distance education would be directed towards illustrating how such principles apply and how practices might be judged according to their impact upon 'approaches to learning'.

Not surprisingly the matter of 'approaches to studying' has been addressed within the specialist literature of distance education. Kember and Harper (1987) first demonstrate the applicability of Ramsden's Approaches to Study Inventory to distance education and then evaluate the significance of the constructs' 'deep and surface approach' to persistence (those completing and obtaining a passing grade). In addition, they point to possible links between approaches to studying and variables such as instructional message design, provision of tutorials or residential schools and quality of assignment feedback. In short they find these constructs a fruitful source for further investigation about the way that practices within distance education might condition students to adopt either deep or surface approaches. Given this initial paper it is surprising that practitioners have not followed up this initial review from Kember and Harper with a flurry of studies about the significance of deep and surface approaches. Ramsden, for example, notes,

> Perceptions of assessment requirements, of workload, of the effectiveness of teaching and the commitment of teachers, and of the amount of control students might exert over their own learning, influence the deployment of different approaches, which are very clearly adaptive responses to the educational environments defined by teachers and courses. Students' perceptions are the product of an interaction between those environments and their previous experiences, including their usual ways of thinking about academic learning. Adaptation may lead to a student understanding the topic or subject, or to learning merely a counterfeit version of it.

> (Ramsden 1992: 84)

That this area is significant is underlined by the sustained interest of other educationists in this area. Entwistle (1991) provides a review of over a decade of research, noting the introduction of new investigations exploring relationships between learning approaches, perceptions of the learning environment, and learning outcomes. Surely such relationships are vitally important for distance education and warrant detailed investigation – how, for example, might researchers approach obtaining information of external students' perceptions of their learning environment?; how might researchers explore the link between how a student learns and his or her perception of the learning environment?

Curriculum theorists and practitioners within distance education have realized the importance of ideological factors and the 'hidden curriculum' in influencing what students value within a teaching and learning situation and have also recognized the importance of the learning environment of the student, the need for supportive mechanisms which acknowledge the reality of this environment, and the need for learning interactions to be seen as central to determining what is meant by distance teaching and learning. What is surprising is that more practitioners have not re-worked and extended this starting point to answer questions posed by any of the four value positions which might characterize distance education. For example, if it is accepted that deep approaches are encouraged by opportunities to exercise responsible choice in the method and content of study, how does this relate to implied and perceived power relations between student and lecturer and the opportunities for students to exercise 'responsible choice'? Is it the case that distance education is framed from answers 'how do adults learn?' or, more importantly, 'how do women and men learn?'; how is choice expanded or diminished by the sorts of processes and procedures used in designing an approach to learning? That is, general educational positions and constructs might well be explored in an attempt to answer questions both of fact and of value.

Thus the debate that would emerge from interpreting and applying core values would acknowledge key educational constructs and be able to interpret, articulate, and appraise their importance for key areas of debate within distance education. The use of such constructs would encourage the explanation of phenomena of distance teaching and learning and where necessary suggest that development of other related but specialist concepts for distance education. The previous example is but one illustration of the situation which would arise where there was a fuller exploration of mainstream educational concepts applied within a value framework which characterizes the nature of distance education.

It is the contention of this chapter that the field of distance education is yet to explore fully its territory through structures which are applied in broader educational debate. Typically, initial work is stated and applications are identified but little further explication of issues through grounded practical exploration follows. This is not surprising as the number of researchers interested in such issues within distance education are few – further, fundamental work on distance teaching and learning must be about teaching and learning in something and consequently researching is often a collaborative effort thereby introducing further practical difficulties with its implementation.

## CAN WE CHARACTERIZE DISTANCE EDUCATION AS AN EDUCATIONAL SUB-CULTURE?

The starting point of this chapter was to attempt to identify the nature of distance education through common beliefs held by a sub-group of educators. The mechanism has been to explore certain key concerns which have underlying values attached to them – the key concerns themselves can be quite easily identified but the extent to which their resolution in practice reveals common beliefs is problematic. At one level there is no doubt that it is possible to characterize distance education as an educational sub-culture – there are those, of course, who would go further and assign discipline status! If distance education is what distance educators do then clearly there is a work-related sub-culture which involves the common concerns of workers. If distance education is an educational position about social values then the answer to our question is not clear. The chapter has explored four central statements containing value positions which, it has been claimed, are pivotal to identifying distance education. Interestingly, the first three of the value positions are continually subjected to revaluation and interpretation by practitioners of distance education in their work – they also are subject to contestation by other educationists whose values reflect their different practices and educational positions. Further, it is significant that the first three value positions are concerned with fundamental and often unresolved issues within other educational sub-cultures. Social justice and equity and power relations conveyed through teaching processes and design for learning are at the heart of identified educational orientations such as vocational/neo-classical, liberal progressive or socially critical.

Characterizing distance education by attempting to understand what distance education means for practitioners or what it 'stands for' in social and educational terms is essential if it is to have meaning beyond technique. This is clearly evidenced by the open learning movement whose propagandists point to their value position about 'openness'. The existence of these values (however potentially contradictory) has enabled the movement to capture parts of educational agendas which are seen to have political and social worth. Distance educationists should more clearly articulate 'what they stand for' and to do this there is a need to explicate the values surrounding the four core values identified in this chapter. At this stage of the development of distance education it seems there is a willingness to explore the issues raised within these value statements but insufficient consistency and coherence in value resolution to claim that distance education is an independent 'construction' of education.

## NOTE

I wish to thank Bruce King and Rosemary Luke for their advice and comments on earlier versions of this chapter.

## REFERENCES

Arger, G. (1987) 'Promise and reality: a critical analysis of literature on distance education in the Third World', *Journal of Distance Education* 2(1), 41–58.

Bagnall R. (1989) 'Educational distance from the perspective of self-direction: an analysis', *Open Learning*, no. 4, 21–6.

Burge, E. and Lensky, H. (1990) 'Women studying in distance education: issues and principles', *Journal of Distance Education* V(1), 20–37.

Devlin, L. (1989) 'Distance education as a discipline: a response to Holmberg', *Journal of Distance Education* IV(1), 56–9.

Entwistle, N. (1991) 'Approaches to learning and perceptions of the learning environment', *Higher Education*, vol, 22, 201–4.

Evans, T. (1989a) 'Taking place; the social construction of place, time and space, and the (re)making of distances in distance education', *Distance Education* 10(2), 170–83.

—— (1989b) 'Fiddling while the tome turns: reflections of a distance education development consultant', in M. Parer (ed.), *Development, Design and Distance Education*, Churchill, Victoria: Gippsland Institute.

—— (1991) 'An epistemological orientation to critical reflection in distance education', in T. Evans, and B. King, *Beyond the Text: Contemporary Writing on Distance Education*, Geelong: Deakin University Press.

Foks, J. (1988) 'Distance education – a developing concept', in D. Sewart and J. Daniel (eds), *Developing Distance Education – Papers Submitted to the 14th World Conference in Oslo*, ICDE, 37.

Fox, S. (1989), 'The production and distribution of knowledge through open and distance learning', *Education and Training Technology International*, 26(3), 269–80.

Gawthorne, G. (1990) 'Is distance education outmoded'?, Paper to National Distance Education Conference (Roneo).

Gibson, R. (1986) *Critical Theory and Education*, London: Hodder & Stoughton.

Gillard, G. (1991a) 'Deconstructing distance', Roneo, 10 July.

—— (1991b) 'Reconstructing independent learning', Roneo.

Gottlieb, E. (1989) 'The discursive construction of knowledge: the case of radical education of discourse', *Qualitative Studies in Education*, 2(2), 131–44.

Gupta, A. (1989) Instructional design in distance education: promises and pitfalls', in M. Parer (ed.) *Development, Design and Distance Education*, Victoria: Gippsland Institute.

Haughey, M. (1991) 'Confronting the pedagogical issues', *Open Learning* 6(3), 14–23.

Holmberg, B. (1989a) *Theory and Practice of Distance Education*, Routledge: London.

—— (1989b) 'Further to the question of whether distance education is a discipline', *Journal of Distance Education*, IV(1), 62–4.

Juler, P. (1990) 'Promoting interaction; maintaining independence: swallowing the mixture', *Open Learning* 5(2), 24–33.

—— (1991a) 'The nature of distance education' in P. Juler and I. Mitchell *Introduction to Distance Education: Study Guide*, Geelong: Deakin University and The University of South Australia.

—— (1991b) 'Discourse or discord? A dilemma for distance education', Paper for Research in Distance Education 91, Geelong: Deakin University.

Kember, D. and Harper G. (1987) 'Approaches to studying research and its implications for the quality of learning from distance education', *Journal of Distance Education*, 2(2), 15–30.

King, B. (1991) *Distance Teaching and Learning 1, Study Guide*, Geelong: Deakin University and The University of South Australia.

Moore, M. (1990) 'Recent contributions to the theory of distance education', *Open Learning* 5(3), 10–15.

Nunan, T. (1991) 'Responding to the Dawkins revolution – the case of distance education in Higher Education', *Unicorn*, 17(3), 146–52.

Parer, M. (ed.) (1989) *Development, Design and Distance Education*, Victoria: Gippsland Institute.

Peters, O. (1991) 'Towards a better understanding of distance education: analysing designations and catchwords' in B. Holmberg and G. Ortner (eds), *Research into Distance Education*, Frankfurt am Main: Peter Lang.

Ramsden, P. (1992) *Learning to Teach in Higher Education*, Routledge: London.

Riley, J. (1984) *The Problems of Writing Correspondence Lessons*, DERG Papers No. 11, Milton Keynes: Open University.

Robinson, R. (1992) 'Andragogy applied to the open college learner', *Research in Distance Education* 4(1), 10–13.

Rumble, G. (1988) 'Distance education as a discipline: a response to Holmberg', *Journal of Distance Education* 3(1), 39–56.

Selman, M. (1989) 'Values and the disciplinary status of distance educations, *Journal of Distance Education* IV(2), 86–7.

Shale, D. (1988) 'Towards a reconceptualization of distance education', *The American Journal of Distance Education* 2(3), 25–35.

Sharma, M. (1987) 'Issues in distance education', in *Distance Education, Vol. 1*, Asian Development Bank, Manila, 45.

Walker, R. (1991) 'Open learning and the media: the transformation of information in times of change', Paper for Critical Reflections Distance Education, Roneo.

# Part V
# Technological underpinnings

# 13 Theory and practice in the use of technology in distance education

*Tony Bates*

## THE IMPORTANCE OF TECHNOLOGY

At the end of the 1980s, the vast majority of distance education throughout the world was still primarily print-based. Print itself is, of course, a technology, and one subject to considerable technological change. Few institutions rely entirely on print, and several of the more influential institutions made considerable use of other media, such as television and audio. Nevertheless, from a student perspective, the bulk of their studies, and at least their perceived main source of material for assignments and examinations, was the printed word.

By the year 2010, this will have changed in most developed countries, and in many of the newly emerging economic 'dragons' of South-East Asia. In particular, telecommunications-based technologies will have become the primary means of delivery of distance teaching.

The main reasons for the increasing importance of technology in distance education can be summarized as follows:

- a much wider range of technology is becoming more accessible to potential distance education students;
- the costs of technological delivery are dropping dramatically;
- the technology is becoming easier to use, both by teachers and learners;
- technology is becoming more powerful pedagogically;
- distance education institutions will find it increasingly difficult to resist the political and social pressures of the technological imperative.

With regard to the last point, distance education is no more immune than any other social system from the rapid technological changes occurring in late-twentieth-century society. Peters (1983) had made a convincing case that the birth of modern distance education systems reflected for the first time the *systematic* application of industrial processes to education. We are, though now living in what is termed a *post*-industrial society, dependent increasingly on knowledge-based industries, information technologies and communications. The successful distance education institutions wil be those that *systematically* adapt to and embrace these trends; these can perhaps be best identified as *third-generation* distance teaching institutions (the first being primarily correspondence schools, and the second large, autonomous, institutions using a wider variety of media – see Keegan 1980, for a general definition of distance education, and Pelton 1991 and Bates 1991a for a discussion of third generation distance education).

This is not to argue that this inevitable trend is necessarily in the best interests of learners; whether or not third-generation institutions are effective will depend not so much on *whether* they use new technologies, but on *how* those technologies are applied. For these reasons, then, it is necessary to examine carefully the role and functions of technology in distance education.

## DEFINING TECHNOLOGY

I find it useful to make a distinction between media and technology. By 'media' I refer to the generic forms of communication associated with particular ways of representing knowledge. Each medium not only has its own unique way of presenting knowledge, but also of organizing it, often reflected in particular preferred formats or styles of presentation. In distance education, the most important four media are: text, audio, television, computing.

While certain technologies are closely associated with each medium, a variety of different technologies may be used to deliver these media, as Table 13.1 indicates. This table is illustrative rather than exhaustive. It can be seen that media can usually be carried by more than one technology, and certainly these distinctions will become less meaningful with greater integration of media and technologies. Nevertheless, there are still significant differences in the bandwidth required for different media (uncompressed television requires 1,000 times the bandwidth capacity of an audio telephone call) and the educational applications associated with different technologies, so these distinctions will remain valid well into the future.

A second major distinction that needs to be made is between

*Table 13.1* The relationship between media, technology and distance education applications of technology

| Media | Technologies | Distance education applications |
|-------|--------------|-------------------------------|
| Text (including graphics) | Print | Course units<br>Supplementary materials<br>Correspondence tutoring |
| | Computers | Databases<br>Electronic publishing |
| Audio | Cassettes, radio<br>Telephone | Programmes<br>Telephone tutoring<br>Audioconferencing |
| Television | Broadcasting, video-cassettes, videodiscs<br>Cable, satellite, fibre-optics, ITFS, microwave | Programmes<br>Lectures<br>Videoconferencing |
| Computing | Computers, telephone, satellite, fibre-optics, ISDN, CD-ROM, videodisc | Computer-aided learning (CAI, CBT)<br>E-mail, computer-conferencing, audio-graphics<br>Databases, multi-media |

*Table 13.2* One-way and two-way technology applications in distance education

| Media | One-way technology applications | Two-way technology applications |
|-------|-------------------------------|-------------------------------|
| Text | Course units<br>Supplementary materials | Correspondence tutoring |
| Audio | Cassette programmes<br>Radio programmes | Telephone tutoring<br>Audioconferencing |
| Television | Broadcast programmes<br>Cassette programmes | Interactive television (TV out; telephone in)<br>Videoconferencing |
| Computing | CAL, CAI, CBT<br>Databases, multi-media | E-mail<br>Computer-conferencing |

technologies that are primarily *one-way* and those that are primarily *two-way*. Table 13.2 summarizes the distinctions.

The significance of two-way technologies is that they allow for interaction between learners and instructors or tutors, and perhaps even more significantly, in some cases amongst distance learners themselves.

Despite a widespread belief, particularly in the USA (see Clark 1983), that there are no significant pedagogic differences between media (for instance, a lecture delivered by television is just as effective as if delivered face-to-face), shifting even the same medium (e.g. television) from one technology to another (e.g. from broadcast to videocassette) has significant pedagogic implications.

## TEACHING WITH TECHNOLOGY

While there is an infinite variety of ways in which technology can be used for teaching at a distance, several relatively distinct approaches have been adopted.

### Extended classroom teaching

The first is to use technology to extend the classroom lecture beyond the walls of a single institution. This form of distance teaching is perhaps the oldest. Its original format was the use of extended lecture notes, or audio recordings of lectures, combined with set or recommended readings, mailed to off-campus students, with students sending in assignments for marking. This form of distance teaching can still be found in many 'dual-mode' institutions, i.e. institutions where the bulk of the teaching is done on-campus but which also have some extension services for off-campus students.

The most popular medium for doing this today, particularly in the United States of America, is through television, although the University of Wisconsin and several other mid-west universities and colleges have a long history of using telephone teaching, increasingly supplemented with audio-graphics, in this way. Reception sites are usually in other educational institutions or, in the case of the National Technological University, in corporate locations as well.

There are several advantages in this approach. It requires little change in the behaviour of the teacher; lectures are prepared more or less in the same way as for a classroom, although greater care may be given to the preparation of graphics. This approach can be particularly useful where television is being used to bring in world-wide experts, or to bring latest developments in a particular field to the attention of postgraduate students or corporate trainees, in that there is little delay between the decision to offer a course, and its availability to students.

Such programmes use very simple, and hence low-cost, production techniques, using either fixed or single camera operations, and/or specially equipped 'television' classrooms. Using 'narrowcast' transmission services, such as cable, microwave, or ITFS (a special broadcast bandwidth allocation reserved for educational use in the USA, and requiring decoding equipment at receive sites) also helps to keep costs low, although the technical costs associated with the development and maintenance of an extensive state-wide system, such as IHETS in Indiana, may run into several million dollars. Using telephone links, students at remote sites have the opportunity to ask questions, and 'participate' in the lectures, if broadcast live, so that there is a form of interaction. Local sites may also have a tutor, who can lead discussion or clarify points locally, which may be important if the programme has been pre-recorded. Using satellite transmission, lectures can be delivered into almost any site on a continent-wide or even international basis (as with EUROSTEP and EuroPACE in Europe).

To some extent, the choice of technology for this purpose has few pedagogic implications; what matters most is its appropriateness for reaching the target groups, and the cost. An extension of this kind of service is the use of two-way video links, using either broadband coaxial cable systems or fibre-optics. Livenet, which links together the main teaching hospitals and several university colleges in London, is one example. This enables the teaching to be originated from several sites, and full two-way video participation from each site. However, costs rise in proportion to the number of sites connected this way, both in terms of terminal equipment, and in transmission costs. It also adds considerable complexity to the way teaching is organized, and therefore has more serious pedagogic implications than the more simple 'one-way' televised lectures.

There are two major criticisms of the use of technology for extended lectures in distance education. First, it fails to exploit the unique pedagogic characteristics of each medium; second, it ignores advances in curriculum design associated with the development of integrated, multi-media distance teaching materials.

**Exploiting the medium**

Each medium represents knowledge in different ways. Different technologies have different influences on student access, control and flexibility.

Media differ in the extent to which they can represent different kinds of knowledge, because they vary in the symbol systems that they use to encode information. Salomon (1979) makes a distinction between three kinds of symbol systems: digital, analogic and iconic.

Digital systems follow precise rules and are relatively unambiguous.

Digital systems tend to represent in permanent form fixed or constant relationships. Symbols in digital systems are logically related. Salomon classifies musical notation, mathematical notation, written words and computer languages as digital. Knowledge can be represented exclusively by digital coding systems in both books and computers.

Analogic coding systems are more expressive of emotions and feelings and tend to represent the performance of dynamic activities. They provide an emotive context to knowledge. Performed music, dance and certain non-verbal aspects of speech (e.g. tone) are examples given by Salomon of analogic coding systems. Knowledge can be represented by analogic coding systems in television and audio.

Iconic coding systems depend on pictures, colour and signs for encoding knowledge. Iconic coding systems are able to handle ambiguity and lend themselves to differing interpretations of the meanings they contain. Knowledge can be represented by iconic coding systems in pictures, books and television.

Different media are capable of combining different symbol systems. Books can represent knowledge through both digital and iconic systems but not analogic. In this respect, computers are similar to books, although it is more difficult (or rather more expensive) to represent fully iconic systems through computers. Television and film are the richest media symbolically. They are the only media which can encompass text, still and moving pictures, natural language, natural movement, music and other sounds, and full colour. They are therefore able to represent most closely real experience in all its facets.

Differences between media in the way they combine symbol systems influence the way in which different media can represent knowledge. Thus, there is a difference between a written description, a televised recording, and a computer simulation of the same experiment. Different symbol systems are being used, conveying different kinds of information about the same experiment. This is significant for media selection, because different subject areas (e.g. art, history, science, mathematics) have different requirements for the representation of knowledge, or rather place differing emphases on the importance of different ways of representing knowledge.

Media also differ in the way they structure knowledge. Books, the telephone, radio, audiocassettes and face-to-face tuition all tend to present knowledge linearly or sequentially. While parallel activities can be represented through these media (e.g. different chapters dealing with different events occurring simultaneously), these activities still have to be presented sequentially through these media. Computers are more able to present or simulate the interrelationship of multiple variables simultaneously occurring, but only within closely defined limits (because of limitations in symbolic representation, and in some cases lack of processing power). Computers can also handle branching or alternative routes through information, but again within closely defined limits. The limitations of the structure imposed by computing languages on the speed and convenience with which information can be accessed is clearly demonstrated by viewdata systems such as PRESTEL, where very rigid and narrowly defined search procedures must be followed. Information providers similarly are forced to present information within very closely defined limits of both structure and symbol systems.

While television also presents information sequentially, its richness of symbol system and its editing techniques generally encourage both the presentation of a wide variety of simultaneously occurring events and a structure which often is not linear either temporally or logically.

Subject matter varies enormously in the way in which information needs to be structured. Subject areas (e.g. natural sciences, history, etc.) structure knowledge in particular ways determined by the internal logic of the subject matter. This structure may be very tight or logical, requiring particular sequences or relationships between different concepts, or very open or loose, requiring learners to deal with highly complex material in an open-ended or intuitive way. Even within a single curriculum area, subject matter may vary in terms of its required structure (e.g. social theories and statistics, within sociology).

Some media are better than others for certain kinds of representation of particular significance to teaching. In particular, media differ in their ability to handle concrete or abstract knowledge. Abstract knowledge is handled primarily through language. While all media can handle language, either in written or spoken form, media vary in their ability to represent concrete knowledge (examples, demonstrations, etc.). For instance, television can fully represent events that cannot be brought into the classroom or laboratory, and only television can provide full symbolic representation of events or movement. Television in particular is very rich symbolically, able to handle all forms of representation of knowledge, except direct experience.

This has several consequences for teaching. First, most kinds of abstract knowledge can be handled by any medium, but television in particular, and to some extent print and computers, can provide concrete examples. Thus television can:

- demonstrate processes or procedures;
- 'model' or construct concrete examples of abstract ideas;
- demonstrate interpersonal communcation;
- dramatize or reconstruct events through documentary-style production.

These representational possibilities are particularly important for non-academic learners, who often require concrete examples or demonstration rather than abstract theory. However, this form of television is much more expensive to produce than the use of television for relaying lectures. Using television to relay lectures does not fully exploit the unique presentational characteristics of television; indeed, audio plus printed notes is equal symbolically to a televised lecture and is more likely to be effective.

Research has also indicated that media differ in the extent to which they can help develop different skills (Salomon 1979). Part of this relates to the control characteristics of technologies and part to the representational features. For instance, computers are excellent for presenting and testing rule-based procedures, or areas of abstract knowledge where there are clearly correct answers.

Television on the other hand, because of its richness of symbolic representation, and hence the need for interpretation, is better at presenting ambiguous situations where a variety of possible learner responses are equally acceptable. This quality can be particularly valuable for professional updating and training, where trainees already have a good knowledge base, but need to adapt to changing situations. Also, television is valuable for developing mechanical or procedural skills, where it is important to see relationship between parts, and sequencing of activities, for developing interpersonal skills, and for changing attitudes, through the use of dramatization or documentaries with which the student can clearly identify. Television on its own though is unlikely to be sufficient for the development of such skills; some form of practice and feedback on performance, or discussion of various interpretations, are also needed.

Technology then can provide learning experiences not otherwise available even in a face-to-face teaching situation. For Arts students, television and print can provide examples of archive film or photographs, paintings and buildings, and dramatic and musical performance. For science, mathematics and technology students, computers can provide simulations and examples of complex mathematical and physical relationships, and above all, plenty of practice in mastering mathematical techniques.

Using technology to create and deliver experiences essential for different subject areas ties media selection very closely to the kinds of experience considered important in each subject area, and especially to ideas about the best way of teaching a particular subject. One consequence of this is the need for a different balance of media between different subject areas. From Open University experience, it seems that all subject areas for instance can benefit from the use of television, but science subjects above all require large quantities of television because of the importance of laboratory and fieldwork and the need to show experimental evidence, whereas philosophy was not a subject that easily lent itself to television.

If media then do vary both in the way they present information symbolically and in the way they can conveniently handle the structures required within different subject areas, it would follow that one needs to select the medium which best matches the required mode of presentation and the dominant structure of the subject matter. For this reason, it is difficult to produce general rules or guidelines which will satisfy all subject areas; also it seems essential that subject experts take an active role in decisions regarding media selection and use to ensure that the teaching requirements of the subject matter can be met.

Media though are flexible; any single medium can usually handle a variety of symbol systems and knowledge structures. Most media combine at least two of the three symbol systems; computers do not have to be used in highly structured ways; television can 'tell a story' sequentially. We are dealing with tendencies distinguishing between media, rather than hard and fast rules.

## Integrated curriculum development

It can be seen that using technology to relay lectures severely restricts the exploitation of the potential of media, limiting the technology to carrying mainly voice, facial expressions and written symbol systems.

In order to exploit the full potential of media use in distance education, an integrated curriculum development process is necessary. This means identifying the main aims of a course, spelling out in more detail the objectives, assigning teaching roles and functions to different media, and designing the media in such a way as to exploit the advantages (and to avoid the limitations) of each medium. This requires a team approach, calling on the skills of different specialists: subject experts, instructional designers, media specialists.

There are several disadvantages of such an approach: cost; time; the required level of expertise; and lack of empirical evaluation studies indicating the teaching effectiveness of this approach over relayed lectures.

Clearly the cost of developing integrated, multi-media teaching materials will initially be much more than using technology to relay lectures. However, the cost factor is more complex than it may seem. Live, relayed lectures need repeating each year. If levels of interaction are to be meaningful, numbers enrolled must be small, or local tutors employed. The development of integrated curricular materials allows the same material to be used each year, over a number of years. Where student numbers for a particular course are large, it may actually be more economical in the long run to create high-quality teaching materials than to repeat lectures each year.

Second, integrated, multi-media teaching materials take a great deal more time to prepare than relayed lectures. However, while in postgraduate teaching and certain areas of job training, speed in the creation and delivery of learning opportunities is essential; for many others this is not so. Clearly there is a trade-off to be made between speed and the quality of the teaching materials.

Third, integrated multi-media curriculum development changes the role of the teacher from someone totally in charge of the teaching material and the process of teaching, to one who is part of a team. The teacher needs to understand the needs and requirements of different media, and the organizational structure of a conventional institution may not allow or may actively discourage teachers from spending the time required to work in this way.

Last, 'traditional' teachers need to be convinced that the development of integrated, multi-media teaching materials is worth the effort. Certainly, the success of the large, autonomous institutions using a combination of media is impressive; however, the newer interactive technologies allow for easier use of 'on-line' delivery methods that are closer to the traditional role of teachers. The challenge is always to show that new ways of teaching are more effective; rarely is evidence provided of the effectiveness (or otherwise) of more traditional approaches. This kind of thinking militates against the high-cost, high-risk integrated multi-media approach, which requires considerable changes both in the teachers' role, and in the organizational structures of conventional institutions.

## LEARNING FROM TECHNOLOGY

Four hypotheses will be put forward about the special roles that different media can play in learning.

The first hypothesis is that for full understanding of a concept, the concept must be experienced in a variety of independent ways; presentation of the same concept through different media is one way in which deeper understanding can be developed.

The second hypothesis is that full understanding only comes as a result of learners developing skills in using or working on concepts; media though vary in their appropriateness for developing certain specific intellectual, social or operational skills; hence it is important to use different media for developing different skills in using concepts.

The third hypothesis is that certain media can match some of the ways learners need to think about subject matter; in other words there can be an isomorphism between the use of a particular medium and the way a learner needs to think about that subject matter.

The fourth hypothesis is that learners need to interact both with the learning material, and with tutors or instructors, and other students, in order to learn effectively.

Let us take these hypotheses one at a time.

### Hypothesis 1: The need for multiple forms of experience

The first hypothesis is Piagetian in essence. It argues that a wide range of appropriate experiences is required before learners internalize and hence fully comprehend concepts, ideas or principles. For instance, to comprehend fully the concept of heat, one needs to experience it in a number of ways; physically, verbally, numerically, conceptually, symbolically. Thus the concept of heat can be 'experienced' by touch (burning oneself as a child), through words ('that is hot') or numbers (42 degrees centigrade) associated with the physical experience, by abstract definition ('a form of energy arising from random motion of molecules of bodies'), or through symbolism (a man dragging himself through a desert). Each way of 'knowing' about heat is different. Eventually though the learner must integrate all these experiences to understand fully the concept of heat. Different media can provide distinctly different experiences or representations of the same concept, and this becomes especially important for students where important concepts or experiences are not likely to be common in their everyday life.

The hypothesis though raises a number of questions. The first is the extent to which media can substitute for direct experience. Another is the extent to which there is evidence to support the contention that exposure to multiple experiences is necessary for deeper understanding.

It is certainly true in the British Open University that non-print media rarely introduce key new concepts not already covered in the print material, but rather tend to present the same concepts in different ways. Grundin (1980) found that Open University Mathematics students varied in the extent to which they rated the value of television. Although students who went on to get 'A' or 'B' grades watched more of the course television programmes than other students, they tended to rate programmes as less valuable than the borderline students. One explanation of this is that the 'A' and 'B' grade students were generally able to comprehend principles mainly from the text, and therefore the television programmes were perceived as being redundant. (It is still possible that viewing these programmes nevertheless increased the depth of these students' understanding without them being aware of the effect.) On the other hand, the 'C' and 'D' grade students were struggling with the texts, and therefore clearly perceived the alternative presentations on television to be much more helpful than did the 'A' or 'B' grade students. However, much more empirical research is needed to confirm this hypothesis. If it is valid, though, it is a strong argument for a multi-media approach to education.

### Hypothesis 2: Media are 'neutral' regarding content, but specific regarding skills

The second hypothesis derives from work by Salomon (1979), who in turn was influenced by Olson and Bruner (1974). Olson and Bruner make a strong distinction between knowledge and skills. They argue that learning involves two distinct aspects: first, acquiring knowledge of facts, principles, ideas, concepts, events, relationships, rules and laws; and second, using or working on that knowledge to develop skills. Salomon suggests that acquisition of knowledge may be independent of the medium of presentation, but the development of skills may be dependent on the media used. In other words, some media will assist the development of some skills, but not others.

Gagné (1974) drew attention to different levels or kinds of learning, as also did Bloom *et al.* (1956). Perhaps the simplest level is aesthetic appreciation or enjoyment. It may be sufficient that learners merely learn to enjoy reading books or watching or listening to dance or music performance. In some instances, it may be sufficient to raise learners' awareness of an issue. For instance, if the learners are already well trained or qualified, it may be enough to alert them to new developments, because once alerted, they already have the skills to cope. However, comprehension is likely to be the minimal level of learning objective for most education courses. Some researchers (e.g. Marton and Säljö 1976) make a distinction between surface and deep comprehension. Surface comprehension could be linked to presentation through a single medium; deep comprehension for many students may require presentation through several media. What is clear though is that transient media, such as broadcasting, are less powerful for achieving detailed or deep comprehension than more permanent media such as print. Lastly, at the highest level comes the application of what one has comprehended to new situations. Here it becomes necessary to develop skills of analysis, evaluation, and problem-solving. There will be advantages here in using media which can best represent the 'new' situations to which learning must be applied. Thus television can be particularly useful in helping students develop skills of analysis, or apply knowledge to new events, or evaluate how well theories apply to real situations.

Again, there are several open questions regarding this hypothesis. I would challenge the statement that acquiring knowledge is independent of the media used, since this seems to conflict with the first hypothesis, and the idea that different media represent knowledge differently.

Second, there is little empirical evidence to date to suggest which skills are best developed through which media. In support of the hypothesis, Salomon (1979) reported a series of ingenious experiments which indicated that certain features of television (zooms, camera movement, etc.) could facilitate the development of perceptual skills (identification of foreground from background, story sequencing, etc.) in young children. Since Salomon was investigating perceptual skills in young children who were still maturing, it is not perhaps surprising that he found a correlation between televisual techniques and perceptual development. It is difficult though to generalize from this research on the perceptual development of young children to other areas of skill development or to adult learners.

Perhaps more relevant is the relationship between media use and the development of intellectual skills. Research at the British Open University (Bates and Gallagher 1987) showed that while documentary-style television programmes covered the same content areas as the printed material, the television programmes were being used to try and develop skills of application, evaluation and analysis of concepts developed in the texts. However, the research also showed that many students had difficulty in using television in this way (although those that were successful went on to get the highest end-of-course grades).

The distinction, though, between content and skills does seem to be useful in pointing attention at the importance not just of transferring information (which all media seem to handle reasonably well) but also at using information. There are some suggestions that media differ in the learning skills that they best develop, but again there is very little empirical evidence to relate particular media to particular learning skills. It does though seem a promising area for future research and experimentation, and the distinction between content and skills is certainly something that curriculum planners and course designers need to keep in mind when designing course materials.

### Hypothesis 3: Media can be matched to appropriate conceptual models of thinking

The third hypothesis, again arising from the work of Salomon (1979), argues that certain ways of thinking about subject matter can best be represented through one medium rather than others, and this facility can help unblock certain conceptual difficulties which students would otherwise encounter.

In practice, what this means is that while print is a very powerful medium for dealing with abstract ideas, other media can sometimes provide insight where print alone would be insufficient. This is done by providing appropriate mental images which assist cognitive processing. Paivio, for instance, argues that: 'Mental images are conscious representations of our knowledge of the world. Like audiovisual aids in instructional programs, they can be intentionally and systematically used as the informational base for cognitive operations and as an aid to new learning' (Paivio 1980: 295).

What media such as television and computers can do is to provide appropriate images where learners would otherwise be unable to generate appropriate images for themselves. Salomon (1983) suggests at least three ways in which television can help cognitive processing in this way.

The first is through visual illustration: television can provide powerful audio-visual images symbolizing important concepts or ideas which can imprint themselves in the learner's memory, and thus act as referent points for more general abstract ideas. He states: 'the unique attribution of illustration is that it is a private case, hopefully a typical one, of a relatively abstract class or category . . . it is a representation of a single case representing a general class' (Salomon 1983: 9). This definition of course is not specific to television; imagery in print is also common. Television's power though is that it can create easily recognizable images which are striking because of their richness of symbolism; television images map directly to the internal mental images that Paivio describes as our internalized audio-visual library.

Salomon adds an important warning about the dangers of illustration as well. Here he is talking about an Open University programme, D102, TV1, on vandalism, in which three teenagers smash up a telephone box, to illustrate that even in such a situation, their behaviour is governed by certain rules or codes of behaviour:

> What the students see is, say, three aggressive youngsters . . . but do they understand that the real referent of this illustration is not the three youths, but 'vandalism'?. . . . There is a fair likelihood they do not. It is quite possible that for a number of students such illustrations are misperceived as they are not seen as illustrating what they're supposed to but rather far more concrete (and somewhat irrelevant) referents . . . the relationship between the illustrator and the illustrated needs to be made specific.
>
> (Salomon 1983: 9)

This raises the important issue of the relationship between concrete experiences and abstract ideas. One view is that learning is very much facilitated if learners can place abstract ideas in the context of concrete examples. Several researchers (e.g. Trenaman 1967, Salomon 1979, Belson 1952) have found that broadcasting is most effective for purposes of comprehending messags when it deals with concrete, specific instances, when it provides striking visual images which symbolize or represent abstract ideas, or uses drama and personification, i.e. people and their interrelationships, to present 'real-life' instances of general or abstract principles.

Again, this is a function not unique to television. Computers can also provide, through animation and graphics, a midway point between fully concrete and totally abstract representation. However, television has currently a major advantage over computers: not only can it fully represent images, it can also use simultaneously the spoken word to make the link between the concrete example and the abstract idea.

At the same time, it is not always necessary to make this link verbally; Salomon also makes the point that learning requires effort, and providing over-explicit links at the wrong time can be counter-productive. Salomon argues that the links need to be made explicit if viewers are meeting new ideas or concepts for the first time; after some familiarity with a concept, it may be enough to give a little help without being too specific; once familiar with a concept, it may be better to allow the learners to try and make the links for themselves. Again, the 'right' approach may depend on whether the main aim is comprehension, or applying knowledge.

Media can also create appropriate images which assist the learning process through modelling. Bandura (1977) argues that one function of teaching is to provide a model of thinking about an idea or concept which acts as a bridge between the learner's original position and the acquisition of deeper knowledge or understanding. For instance this can be done by a teacher modelling how to solve a particular kind of mathematical problem. Salomon uses the term more specifically though. Television in particular can present physically concrete models which represent abstract ideas. A clear example is the use of a cube in an Open University Mathematics programme (M101, TV2) physically to model the formula $(a + b)^3$. The overall cube was then physically broken down into smaller shapes representing parts of the formula (this is a good example where you need a concrete, televisual example of what I am discussing!)

Salomon also uses the term 'supplantation' to describe the way in which media can be used to generate ways of thinking about subject material which students may find difficult to generate for themselves. To quote Salomon:

> supplantation is perhaps the most important, yet least self-evident function of TV's pictorial representation . . . when complex new ideas, constructs and processes are verbally introduced, students neither have appropriate corresponding images nor can they generate them on their own. TV can accomplish the critical function of explicitly providing the students with appropriate images as substitutes for the ones they would benefit from but could not generate on their own.
>
> (Salomon 1983: 11)

The important point here is that television, and to a lesser degree computers, can be used to generate images which are then internalized as mental images to help in the way learners can think about abstract ideas and principles. This is not a unique function of television, but television's richness of symbol system makes it much easier to create striking and relevant images than through other media.

## Hypothesis 4: Learners need to interact both with the learning material, and with tutors or instructors, and other students, in order to learn effectively

Another important criterion influencing choice of technology is the control over the medium available to the learner. For instance, lectures or broadcasts (terrestrial, cable or satellite) are ephemeral technologies. However, the value of permanent technologies such as books, cassettes or computers lies not just in their ability to allow students to view or listen to material at more convenient times. They also enable learning from media to be much more effective.

Research has indicated that learning from ephemeral media is much more difficult than learning from permanent material (Bates *et al.*, 1981). Furthermore, there are design implications once material is available in permanent form. Television material for use on cassette for instance does not have to resemble the continuous, lengthy broadcast format. Videocassettes can contain short, unlinked sequences, with activities following each sequence, and feedback provided on the activity, either on the cassette itself, or in notes. Videocassettes in particular lend themselves to group use, because of the need for interpretation and discussion of video examples. This can increase the activity and participation of the learner.

Interactivity – the ability for the learner to respond in some way to the teaching material and obtain comment or feedback on the response – considerably increases learning effectiveness. There are two very different kinds of interactivity (see Bates 1990 for a fuller discussion of this issue). One is interaction between people, and in particular between the student and a teacher or tutor, although interaction between students is also valuable. The second is the interaction between the learner and the teaching material. Media again differ in their ability to provide these two types of interaction.

'One-way' media, such as print and broadcasting, require supplementing by 'two-way' interaction with tutors, through correspondence, telephone or computer communication. Some technologies make it easier to provide feedback on student responses to the teaching material. This is at its strongest in compuer-based learning, where learners can be tested, corrected, or given remedial activities by the computer. The attraction of computer-controlled videodiscs or 'multi-media' computer learning is that they combine the strong interactivity of computers with the powerful representational qualities of television. However, even these technologies have great difficulty in handling teaching contexts where individual interpretation or the development of argument is needed. Audiocassettes and video-cassettes can be designed to increase learner interaction, and do allow for more open-ended and interpretative responses than computer-controlled learning, but still need supplementing with some form of two-way interaction with people.

Perhaps the most important element of control then is the ability for open-ended two-way communication *under the students' control*, allowing students to interact easily not only with tutors, but also with other students. Until recently, the telephone has been the only means of doing this for students at a distance, and costs have been high. Computer-mediated communication though now enables two-way communication at a distance, at asynchronous times, at relatively low cost, between students, and between students, regional tutors or even central academic staff. This could have revolutionary implications for distance education, providing the means to free students from the centralized control of pre-prepared and constricted curricula (see Mason and Kaye 1989 for more information).

The extent to which any particular medium encourages interaction or active learning depends to some extent on the way it is designed, but is also determined to some extent by the nature of the medium. What is clear is that the design of multi-media distance learning materials which encourage active learning requires considerable instructional as well as programming expertise. An understanding both of media and learning is required.

These are only some of the pedagogic differences between media, but it does indicate the importance of course designers identifying clearly not only the content of a course, but also how best to present knowledge in a particular subject area, and what kinds of learning (comprehension, analysis, application of principles to actual cases, problem-solving, interpersonal skills, mechanical skills, attitude change, etc.) are required. This means that a good understanding of what is required to teach a particular subject needs to be combined with good knowledge of the pedagogic strengths and weaknesses of different media.

## TRENDS

As pointed out at the start of this chapter, we shall see increasing use of new technologies in distance education. Within this overall increase in the range of technologies, we shall see certain trends.

## Lower cost

One of the main factors which influences an institution's use of technology is the access to that technology by students. To date, many distance teaching institutions have been committed to home-based delivery, and equal access to all. This means that whatever technology is used, it must be available in nearly every home within the orbit of the institution. Until recently, this has restricted technology, even in developed countries, to print delivered via mail services, broadcast television, radio, and audiocassettes. Telephones have become increasingly available to most homes over the last few years, but long distance charges are an inhibiting factor.

Videocassettes are now common in most homes in the more advanced developed (and developing) countries. The big explosion though will be in computers and telecommunications, where costs are dropping dramatically. In computing, while the minimum cost of a complete workstation (computer, modem, printer) suitable for study is unlikely to drop below US$1,000, the power that one can buy for that price is increasing all the time. The introduction of fibre-optics, cellular telephones, ISDN, and data compression will also dramatically reduce the cost of transmitting information. Thus not only will the cost of (audio) telephone calls drop, so will the cost of sending data and images.

This means that already a much wider range of technologies is becoming available to distance teaching institutions. This trend is compounded by the move to collaboration between conventional and distance teaching institutions, the development of state or province-wide consortia or networks for distance education, workplace-based training, and the development of local learning centres, all creating increased opportunities for the sharing of equipment.

## Media integration

The barriers between different media and technologies are coming down. We are seeing the integration of computing, television and communications technologies. Already, the integration of videodisc or CD-ROM with computers has led to the creation of 'multi-media' workstations. With the introduction of ISDN, which digitizes and integrates sound, data, and graphics for transmission through the standard 'copper-wire' telephone system, we shall see multi-media integrated with telecommunications. Combined with cellular telephony and miniaturization, we shall see by the end of this century the

232  *Technological underpinnings*

development of cordless, easily transportable workstations combining computing, telecommunications and television, at relatively low cost.

**Easier use**

The technologies are also getting easier for both teachers and students to use. More powerful 'front-end' software, using menus, icons and 'intuitive' procedures, will enable teachers to seek, select, download and re-edit materials themselves, and students to access materials, communicate with other students and tutors, and store information all within the same workstation environment. These developments are not being made primarily with education in mind (although it is becoming recognized as a significant market in its own right) but for business application as well.

What will not get cheaper is the cost of producing good quality distance teaching materials. This will require people who can combine good pedagogic practice with an understanding of the strengths and weaknesses of different media and technologies. Also needed will be stronger procedures and methods for making decisions about technology use in distance education as the range of technologies and their complexity increases (see Bates 1991b for one possible approach to the selection of technologies for distance education).

The psychologist Kurt Lewin once said: 'There is nothing more practical than a good theory.' It will become increasingly important to develop a good theoretical basis for the applications of media and technology in distance education as the new technologies come to play a more central role in distance education.

**REFERENCES**

Bandura, A. (1977) *Social Learning Theory*, Englewood Cliffs, N.J.: Prentice-Hall.
Bates, A. W. (1990) 'Interactivity as a criterion for media selection in distance education', in Asian Association of Open Universities, *Interactive Communication in Distance Education*, Jakarta: Universitas Terbuka.
—— (1991a) 'Third generation distance education: the challenge of new technology', *Research in Distance Education*, 3(2), 10–15.
—— (1991b) *Technology in Open Learning and Distance Education: A Guide for Decision-Makers*, Vancouver: Commonwealth of Learning/Open Learning Agency.
—— (1981) *Radio: The Forgotten Medium*? Milton Keynes: The Open University Institute of Educational Technology (mimeo).
—— and Gallagher, M. (1987) 'Improving the educational effectiveness of

television case-studies and documentaries', in O. Boyd-Barrett and P. Braham (eds), *Media, Knowledge and Power*, London: Croom Helm.

Belson, W. (1952) '"Topic for Tonight": a study of comprehensibility', *BBC Quarterly* 5(2).

Bloom, B. *et al.* (1956) *Taxonomy of Educational Objectives: The Classification of Educational Goals, Handbook 1: Cognitive Domain*, New York: David McKay.

Clark, R. (1983) 'Reconsidering research on learning from media', *Review of Educational Research* 53(4), 445–60.

Gagné, R. (1974) *The Condition of Learning*, New York: Holt, Reinhart & Winston.

Grundin, G. (1980) *Audio-visual and Other Media in 91 Open University Courses*, Milton Keynes: The Open University Institute of Educational Technology (mimeo).

Keegan, D. (1980) 'On defining distance education', *Distance Education* (1), 13–36.

Marton, F. and Säljö, R. (1976) 'On qualitative differences in learning: outcome and process', *British Journal of Educational Technology*, vol. 46.

Mason, R. and Kaye, A. (1989). *Mindweave: Communication, Computers and Distance Education*, Oxford: Pergamon.

Olson, D. and Bruner, J. (1974) 'Learning through experience and learning through media', in D. Olson (ed.), *Media and Symbols: The Forms of Expression (73rd NSSE Yearbook)*, Chicago: University of Chicago.

Paivio, A. (1980) 'Imagery as a private audio-visual aid', *Instructional Science* 9(4), 285–304.

Pelton, J. (1991) 'Technology and education: friend or foe?', *Research in Distance Education* 3(2), 2–9.

Peters, O. (1983) 'Distance teaching and industrial production: a comparative interpretation in outline', in D. Sewart, D. Keegan and B. Holmberg, *Distance Education: International Perspectives*, London: Croom Helm.

Salomon, G. (1979) *The Interaction of Media, Cognition and Learning*, London: Jossey-Bass.

—— (1983) *Using Television as a Unique Teaching Resource for Open University Courses*, Milton Keynes: Open University Institute of Educational Technology (mimeo),

Trenaman, J. (1967) *Communication and Comprehension*, London: Longman.

# 14 A theory of distance education for the cyberspace era

*Gary Boyd*

## INTRODUCTION

Distance education is nicely characterized by Keegan (1990) in terms of five defining conditions: quasi-permanent teacher-learners separation; the central involvement of a formal (bureaucratic?) organization; the use of technical media; the provision of two-way communication; and quasi-permanent separation of the learner from a learning group. The quasi-permanent separation of teacher and learner is, as Keegan has demonstrated, where the crux of the problem and the opportunity in distance education lie.

The problem is to reintegrate teaching and learning without losing the great economies of scale which are possible through well-designed pre-packaged materials and mass-distribution (broadcasting etc.) media. Audio, video and computer teleconferencing support the reintegration of teacher and learners at a distance but when they are used for synchronous collaborative learning most of the potential economies of scale are lost. Indeed it is easy to have higher costs per student with these media than in face-to-face teaching institutions. Also, depending on how you define the 'learning group', the last of Keegan's defining characteristics may need further consideration and revision in the age of cyberspace.

The others are taken, here, to be less problematic defining characteristics of distance education. Clearly it is agreed that distance education involves specialized institutional arrangements as well as distinct forms of teaching and learning.

A theory of distance education has to be a (preferably systemic) theory of organization as well as an embedded theory of instruction if it is to be helpful for the development of concerted public education based on modern communications media.

## Learning networks

The core idea here is that the development of communication and control technology from print and mail, to quasi-intelligent multi-modal (image, voice, kinetics) computer-communications offers distance education this opportunity to evolve from being mainly a way of providing access to knowledge and credentials for highly motivated, scattered, or otherwise isolated, students, into the paramount means for building pluralistic, geographically extensive networked learning communities of complementary human capabilities which can work together in mutual appreciation to improve our world.

Education is not just the self-involvement of individual learners, it is an intrinsically organizational and communal enterprise. Human capital is not just a collection of capable individuals, rather it is networks of people who appreciate one another's skills, knowledge, and motivations, so that continually evolving collaborative ventures are readily accomplished by them.

## The inseparability of organizational development theory and instructional systems theory

It usually seems to be assumed that conventional Weberian bureau-cratic-industrial organization methods are good enough for distance education institutions. There are certainly notably successful institutions (e.g. the Open University of the United Kingdom; International Correspondence Schools) which in general form appear like conventional industrial organizations. However, under closer inspection the successful ones usually turn out to have exceptional capabilities for learning to reorganize themselves flexibly as opportunities and resource availabilities change.

At first, ordinary bureaucratic organizations often are effective and efficient, and even pleasant workplaces. This is because at the outset, for reasons of political popularity, they tend to be well funded, and, as Stafford Beer has shown, when they are first created their role and task definitions on paper tend to fit well with the actual job at hand. But as time goes on, the surrogate (rules, contracts and conventions) world of the institution becomes ever more oriented towards security and equity. The entrepreneurial people tend to move on to greener pastures and leave a stagnant pool of security seekers behind. The conventional bureaucratic institution eventually becomes mainly concerned with merely producing itself rather than with its service output, which then deteriorates as does the quality of life within.

Another reason why conventional organizational models are inadequate for distance education is that the quality of the teaching–learning process is deeply affected by the institutional support structure. The Open University of the United Kingdom's regional tutorial services appear to be one of the main reasons for the high completion rate achieved at the Open University, while from a hard-nosed business standpoint they appear to greatly reduce the economies of scale achievable. It is really very difficult to develop and sustain optimal distance learning activities in a structure constructed on old hierarchical industrial preconceptions, ones borrowed from altogether other kinds of enterprise. Probably much of the reason for the weakness of hybrid distance education institutions when they attempt to do much more than be a means for recruiting people into the conventional programmes, is due to the overhead of the autopoietic regulations and structures of conventional institutions. ('Autopoietic' means actively self-producing or survival and reproduction oriented.)

## New technology

Today telecommunications and computer technology is coalescing into one cybernetic global medium. Sight, sound and motion are all communicated and manipulated, stored and routed by digital electronics/photonics. More and more appliances from TVs to automobiles of the current generation have microprocessor controllers embedded in them. Our common-sense 'real' world is being paralleled by ever more realistic models and simulations culminating in the so-called 'virtual realities' of 'cyberspace' (Benedikt 1991) into which people can enter and interact by wearing electronic helmets, suits and gloves. Perhaps for the time being, distance educators can ignore more of these developments, but an adequate general theory of technology-based distance education ought to embrace them just as well as the more traditional print and broadcast educational media.

The skeleton of an integrated theory of viable organization and effective instruction applicable to the age of cyberspace ('The parallel universe created and sustained by the world's computers and communications lines' – Benedikt 1991) is what I have attempted to construct here. The basic philosophical position is a combination of Nicholas Rescher's Methodological Pragmatism and Roy Bhaskar's Critical Realism.

The organizational part of the theory is an adaptation of Stafford Beer's Viable System Theory, combined with Habermas's discursive legitimation theory. The instructional systems part of this theory owes a good deal to Helmar Frank, Gordon Pask, Jerome Bruner, Sheila Harri-Augstein and Laurie Thomas, and to Robert Boyd.

The essential, underlying theory of human nature derives from Karl Jung, P. F Strawson, Ernest Becker, Rom Harré and Amelie Oksenberg Rorty.

Aside from the novel combination of other people's work, my own unique, and controversial, contributions are: the recognition of the defining human imperative ('The ought that is') to propagate identity, the elucidation of the Relevant Credibility Status Knowledge Development game, and the elucidation of education in terms of the development of various transbody and intrabody autopoietic virtual organisms, and the derived imperative to foster cultural symbioses among them.

## DISTANCE EDUCATION GOALS

As a starting point, one might assert that good education is the systematically effective and efficient transmissive re-creation of the most adaptively potent (indefinitely viable), and yet traditionally rooted, elements of a culture that the people involved can be happily capable of enjoying, of using practically, and of propagating. Good distance education is, in addition, particularly concerned with the linking in teaching–learning experiences of people with complementary educative interests and capabilities who are geographically separated, or are otherwise constrained (infants, money, etc.) from attending regular classes.

The thesis is that cultivation of: (a) potency to cultivate autonomy and 'Self-integration', (b) collaborativity, and (c) traditional rooted-ness, are the core of good education, can be legitimated discursively (Boyd and Myers 1988), and also historically (e.g. Matthew Arnold's Rugby, Victor Gollancz's Repton, Methodist Sunday schools, The Mechanics Institutes, and the Workers Educational Association, the United Kingdom Open University).

The heart of the matter, as I see it, is that responsible creative free-willed selves are struggling to reach one another, in order to help, despite constraints not just of ignorance, distance and noise, but of unexamined ideologies, and the obstructions of a vast and dense crowd of busy robots which they enlist.

Both our 'selves' and the robots or 'virtual organisms' share space in our humanimal brains. Our robotic habits save time and effort when they are appropriate to the tasks at hand, and are therefore indispensable. But these habitual automatisms or 'task robots' and 'learning robots' as Harri-Augstein and Thomas (1991) call them, are continually pre-empting control of our actions, and often by acting in concert, as well as in competition to propagate themselves, reduce our viability and happiness. Public and commercial communications space/media are also largely pre-empted by parasitic autopoietic modulations generated by and generating these virtual organisms.

If technology is to be really educational and really effective, whether at a distance or face-to-face, it must serve as a powerful aid to selves in collaborating to manage those parasitic and dominative virtual organisms which infect us, and limit our learning capabilities.

It is not usually possible for an individual to overcome deeply ingrained habits and addictions unaided. The help of others is indispensable. Usually we think of such help in terms of face-to-face counselling or group work, but it is equally possible to provide it via any of the modes of teleconferencing.

Our twentieth-century western society has tended to make a fetish of providing the means (land, food, clothing, shelter, transport, medicare) to survival and reproduction, without much considering the means to sustain the desire to survive. Whereas, as Albert Camus pointed out, for anyone who can see what we have to contend with, the first question to be answered is 'Why not commit suicide?'. The desire to go on desiring and being hopefully alive is largely sustained by beauty (flowers, music and art are very practical things), and whatever indicates that there may be an opportunity for us to propagate parts of our identity.

Much distance education is therefore concerned with providing hopeful opportunities to alienated people who otherwise might feel desperately cut off.

## CULTURAL SYMBIOSIS

The highest level goal possible for distance education is probably to promote symbiosis among the various cultures of the world, between people and between them and the rest of the living mantle of our little planet.

Symbiosis is living together in a mutually supportive relationship, yet retaining one's own distinct identity and identity propagation continuity. The extreme alternatives are assimilation or annihilation. Both destroy the identity-variety which is really our most crucial requisite for the long-term survival of life on earth. Some cultural competition is beneficial. Some lingua franca is essential. But beyond that the more variety that we can conserve the better, especially for sustaining our desire as well as our ability to go on indefinitely.

## DEFINITIONS

### Theory

A *good* theory is predictive, heuristic, economical, understandable, and largely coherent with existing scientific knowledge. Viewed as a work of art, a good theory is one which seduces people into propagating it. A theory may succeed as a virus/art for the above substantive reasons, or merely because it is aesthetically attractive, or nicely fits the potential carriers' existing prejudices.

It may seem odd that I put understandable *after* predictive and heuristic, but there are examples of theories with outstanding predictive power such as Quantum Mechanics, which are not really understandable. To demand predictivity is to require that a good theory enables one to determine what is possible and what is likely (not necessarily certain) to occur in a given system, under specified conditions. Possibilistic predictivity is the minimum demand for a practically useful theory. Plausible explanatory power actually requires possibilistic prediction. (An 'explanation' which does not constrain, is merely a rationalization.) Obviously, without some predictive power an educational theory is useless for designing distance education. Less obviously, even to criticize existing distance education projects we need a theory with causal relationships, otherwise the bad outcomes that we see, or foresee, might merely be due to chance, not to the features of the system which we assert should be changed.

To demand heuristic power is to require that a good theory leads on to possibly better theories, that it be oriented towards progress not merely towards description and prediction.

The demand for coherence with our best evolved existing theoretical and empirical models of reality is what separates scientific theories from mere *ad hoc* creations. The demand for coherence is not a demand for total logical consistency, since complementary incompatible theories may be needed to cover reality – as is the case with the Bohr complementarity between wave and particle theories of radiation.

An economical theory is one which with a few definitions, axioms and theorems, covers an immense variety of actual cases. There must be real similarities and real recurrences for a theory to be possible. People's lives are unique and in detail never repeat. Unique situations and events in their uniqueness are not amenable to theory (they are the ineffable stuff of art). However, since the detail with which we can discriminate situations is limited, and the languages with which we think and communicate always deal with regularities, this demand does not rule out our making good theories about people.

## Culture and community

Whatever else it is, institutionalized education is the organized transmission of culture. Distance education sytems are cultural propagation sub-systems.

Culture may be defined as whatever is transmitted on from generation to generation of human beings by non-genetic means (Shweder and Levine 1984). For example: cuisine, dance, religion, language, archetypal roles, scripts, architecture, tools, maps, books, other recordings. Culture is directly tied to community.

The best definition of community which I have been able to find is that of Cohen:

> The quintessential referent of community is that its members make, or believe they make, a similar sense of things either generally, or with respect to specific and significant interests, and further they think that sense may differ from one made elsewhere. The reality of community in people's experience thus inheres in their attachment or commitment to a common body of symbols.
>
> (Cohen 1985)

Cultural potency is the power of cultural agents to seduce and captivate people into preserving, transmitting, and elaborating a common body of symbols and some common associated meanings behind them, which creates and maintains community.

Cultural potency has conformative, aesthetic, technical, and majoritarian dimensions. The conformative dimension is to do with how well it fits with the world view/cultural identity that you have already espoused (or been deeply infected with). The majoritarian dimension is the bandwagon effect of wanting to be with what seems likely to be an overwhelming majority.

Clearly, to be legitimate and effective, and therefore viable, distance education systems need to be concerned with cultural potency.

## Education and distance education

Education is the systemically (institutionalized), and more or less systematically organized, transmission of selected elements of culture to be internally carried and used by people. These elements can of course include techniques for radical creativity, not just those elements involved in the reproduction of traditional forms. What is actually transmitted includes hidden curricula addressed to the unconscious as well as (or better than!) the overtly declared curriculum.

Distance education is that sector of education where teachers and learners are separated physically but connected by various communications media.

The big difference between training and education is that training is concerned mainly with ensuring that someone shall soon be able and motivated to quite adequately do some specific job; while education is broadly concerned with human fulfilment, with confluent multi-sensory learning, and with meta-cognitive skills such as learning how to effectively organize and manage further learning.

Whatever the specific practical instructional objectives happen to be, distance education should also have the meta-objectives of promoting the abilities, desire, and will to carry out ongoing collaborative autonomous learning.

## People as participants in distance education

One of the main weaknesses of most educational theory lies in the rather simplistically narrow models of human nature which are usually employed (Berry 1986, Harré 1985).

Probably the behaviourists were the worst in this respect, and much educational technology is still based on a behaviourist model of man. But even the currently fashionable cognitive psychology movement tends to focus on rational conscious cognition of one individual, largely ignoring affective kinesthetic and social dimensions of learning.

By contrast, in this theory people are defined as *Homo Sapiens* (humanimals) which have learned, both unconsciously and consciously, socially constructed ways of thinking and behaving, and have a vested interest in the continuing evolution and propagation of those action programmes.

More precisely, in order to become human each biological individual has acquired and/or created a number of intrabody and transbody autopoietic virtual organisms, or in Strawson/Pask terms 'p-individuals', which transact life mostly according to the mores of the given society.

In particular the transbody Distributed Autopoietic Virtual Organisms (DAVOs) are such 'creatures' as languages and religions, and mythologies/ideologies, 'group-identity' or 'team spirit' or family solidarity, or the madness of crowds, all of which function largely subconsciously in all the members of each collectivity to preserve themselves.

Unfortunately the growth of conflicting habits or 'DAVOs' is more usual than otherwise in the contemporary world. And it leads to weakness of will, or self-defeating activity (Oksenberg-Rorty 1976).

The intrabody Personal Autopoietic Virtual Organisms (PAVOs) certainly include the conscious ego, and various personae which it can deliberately deploy and/or orchestrate, but also very important unconscious entities such as (probably/possibly): the animus, the anima, the id, the super-ego, shadow, etc. Again in modern persons there is frequent conflict among PAVOs which can and do from time to time pre-empt control from the self and often twist or sabotage its efforts.

Of course PAVOs and DAVOs can and do both collaborate and compete (often disastrously) for life expression time and resources.

The pyscho-philosophical-moral question as to just what combination of the above intrabody and transbody virtual-organisms constitutes the free-willed, creative responsible self (if any?) has not yet been satisfactorily answered as far as can be made out (Dennett 1991).

For the purpose of improving distance education, it is enough to recognize that there is a diversity of conscious and subconscious auto-poietic actors in each distance learner, and in networks of teachers and learners and administrators, which from time to time participate both constructively and inhibitively in the distance education process.

## Legitimate education

As Habermas demonstrated, education can be legitimated in three ways:

- Historically: what we were taught is what our children should be taught!
- Quasi-scientifically: whatever the theories and empirical findings of authoritative professional experts somehow add up to is legitimate.
- Discursively: what all stakeholders, after hearing all the arguments, and conducting non-dominative discourse, agree upon is thereby made legitimate.

At first understanding 'discursive legitimation' seems obviously the best sort, especially in a turbulent multi-cultural world. The really tricky thing about discursive legitimation however, and the consideration which may indeed be the aporias of Habermas's theory, is that because the conscious ego is only one part of the self, any deliberations or commitments it makes have no guarantee to be beneficial for the whole person, let alone for the whole community. This is obvious with children. But even adult distant learners may think what they want is a B.Comm. when what their subconscious wants of the educational contract is some particular kind of human intercourse (e.g. *Educating Rita*). Consequently, both 'expert' and even 'historical' legitimation still have valid roles to play in conjunction with discursive legitimation mechanisms.

### Viable system theory

The organization theory which I think is most appropriate is a tailored version of Stafford Beer's recursive five-level Viable System Theory (Espejo and Harnden 1989). What Beer did was look at what functional sub-systems a living organism must have in order to continue to be viable. Then he looked at various corporations and schools to see how to conceive organizational analogues of the essential vital sub-systems. Finally, Beer and other operational researchers tried out the Viable System Theory methodology in many institutional settings and modified it on the basis of experience, and published the modified theory.

The essential core of the theory is that to be viable any organization must have five functional sub-systems each of which in a sense re-capitulates the whole structure. This is why it is called a recursive theory.

Figure 14.1, based on Beer's diagrams, gives an indication of the whole scheme. At the top, System V is concerned with matters of life and death of the organization. It is the constituting body, the internal supreme court, and the body responsible for divisions and mergers. All members of the organization and other principal stakeholders (students, employers, governments) should participate in or be represented in System V.

System IV is concerned with options and 'visions'. It looks outside and to the future in trying to come up with alternative ventures and strategies such as new academic programmes, new media, etc. It exhibits possibilities in terms of academic, ethical, aesthetic, and resource requirements, and coherence with the existing organization.

System III is everyday management of human and material resources and service and career opportunities across the whole institution.

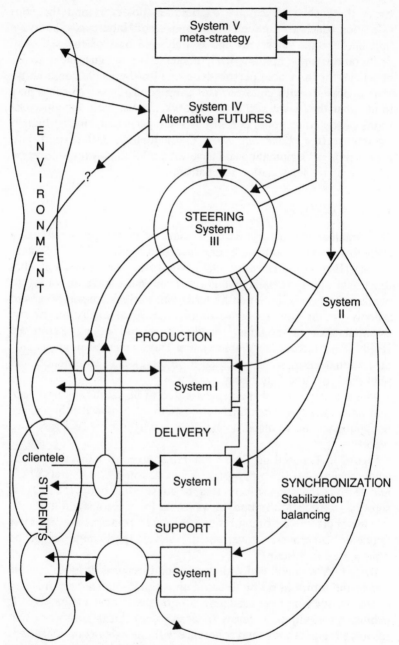

*Figure 14.1*   Restructuring as a truly viable system
*Source:* After Stafford Beer (1985).

System II is a synchronizer and balancer, concerned with the adjustment of timing and reallocation of tasks and resources among the System Is.

The System Is are the basic marketing, materials-production, distribution, broadcasting, communicating, teaching, tutoring, learning, testing, diploma-awarding, units of the organization.

It is to be noted that any given person may (e.g. from time to time) be a participant in many or even all of the functional systems.

## Cyberspace

Radio, television, the telephone, and computer communications are coalescing into one universal digital photonic/electronic medium.

The term 'cyberspace' was invented by Gibson in his novel *Neuromancer* (1984) to describe this new encompassing medium of communication and control. He described it as: 'A consensual hallucination experienced daily by billions of legitimate operators, in every nation, by children being taught mathematical concepts etc . . . A graphic representation of data abstracted from the banks of every computer in the human system.' Gibson's allusive definition has been much refined by McFadden and others in Benedikt's (1991) book on cyberspace. This states that 'Cyberspace will be an inhabitable new parallel universe created and sustained by the whole world's computers and telecommunication networks.'

Cyberspace can be seen as an alternative (eventually maybe the main?) embodiment of Karl Popper's third world. It will contain numerous virtual sub-worlds with more or less limited access.

Cyberspace will contain virtual realities which are sensuously and dynamically inhabitable by suitably garbed and 'jacked-in' persons. To others, in the cyberspace you will appear as any sort of android being, or multiple beings that you choose.

Cyberspace is obviously problematical as it will offer not only surrogate worlds for neurotic retreat into vicarious living, but also serious dominative-game-playing fields.

For millions of people some of the most important parts of cyberspace will be the worlds of on-line distance education institutions, which will make use of gateways to other organizations' cyberspace-worlds to provide observations of people at work, and apprenticeship–internship situations.

## PRESCRIPTIVE THEORY

### Systemic structure for viable distance education systems

In order to make a prescriptive theory for distance education systems I have modified Stafford Beer's Viable System Theory to accommodate Habermas's (1987) prescriptive desiderata for democratic systems aimed at promoting human understanding, and to emphasize the ongoing learning activity which needs to occur at every level of a viable organization.

A viable system is one which possesses a determination to be viable, and the requisite control variety capability to sustain that determination. If the system involves people, then politics, in the sense that some people getting what they want precludes other people getting what they want, arises. Democratic politics requires protected non-dominative discourse spaces (the most rudimentary of which is the secret ballot). Consequently a viable system involving people must have a number of such system-steering discourse spaces. Here, new technology should enable the extension of the concept of a secret ballot into a broader channel of exchange for arguments circulating among hundreds or even thousands of people who are seeking the most generally beneficial course of action without being dominated by vested interests. The new learning discourse spaces still need to carry out Beer's five vital functions, which may be further particularized for distance education institutions as follows:

- System V discourse spaces: a constitutive discourse space to set the organization up (and split or dissolve it); and a judiciary discourse space to deal with infringements of regulations.
- System IV discourse spaces: an anticipatory-intelligence discourse space to look outside and into the future;
- a synectics or creative brainstorming discourse space to formulate evolving visions of system identity and ventures; and educational technology research project systems.
- System III: a task allocation and monitoring system; a recruitment/ marketing system to recruit students and staff, and market course-ware; and a resource (hekergy = information, energy, money, materials, etc.) acquisition, and waste disposal system.
- System II: the resource allocation, monitoring and balancing system.
- System I: instructional design and production systems; teaching broadcasting/publication distribution systems; learning–teaching conversation discourse–space systems; and learner support discourse sub-systems.

All of the above need to carry learning conversations in which the aspirations, anxieties and arguments of all the stakeholders can be combined for democratically optimal practice and evolution.

With the possible exceptions of the judicial and task/time allocative (II) sub-systems, all of the sub-systems must carry on transactions with wider societal systems.

### Essential focal system dimensions

*Eight descriptive and prescriptive dimensions of the constitutive sub-systems*

The work of Helmar Frank has been most helpful as a basis for determining the necessary and sufficient dimensions, or classes of

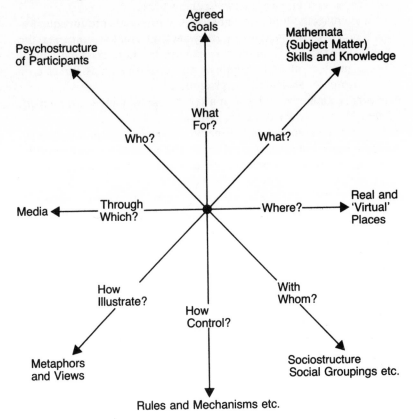

*Figure 14.2* Eight necessary focal system dimensions
*Source:* After Helmar Frank (1974).

variables to be considered in understanding and developing focal systems. Frank elucidated six pedagogic variables to specify instructional systems. I have added two more, and drawn attention to the temporal and spatial, and energetic 'backdrop' variables. Figure 14.2 illustrates the eight main dimensions or classes of variables which occur in all the eight functional sub-systems of the augmented viable system structure developed here.

The dimensions are:

- *Psychostructure of participants*. By this is meant all the characteristics of who the participants are, which are relevant to the work of the focal-system (e.g. if we consider a System I devoted to instruction and learning, then Psychostructure of participants equals name, motivations, entry-level knowledge and skills, cognitive style, etc, of each learner and teacher).
- *Goals* equals the mutually agreed-upon products, product quality, and process quality, and delivery/accomplishment dates for the focal systems (e.g. focal system equals instruction then *Goals* might equal mastery of meta-cognitive and cognitive skills for electric circuit problem-solving by a given date).
- *Matter* equals the subject matter to be obtained, developed, learned, or used by the focal system.
- *Media* is the communication media employed (voice, TV, print).
- *Places* equals the places, real (or virtual) where the people in the focal system act to achieve its goals (e.g. study centre, home kitchen, computercations workspace, etc.).
- *Sociostructure* equals who works/performs with whom in what sort of groupings, whenever (e.g. solo learners, dyads, small groups in study centres, etc.).
- *Views (illustrations), examples and metaphors* equals whatever supplementary material is introduced to facilitate motivation, precision, or generalized understanding of the matter being dealt with.
- *Controls* are the means for control of the activities of the focal system. These may be mutually accepted metaphors, game-rules, procedural algorithms, deviation-limiting feedback loops, command languages, budgets and in general all strategies, tactics and actions of a process-steering, cybernetic nature.

Note that in any research or development project in distance education all eight sets of variables really should be specified for all the focal systems involved (for generalizability in the case of research, or for optimizing in the case of development).

## Cybernetic principles

There are a number of general cybernetic (communication and control) principles which apply to the design, development and operation of systems of actors and agents. Five of the most important are:

- The principle of *concentration* of effort; some few product and process goals must be negotiated as paramount, must be well specified and must have the commitment of the principal actors.
- The principle of *requisite control variety*. All seriously possible sources of disturbance variety must be envisaged, and prioritized, and appropriately matched forms of counteracting control variety must be provided for each.
- The principal of *closed feedback loops*; a return message about performance although commonly called 'feedback', does not actually function as feedback control unless it is compared with a set standard, and the difference, if any, is indeed used to activate controlling actions. A looped channel, without a standard, and without triggerable control actions, is not a true 'closed' feedback loop.
- The principle of *collaborative game prescription*; when a system is too complex to understand, then prescribe! Design into the machinery and/or get an agreement by those involved to play by rules which will simplify it to something understandable.
- The principle of *intermittent control*; leave subsystems alone as long as possibly appropriate to get on with their work undisturbed by 'higher' questions or orders.

## Dynamics

There is not space here to consider the activities and processes of all the eight types of focal system in a distance education system. The most interesting systems are, I think, those Systems I devoted to learning activities, System IV devoted to the development of visions and new ventures, and also System V which assures the legitimacy and democracy of the whole.

Let us consider a System I supporting and guiding student learning. The operation of the system amounts to a transformation over time of some of the variables in some of the eight classes (Goals, Psychostructure of participants, Mathemata, Media, Places, Sociostructure, Illustrations and controls), while the others establish the constraints within which the transformations occur.

As Bruner pointed out there is an important distinction to be kept between (descriptive) theories of learning and (prescriptive) theories of instruction. While cognitive learning theories, such as Roger Shanks's Dynamic (linguistic) Memory Theory and William Clancey's Impasse-Driven-Learning Theory, are very helpful for the development of instructional theories, they have been made narrow to be precise, formalizable and testable. They are important, but none the less just parts of what human educational learning involves; parts which must be complemented by reference to the more global insights that have arisen from the reflective practice of gifted teachers and educational researchers in the field.

A. N. Whitehead (1929) has characterized the main sequential phases of significant learning as being three: Romance, Precision and Generalization. He points out that aesthetic factors are very important with respect to motivation in the Romance phase, and are again very important with respect to metaphoric transfer of learning in the Generalization phase.

Whitehead does not, however, address the problems caused by existing human automatic-behaviour complexes (or as Harri-Augstein and Thomas (1991) call them 'task robots' and 'learning robots') which stubbornly resist being displaced by new skills and/or personae. It seems that carefully guided stages of history retelling, discernment, role-play, and grieving are involved in the deeper kind of adult transformative learning needed to achieve self-integration and self-autonomy with respect to internalized robots (Boyd and Myers 1988). Non-verbal communication as well as verbal learning conversations often seems to be needed for such transformative learning. There are some indications that television teleconferences are adequate for the non-verbal communication in some group process learning.

According to this theory, education is concerned with partial reprogramming of what I call AVOs (Autopoietic Virtual Organisms) which subsist in people's nervous systems.

First, we need somehow to recognize and identify the AVOs which we carry. Second, we need to determine where and when some of them function inappropriately. Third, we need with the aid of discernment to work towards deep self-integration, to imagine more appropriate functioning. Fourth, we need to modify the triggering, or the functioning of the relevant AVOs accordingly, and/or train new AVOs by acting out new roles to take the place of inappropriate ones in specific situations.

The sticky bits to all this are that (a) AVOs are autopoietic and so resist any changes being made to them; (b) AVOs are mostly only indirectly accessible to consciousness, and so have to be recognized through recordings and projections, and have to be retrained in dramatic situations rather than by direct command; and (c) that the level of self-understanding, autonomy, friendly support, and personal integration required to do this well is very high.

The good bit is that, as our AVOs are improved or replaced, self-understanding and friendships improve too so that the educational process becomes somewhat easier and more satisfying the more it is engaged in.

Although the importance of education for autonomy and integration has long been well understood by many adult educators, their insights have scarcely penetrated into the educational technology world of distance education. Lack of autonomy, and lack of integration, probably are important causal components of student under-achievement and drop outs.

## APPLICATION TO INCORPORATION OF NEW MEDIA

It is apparent from the foregoing that communication and steering or control of the learning of large complex organizations and large numbers of students is central to the success of distance education. The questions then arise: how can newer technologies help? and how might they hinder such learning?

### Advantages

The areas where help seems most needed and most possible is in the aggregation of contributions and the matching of resources to needs.

- Artificial intelligence applied to discourse recordings and other inputs should be capable of combining thousands of arguments so as to emphasize their common core, and preserve the more interesting variants on it. Some evidence of this capability is arising in the field of knowledge engineering using expert system shells which learn from examples rather than having to be programmed by inserting specific rules. Many commercial products (Lotus Agenda, TTX-Trilogy, etc.) now have rudimentary recognition and linking capability of the kind needed.
- Since motivation and generalization are so heavily dependent on aesthetics, and since many people do primary thinking in visual or oral/aural or kinesthetic modes, it is important that learning conversations should be enabled by visual and auditory and kinetic means not just by alpha-numeric text. Currently available input and

output devices are probably adequate but the cognitive ergonomics needed is at a rudimentary stage of development and there is a formidable welter of unconformable transmission standards for pictures; sounds and manipulations; that is, there is no real international standardization of the kind needed yet.

## Disadvantages

The four main foreseeable disadvantages are: (a) the possibility of drowning in seas of noise; (b) the preferential disadvantage situation for those who have little skill at analysis and argument in abstract terms; (c) possibilities for nasty 'let you and him fight!' situations being set up through pseudonymous computer-communications; and (d) the cost and politics may be such that low-income people may not have access to cyberspace.

## CONCLUSION

The foregoing has been an outline of a prescriptive theory for use by developers of, and researchers into, distance education supported by quasi-intelligent multi-modal computer-communications or 'cyberspace'. The theory is falsifiable in three senses: (a) the norms involved may not be acceptable in a given milieu; (b) it may prove too cumbersome to be helpful to busy practitioners in a hurry; and (c) the prescription may not in fact lead to the predicted desired outcomes. Finally it might be a dead end, leading to no further and better theories.

## BIBLIOGRAPHY

Beer, S. (1985) *Diagnosing the System for Organizations*, Chichester: John Wiley & Sons.

Benedikt, M. (1991) (ed.) *Cyberspace: First Steps*, Cambridge, Mass.: MIT.

Berry, C. L. (1986) *Human Nature*, Atlantic Highlands, N.J.: Humanities Press International.

Bhaskar, R. (1989) *Reclaiming Reality*, London: Verso.

Boyd, G. (1991) 'R-places', *Education and Training Technology International* 2(3), 271–5.

Boyd, R. D. and Myers, J. G. (1988) 'Transformative education', *International Journal of Lifelong Education* 7(4), 261–84.

Cohen, A. P. (1985) *The Symbolic Construction of Community*, Chichester: Ellis Horwood.

Dennett, D. C. (1991) *Consciousness Explained*, Boston: Little Brown & Co.

Douglas, M. (1985) *How Institutions Think*, Syracuse: Syracuse University Press.

Espejo, R. and Harnden, R. (eds) (1989) *The Viable System Model: Interpretations and Applications of Stafford Beer's VSM*, Chichester: John Wiley & Sons.

Flood, R. L. (1990) *Liberating Systems Theory*, New York: Plenum Press.

Frank, H. (1974) *Kybernetische Padagogik* Vol. 5, Stuttgart: Verlag W. Kohlhammer.

Habermas, J. (1987) *The Theory of Communicative Action* (2 vols), Boston: Beacon Press.

Harré R., Clarke, D. and DeCarlo, N. (1985) *Motives and Mechanisms: Introduction to the Psychology of Action*, London: Methuen.

Harri-Augstein, S. and Thomas, L. (1991) *Learning Conversations*, London: Routledge.

Keegan, D. (1990) *Foundations of Distance Education* (2nd edn) London: Routledge.

Oksenberg-Rorty, A. (1976) (ed.) *The Identities of Persons*, Berkeley: University of California Press.

Pask, G. (1984) 'Review of conversation theory', *Educational Communication and Technology Journal* 32(1), 3–40.

Ramos, A. G. (1984) *The New Science of Organisations*, Toronto: University of Toronto Press.

Restivo, S. (1991) *The Sociological Worldview*, Oxford: Basil Blackwell.

Shweder, A. and Levine, R. A. (1984) (eds) *Culture Theory*, Cambridge: Cambridge University Press.

Whitehead, A. N. (1929) *The Aims of Education*, New York: Macmillan.

# 15 Distance training

*Tony Devlin*

## INTRODUCTION

The first and most important feature of distance training as it is understood today is its essential difference from the broader concept of distance education. This difference is one of focus.

Distance *education* is, typically, student centred. Learners are encouraged and facilitated to pursue their own needs and preferences within the subject matter under study, enabling a broad range of learning outcomes and substantial tolerance of individual differences. Distance *training*, conversely, is driven and controlled principally by the needs of the organization. These needs, expressed simply, are to have effective, generally task-oriented skills acquired by trainees in the most cost-efficient manner possible. The role of defining the student's learning and competence needs is assumed by the organization.

This chapter examines the nature and particular characteristics of distance training in large organizations, whether governmental or commercial. The specific circumstances of transnational and multinational organizations are also considered.

The critical importance of design factors in distance training, issues of standardization, and what may be called the 'productification' of training are explored, together with factors affecting the justification, inefficiency and effectiveness terms of distance training in organizations today.

The characteristics and situation of today's organizational learner are examined as is the pivotal importance of motivation in the effectiveness of current forms of distance training.

Distance training has been, and to some extent remains, disputed territory for many organizations. Some typical problem areas and contentious issues are presented here together with the growing influence of the rapidly changing media and communications components of distance training systems.

The chapter concludes by considering the relationship between distance training and emergent embedded training and performance support technology leading to the prediction of the inexorable growth of distance training to become the dominant form of competence development in large multinational organizations.

## CHARACTERISTICS

Organizations develop and implement training strategies and programmes specifically and solely to improve their own performance. Training is evaluated in terms of its effectiveness, that is the extent to which it generates performance improvement and efficiency, and in terms of the cost associated with this performance improvement.

In practical terms, the evaluation of organizational training is criterion-referenced with organizations frequently employing precise performance measures and testing techniques to establish that trainees have reached required competence levels. Allied to this, organizations place limited value on the achievement of performance above or outside the criterion level; there is a general desire that trainees should learn what they need to know and so demonstrate required levels of proficiency, but, conversely, there is a perception that efficient training minimizes the 'nice to know' components and avoids wasteful investment in training beyond required proficiency levels. An important corollary of this criterion-referenced approach is that there is no acceptable level of failure or no tolerable drop-out rate. Unlike distance education, distance training is, for most organization members, not an optional activity but a critical job component. For trainer and trainee alike the achievement of targeted competence levels is mandatory for all participants and this has implications, in particular, for the design and application of remediation systems.

Where organizations implement distance training strategies, then, it is normally with efficiency in mind. While training effectiveness to the relevant criterion level is an essential requirement across all organizational training activity, distance training is favoured on grounds of cost, flexibility and accessibility – all purely efficiency factors.

In multinational companies, for example, with operational units scattered over the globe and with complementary and interdependent manufacturing, adminstration, marketing and support staff located in many different countries, there is a tendency to employ a 'competence centre' concept. These competence centres address areas such as research and development, administration of business procedures, strategic marketing, and competence development.

The implication of the competence centre concept for training is that training activity will tend to be concentrated on a small number of well-developed, highly competent locations whose brief is to serve the diverse needs of a widely dispersed organization. In turn, this concentration, for reasons of efficiency, leads to a standardization of training products and programmes together with the growth of an infrastructure for the distribution of these programmes. Increasingly, distance training offers these competence centres an efficient mechanism to balance the twin imperatives of distribution and control of the organization's training.

A further factor of importance in larger organizations, even those which are not especially engaged with complex technologies, is the accelerating rate of change in their operating environments. Technological change, increased competition, the globalization of organizations, all contribute to increasingly rapid turnover of the knowledge and skills base of organizations today. This turnover generates a need for continuous learning, adaptation and retraining for many if not all organization members throughout their organizational lives. Increasingly this adaptation and retraining must be delivered ever more frequently, in shorter time-scales and directly at the point of need.

As in manufacturing, where the concepts of ship to stock, ship to line and Just in Time delivery have transformed traditional production processes, so a concept of Just in Time training is emerging to underpin the structure and processes of ongoing competence development in the large distributed organization.

The implications for the use of distance training are twofold. First, organizations expect distance training to provide the means of delivering effective training in a timely manner directly to the point of need – this training is no longer a discrete, typically centralized *event*, it is a continuous *process* driven by competence centres organized to provide a controlled and standardized training 'flow' to all parts of the dispersed organization structure. Second, there is an underlying need for organization members, at virtually all levels, to go beyond task-based, procedural learning towards a flexible, problem-solving orientation based on the continuous acquisition and integration of new knowledge. Organizations expect distance training to address this underlying process also. The increasing importance of the individual learner is recognized as is the need for this individual learner to acquire and enhance a range of enabling knowledge and skills which constitute a competence platform on to which the organization can deliver its continuous flow of new material. The challenge for the training system and for distance training in particular is to engage the unique capabilities, background and motivational levels of the individual learner and to form and direct them towards the establishment of a common competence platform.

In summary, distance training is perceived as an efficiency driven imperative for the large dispersed organization today. It must therefore adapt its forms, structures and strategies to maximize training effectiveness. The productification of training is a key condition for such effectiveness.

## PRODUCTIFICATION OF TRAINING

All forms of distance learning are characterized by a relatively high level of investment in the design and packaging of the course of study and its associated learner, tutor and support materials. In the particular case of distance training, standardization and instructional design factors are of major importance. The task of distance training units in large organizations has three major components: development of appropriate training materials, delivery and administration of these materials across the organization, and certification of the achievement by trainees of the appropriate performance and competence levels. The distance factor, together with the increasing identification of the learner as an autonomous and responsible participant in training, has led to a shift in training design from a behavioural to a cognitive emphasis. There is a clear need in the distance training scenario to de-emphasize models which structure training as information accompanied/followed by behaviourist reinforcement. Instead, a new emphasis is required on the delivery of information accompanied by appropriate levels of psychological support for learning. The implications for training design are significant. It is appropriate to discuss some of them here.

First, a cognitive orientation places increased emphasis on the *engineering* of training products – that is, the creation of training which is precisely calibrated and assembled from clearly specified components, each with its own embedded instructional design. In this context, Component Display Theory (Merrill 1983) provides one set of prescriptions which can be used to guide the design and development of learning activities. This theory gives rise to the two dimensional performance/content matrix which underpins much of today's design approach in distance training. Using the matrix, knowledge and information to be imparted are structured according to the two broad categorizations of procedural and declarative, and performance objectives are set at the levels of memorize and use, as appropriate.

This scheme is particularly useful to the structuring of training in large commercial and service organizations. For example:

- action procedures support many of the routine mechanical tasks which arise in industrial and manufacturing settings;
- decision procedures support many of the diagnostic activities involved in service provisioning and maintenance tasks;
- process procedures provide support for declarative knowledge in the understanding and control of large technical systems such as computer networks.

Again, the subdivision of declarative material into facts, concepts and principles provides a method of organizing knowledge for delivery using prescribed instructional strategies.

The principal performance categorizations are also subdivided: memory performance may be evoked in terms of recognition or recall, and use performance in terms of near and far transfer. The concept of far transfer – that is, the application of knowledge and skills in situations significantly different from those in which the learning takes place – is particularly relevant to today's organizational context where emphasis is increasingly placed on the capacity to adapt to a rapidly changing task environment and to exhibit appropriate adaptive problem-solving skills.

A working model of the performance/content matrix in distance training is illustrated in Figure 15.1. Strong adherence to this or an equivalent model results in a highly systematic approach to distance training development and aids the productification process.

A second important factor is the strong emphasis on testing in distance training. A rigorous approach to the definition and structuring of training objectives based on the Action, Condition, Criterion Model (Mager 1986) ensures that an explicit basis for the creation of objective linked tests is available to the developer. The Mager model emphasizes the testing of precisely defined performance (the action) to a measurable level of success (the criterion), subject to a tightly controlled enabling and support environment (the condition). Where such testing is comprehensive and experience-based, using real or simulated practice scenarios, a high rate of learning transfer to the job situation may be expected. However, the relative scarcity of certification systems outside the traditional trade and professional membership structures leaves room for substantial improvement in this area.

Again, the structuring and standardization of testing promotes the productification process but a broader-based certification system

## TYPES OF CONTENT

| LEVEL OF PERFORMANCE | | | PROCEDURAL | | | DECLARATIVE | | |
|---|---|---|---|---|---|---|---|---|
| | | | ACTION | DECISION | PROCESS | FACT | CONCEPT | PRINCIPLE |
| | MEMORIZE | RECOGNIZE | | | | | | |
| | | RECALL | | | | | | |
| | USE | NEAR | | | | | | |
| | | FAR | | | | | | |

*Figure 15.1* A working model of the performance/content matrix in distance training

would be required to exploit fully the potential benefits. For example, current once-off certification of electronic engineers at third level can be extended to include ongoing testing and certification of competence in specific new hardware, software, systems and processes. Such an increase in the frequency and range of testing can, in part, compensate for the difficulty of carrying out ongoing formative evaluation of students in distance training over time. The proliferation of testing and certification activities can transcend conventional summative evaluation and become a form of continuous assessment of trainee progress.

Third, there is an increasing emphasis on the imparting of more generalized coping skills such as problem-solving ability to trainees in organizations which experience rapid rates of technological change.

Extensive use of context-setting components in task training and the promotion of system level knowledge of technical processes are consciously engineered into the distance training products of these technology driven organizations. The aim is to achieve a broad-based and flexible transfer of knowledge and information to the task environment, where the trainees are required to apply that knowledge in contexts which are sometimes radically different from those presented during training.

The cumulative effect of productification for the training organization is that operational management can measure with some precision the extent and level of competences present in their working populations. Such quantitative information can be collected and analysed to facilitate the harnessing and deployment of skills and knowledge across the widespread and disparate units of the organization.

Discussion of distance training in terms of its productification leads naturally to an examination of the consumers of these training products, today's organizational learners.

## THE ORGANIZATIONAL LEARNER

The first point to consider is that today's employees are, in large measure, engaged in a continuous process of knowledge and skills acquisition throughout their working lives. Rapid decay and obsolescence of knowledge and skills are features of the environment, and organizations are striving to establish a learning, knowledge acquisition culture in their work-forces.

Today's learner, the typical participant in distance training, is increasingly adept in the process of knowledge and skills acquisition. This learner has acquired, through successive training experiences, a learning tool kit, a metacognitive (Corno and Mandinach 1983) scheme for planning, connecting and monitoring throughout the learning process. Such learners are very effective in the processing of new information and often do not perceive the process as training in the traditional sense at all. They are committed to the concept of competence development and represent a richly receptive target population for the developer of distance training. Increasingly, developers are motivated to provide 'browsing' capabilities for these learners, means whereby maximum use of existing capabilities may be made so as to minimize the time spent in acquiring new knowledge – that is, to minimize the core training time. For example, a learner with extensive and well-developed knowledge of a particular technical system (say, a radio transceiver in telecommunications) may achieve the learning objectives of an introductory course for a new model or type of transceiver with minimal immersion in the training package. The developer will be sensitive to this situation and will so structure the package's mastery tests as to afford the learner a short but adequately certified path to the completion of the course.

This capacity to isolate and consume only the new/unique components of the learning materials is an essential design factor in distance training, recognizing the heterogeneity of the trainee population and the potential for efficiency gains in the absorption of new knowledge.

Clearly, not all learners will take the shortest, most 'expert' path through course materials. Many will need to complete the programme in more manageable steps and here again the engineering approach proves helpful to the developer. Building on the performance/content matrix a further learner-centred design strategy is offered by Elaboration Theory (Reigeluth 1979). Elaboration theory stresses the instructional importance of using structured elaboration sequences in the presentation of new knowledge. Progressions from simple to complex, general to detailed, and abstract to concrete, characterize the training packages developed to exploit the potential of elaboration theory and effectiveness can be maximized where the learner is afforded control of content, rate of delivery and choice of instructional strategy.

Perhaps, the most important learner characteristic of relevance to distance training however, is motivation. Motivation is the critical component in learning effectiveness for a number of reasons which are worth elaborating.

## MOTIVATIONAL ISSUES

If, for the purpose of illustration, training is taken out of its normal organization context and placed into hypothetical extreme scenarios, the true influence of motivation becomes easier to visualize. Say, for example, a group of learners is placed in a situation of exaggerated opportunity or threat. Consider this scenario:

The organization has installed a new type of computer system. The trainees must become competent in the operation of the new system and to achieve this competence will have access to a number of documented handling procedures in the form of job aids and a collection of operational descriptions and instructions in handbook/user manual form. There will be no access to formal training or to sources of expert advice. Suppose further that at the end of a finite learning period the trainees will have their competence tested in hands-on sessions with the new system. Those who achieve the criterion level will be promoted, those who do not will be redeployed to other, less desirable, positions.

Clearly, an extraordinarily high level of motivation will exist in such a hypothetical learner population. It is almost certain that, assuming the materials provided contain enough information to enable competence in operating the new system to be achieved (in other words provided it is actually *possible* to achieve the competence by using the information available), all of these learners will achieve the criterion level in their tests. Motivation will compensate for all inadequacies in learning material and in associated support. It is useful to keep this extreme scenario in mind when considering the relative importance and influence of some of the distance training components discussed later in this chapter (for example, media, interaction, tutor support, etc.). Motivation, where present in sufficient intensity, compensates for a range of structural and design deficiencies, and investments in learner motivation have enormous payback potential.

In the area of motivational design in training one may consider four motivational components (Keller 1983) of significance to the training developer – namely, interest, relevance, expectancy and outcomes. In the distant training context these components influence training design in a number of ways.

First, the interest component is typically addressed through the design of 'hooks' (such as visually attractive presentation elements, frequent changes of pace, and variations in instructional strategy) to arouse and maintain the learner's interest. Again, however, external factors may intervene and the subject matter of the training (a new state-of-the-art technical product, for example) may generate sufficient interest to render consideration of this component in the training design superfluous.

Second, the relevance component may be promoted through the instructional material to a limited extent only. Perceived relevance must be mediated through the trainee's local management and, for maximum effectiveness, must be expressed as instrumental in the achievement of valued job or personal goals.

The expectancy component can be facilitated through the use of elaboration theory in the training design, and by close attention to support and remediation (so as to convey a high expectation of successful outcome and a low perception of the learning task difficulty) across all levels of learner competence. The provision of access to some relevant components of conventional training (such as a teacher-equivalent in the form of tutor or expert support) may also help to overcome difficulties in this area.

Fourth, the outcome component is to some extent a behaviourist notion employing contingent reward and reinforcement to encourage increases in trainees' effort and involvement in the training process. Post-course certification is a valuable strategy here as are the inclusion in the training materials of explicit recognition for successful progress nd positive feedback in response to acceptable test scores.

A further consideration of relevance to the distance trainer is the influence of personality type on receptiveness to self-paced learning experience. Kern and Matta (1988) have identified evidence that, using the Myers–Briggs Type Indicator (Myers 1980) of Jungian typology, trainees who are high on the thinking/sensing preference scale perform better with self-administered training than colleagues rated high on feeling/intuition. Where such preferences are evident it may be desirable to provide support components which compensate for the relative lack of appeal of distance training to the high feeling/ intuition class of trainee.

Trainee motivation is of major significance in distance training. No less significant however is the motivation level of the user organization – the designers, implementers and administrators of the training. These motivation levels are heavily influenced by the ebb and flow of a continuing debate around a number of contentious issues in distance training.

## CONTENTIOUS ISSUES IN DISTANCE TRAINING

A major issue in distance training is the extent to which the training itself is necessary. Professional trainers have a tendency to define all performance problems as training needs, whereas clearly much can be achieved simply by providing better access to information and by working with motivation levels. There is an obvious growth in the use of distance training techniques in large dispersed organizations in recent years (ETTE 1991) to the extent that in some economies (the US for example), we can predict that this form of training can outstrip traditional methods to become the dominant form of intraorganizational competence development.

There occurs an inevitable blurring, however, of the distinction between training and information supply in these contexts and many organizations appear consciously to be winding down their large training infrastructures and relying on the learning capacities and motivation levels of staff continuously to enhance competence. Without rigorous testing and certification it is difficult to see how this approach can assure reliable knowledge transfer to the job situation.

Allied to this erosion of commitment to training is the gradual bridging of the competence gap between the user and the technology in today's organizations. Training mediated on-site and over distance has been the traditional method by which users are interfaced with the technology. Training design has been aimed at compensating for deficiencies in user skills and knowledge and for deficiencies in the design and usability of the technology itself. Increasingly, the technology is being engineered with usability in mind and this factor, taken together with increasing levels of expertise and adaptability in the user population, is squeezing training in an ever-decreasing competence gap. The logical conclusion is the end, the elimination of training, made obsolete by users who, at most, simply learn how to learn and by technology which comes embedded with such sophisticated all-encompassing help and performance support systems as to eliminate the need for formal training.

Trends in this direction are already visible in the conventional office products environment where, to take photocopiers as an example, an indexed help guide, supported by LCD display panel and an array of lights, icon buttons and audio tones guides even the novice user through the complexities of conventional copying, reduction, enlargement, double-sided copying, stapling and sorting. Training as such is neither offered not deemed necessary.

Similar trends are becoming evident in office computer systems and in many software products which come embedded with tutorial materials and simulation/practice environments so that many, if not all, users are self-taught through what are, in effect, stand-alone distance training packages.

The biggest area of contention, however, remains the efficacy of the classroom/training centre model of training versus the distance training model. Viewed purely in terms of efficiency, distance training, typically, offers lower unit costs of delivery and should therefore be favoured by the commercial organization. The picture becomes more complex, however, when learning effectiveness is considered.

The classroom model offers advantages in respect of immediacy, direct access to the trainer, and the capacity to share the experience of fellow trainees. In a well-managed environment, where the quality of instruction is high, the co-operative and supportive aspects of the classroom model are clearly visible. A well-managed environment cannot generally be assumed, however, and, accordingly, the effect of individual differences in instructor technique and competence levels can result in the delivery of a highly variable product. The effect of individual differences (particularly in skill and experience levels) and interpersonal processes among students can also be detrimental.

To some extent, the effectiveness of the classroom model is also influenced by the nature of the training task. It is at its lowest for lecture-based, theory presentations on technical topics where the emphasis is on the presentation of declarative knowledge in settings which require minimal human interaction. Conversely, training tasks which require higher levels of 'hands-on' practice and/or the development of interpersonal skills (that is, procedural knowledge being taught at the use level) will benefit more from the classroom environment.

The choice of model, therefore, should be dictated by the training task and by the efficiency factors valued by the training organization. The Cone of Experience Model (Dale 1969) supports the view that training intervention should be at a level not deeper than that required to achieve the desired learning effect. The classification (Gropper 1983) of routine (common to all types of objectives) shaping (graduated, step by step), and specialized (tailored precisely to unique learning requirements) forms of practice further suggests that an early transition from group presentation and learning to individual one-to-one practice and coaching on-the-job is desirable.

Distance training, of course, through the employment of tutoring systems, offers trainees a level of human, 'teacher' support as compensation for the absence of the classroom environment. It is worth examining here a number of aspects of the tutoring role.

## THE ROLE OF THE TUTOR

Tutor support in distance training is designed to provide a mixture of services to the student/trainee. These include

- enrichment of the learning experience through the provision of additional information and contextualization as the trainee progresses through the usually self-paced course materials;
- diagnosis of learning difficulties as the trainee progresses, through a process of monitoring, testing and interpersonal contact;
- remediation of difficulties diagnosed or reported by the trainees themselves;

- practical help for the trainee in administrative matters, access to course materials;
- human support, deemed important by trainees in countering the isolating effects of the distance training environment.

The tutor role is clearly important, and all of the services described are likely to be required by at least some proportion of trainees.

Tutoring, however, is expensive, and training organizations inevitably seek to minimize costs in this area. Savings can be achieved partially through improved training design and packaging, thus reducing the incidence of trainees encountering learning difficulties or other more practical problems in using course materials. A second and potentially more significant source of savings is the increasingly wide range of capabilities offered by the use of technology in distance training. Among these, the use of E-Mail to mediate tutor–student interaction is of major importance.

## E-MAIL AND THE TUTOR

E-Mail is a computer-mediated, asynchronous form of interaction between trainer and trainee and, as such, provides a medium whereby the trainee can develop considerable skill in structured communication and in reflective writing. The asynchronous nature of E-Mail communication provides similar opportunities for the tutor to structure and present constructive and comprehensive feedback to the trainee. Both tutor and trainee can be encouraged to optimize the attributes of the E-Mail medium to improve the clarity, efficiency and effectiveness of their communication. Thoughtful use of the medium can, in large measure, overcome the drawback of weak contextualization in E-Mail systems. This contextualization capacity is a learned component which can, with guidance and practice, be readily acquired by tutor and trainee alike.

The further negative factor of social isolation remains significant of course, yet here we must recall the decisive influence of motivation and the supportive social context of the working environment. The distance trainee typically operates from within the context of the working organization and this factor compensates substantially for the relatively solitary nature of the learning process.

With regard to communication, it is worth noting here that, for effective knowledge transfer, immediate feedback of diagnosis and remediation to the trainee may not always be best. This immediacy, characteristic of the classroom situation, can inhibit the learning which the more reflective context of asynchronous communication can facilitate.

## TECHNOLOGY IN DISTANCE TRAINING

It is worth taking a moment to review the role and importance of technological progression in support and delivery systems for distance training today. Advances in technology hold the key to the resolution of many residual problems affecting the developers and users of distance training materials. The quantum increase in capacity and coverage of telecommunications networks which has characterized the 1980s and 1990s is of major significance – not simply in the areas of E-Mail and computer conferencing but also in the vastly richer and more interactive technology of videoconferencing where the practical effects of this increase can be found. The concept of the Virtual Classroom, where broadband telecommunications links are used to support simultaneous access and interaction for remote and local trainees, is proliferating rapidly, particularly in the larger, technically oriented organizations. The availability of real-time video capacity, supported and augmented by computer links and document transfer technologies, begins to blur the distinction between local and distance training environments.

In the area of self-administered training products, the advent of multimedia (full motion video, stereo quality sound, graphics, animation etc) provides a similarly rich set of trainee facilities, and, again supported by computer communications links, these facilities can provide an exceptionally effective and well-supported distance training environment.

The rapid expansion and growing sophistication of embedded help systems and computer-supported job aids also contributes to training efficiency by increasing on-the-job performance support and hence reducing the need for extensive formal training.

The increasing use, in distance training software, of artificial intelligence techniques for diagnosis, remediation and guidance goes a long way towards reducing the dependence of trainees on the tutor for pedagogic and competence support.

Taken together, all these technological developments assist in different ways in the productification, dissemination and personalization of training at a distance.

## SUMMARY AND CONCLUSION

In summary, organizations view training today largely in terms of efficiency. Learning effectiveness in the training design and in the delivery systems is assumed as an essential prerequisite for any training programme and is not considered negotiable, in effect it is a given. Focus is therefore increased on the efficiency issues and it is to the delivery technology (in particular telecommunications and computer technology) that organizations look to achieve the most efficient learning.

Add to this the cultural dimension of the new learner, ever active, browsing through a continuous stream of new knowledge reflective of rapidly developing technology and a fast-changing task environment, a learner becoming more and more an integrator and problem-solver, and increasingly responsive to cognitive rather than behavioural stimuli.

Taken together, we have, in these factors, the probable future shape of all training, not simply distance training, and we can see the trend line towards the inexorable extinction of today's training, making way for a new order of training through technology where the learner is empowered and where the prime prerequisite task is to learn *how to learn*.

## REFERENCES

Corno, L. and Mandinach, E. B. (1983) 'The role of cognitive engagement in learning and instruction', *The Educational Psychologist* 18(2), 88–108.

Dale, E. A. (1969) *Audiovisual Methods in Teaching* (3rd edn), New York: Holt, Rinehart & Winston.

ETTE Conference (1991) Topic Oriented Meeting: Which Issues Influence Technical Training with TBT?, Vienna.

Gropper, G. L. (1983) 'A behavioural approach to instructional prescription', in C. Reigeluth (ed.), *Instructional Design Theories and Models*, Hillsdale, N.J.: LEA.

Keller, J. M. (1983) 'Motivational design of instruction', in C. Reigeluth (ed.), *Instructional Design Theories and Models*, Hillsdale, N.J.: LEA.

Kern, G. M. and Matta, K. F. (1988) 'The influence of personality on self-paced instruction', *Journal of Computer Based Instruction* 15(3), 104–8.

Mager, R. (1986) in R. Gagné and L. J. Briggs *Principles of Instructional Design* (2nd edn), Holt, Rinehart & Winston.

Merrill, D. M. (1983) 'Component display theory', in C. Reigeluth (ed.), *Instructional Design Theories and Models*, Hillsdale, N.J.: LEA.

Myers, I. B. (1980) *Introduction to Type* (3rd edn), Palo Alto, Calif.: Consulting Psychologists Press Inc.

Reigeluth, C. M. (1979) 'In search of a better way to organise instruction: the elaboration theory', *Journal of Instructional Development* 2(3), 8–15.

# Index